D1155078

Lesbian Panic

Between Men ~ Between Women

Lesbian and Gay Studies

Lillian Faderman and Larry Gross, Editors

Lesbian Panic

Homoeroticism in Modern British Women's Fiction

Patricia Juliana Smith

Columbia University Press

NEW YORK

Columbia University Press
Publishers Since 1893
New York Chichester, West Sussex

Library of Congress Cataloging-in-Publication Data
Smith, Patricia Juliana.
Lesbian panic : homoeroticism in modern British women's fiction / Patricia Juliana Smith
p. cm. — (Between men—between women)
Includes bibliographical references and index.
ISBN 0-231-10620-3. — ISBN 0-231-10621-1 (pbk.)
1. English fiction—Women authors—History and criticism. 2. Lesbians in literature 3. Homosexuality and literature—Great Britain—History—20th century. 4. Women and literature—Great Britain—History—20th century. 5. English fiction—20th century—History and criticism. 6. Woolf, Virginia, 1882–1941—Characters—Lesbians. I. Title. II. Series.
PR888.L46S66 1997
823'.910935206643—dc21 96-48366
CIP

∞ Casebound editions of Columbia University Press books are printed on permanent and durable acid-free paper.

Printed in the United States of America

c 10 9 8 7 6 5 4 3 2 1
p 10 9 8 7 6 5 4 3 2 1

BETWEEN MEN ~ BETWEEN WOMEN

Lesbian and Gay Studies

Lillian Faderman and Larry Gross, Editors

Between Men ~ Between Women is a forum for current lesbian and gay scholarship in the humanities and social sciences. The series includes both books that rest within specific traditional disciplines and are substantially about gay men, bisexuals, or lesbians and books that are interdisciplinary in ways that reveal new insights into gay, bisexual, or lesbian experience, transform traditional disciplinary methods in consequence of the perspectives that experience provides, or begin to establish lesbian and gay studies as a freestanding inquiry. Established to contribute to an increased understanding of lesbians, bisexuals, and gay men, the series also aims to provide through that understanding a wider comprehension of culture in general.

To Kathleen Lanehart,
the very best of sisters

CONTENTS

PREFACE

I SEND THIS BOOK OUT into the world with some sense of trepidation, a trepidation founded upon the cultural overdetermination of a particular word, a key word in the title of this book, a word that informs my day-to-day reality as well as that of the many others who are so labeled. The word is "lesbian."

If many years of living with this linguistic sign had not already convinced me of the dilemma it represents and entails, an incident at an academic conference a couple of years ago presented that dilemma to me as a startling revelation. After a panel, I engaged in the usual chit-chat with a lesbian critic who teaches in a region of the country that would not generally be considered optimal for one whose existence is outside the parameters of institutional Christianity and institutional heterosexuality. I asked her what it was like to be a lesbian critic in such a place. She replied that it wasn't *that* bad; there actually was a thriving local lesbian subculture; but, she added, regarding this populace, "They're kind of primitive. They think lesbianism is about liking girls." I must have realized a priori, at least on some level, that my colleague is of the belief that lesbianism is primarily about ideology, politics, and theory—and, granted, in many ways it is. Still, considering how many untoward things have happened to me and to others like me—and happen to characters in the novels I discuss in this text—as a result of "liking girls" a bit too much, I could not resist the temptation to roll my eyes in mock horror and respond, "Do you mean someone's changed the rules?"

I was later taken aside and scolded for my lapse in decorum by yet another lesbian critic who had witnessed this exchange. I was, in her opinion, not taking myself seriously enough and insulting the intellectual endeavors of those who had my best interests in mind. She was not exactly mollified by my only partially facetious response that being a lesbian has so few rewards in this society that if "liking girls" is no longer part of it, I see no reason to be one.

If I have learned anything from this incident, it is the almost ferocious extent to which the very word "lesbian" is overdetermined—even to the breaking point of Lockean epistemology—among lesbians themselves, much less the general public. Accordingly, I assume that expectations about what this book will be and do will therefore be overdetermined, to some extent and by some readers, even before it is read. For that reason, I would like to clarify at the very outset what this book is and what it is not.

This book does not purport to be a lesbian treatise on narrative theory. In recent years several lesbian critics have produced highly commendable theoretical studies of what is entailed in the narration of lesbianism. These include Judith Roof's *The Lure of Knowledge* and, more recently, *Come as You Are*; Elizabeth Meese's *[Sem]erotics: Theorizing Lesbian: Writing*; Annamarie Jagose's *Lesbian Utopics*; and Marilyn R. Farwell's *Heterosexual Plots and Lesbian Narratives*. All of these works are indispensable to a theoretical understanding of the at best uneasy relationship between lesbianism and the conventions of narratives. While I am deeply indebted to all these critics, I do not attempt to replicate or enlarge upon their work here nor revisit the same fields; rather than being an exploration of lesbianism and narrative *theory*, this book is an examination of the function of lesbianism—or, more specifically, a socially and culturally ingrained *fear* of lesbianism and the stigma pertaining thereunto—in specific narrative *texts*.

Nor is this a Freudian study of lesbianism. This, too, has been the focus of a number of significant works by lesbian scholars in recent years, including Teresa de Lauretis's *The Practice of Love: Lesbian Sexuality and Perverse Desire*, Noreen O'Connor and Joanna Ryan's *Wild Desires and Mistaken Identities: Lesbianism and Psychoanalysis*; and the aforementioned works by Judith Roof. My debt to Freudian theory is, no doubt, apparent; indeed, the perceptions of the authors of and the characters in the texts I examine are in virtually all cases informed by the extent to which Freudian discourse (and the earlier discourses of medical sexology) were internalized by society at the time of their composition. Yet, once again, this is not an attempt to expand or revisit previously explored territory.

Instead, this volume is an exploration of a recurring scenario that I have noted in twentieth-century British women's fictions, a means of representing and narrating those anxieties that inform and thwart erotic desire between women, a desire at times so forbidden, so formidable, and, as I have already argued, so *overdetermined* that many of those who experience it (or narrate or represent it) cannot call it by its proper name, perhaps cannot call it by any name at all. If I may return to my initial story, this is, in a sense, an exploration of the how various British women authors have novelistically calculated the high-risk stakes and the penalties incurred as a result of "liking girls."

That much being said, several other matters remain to be clarified. In Thomas Pynchon's *The Crying of Lot 49*, several characters come across a couple engaged in what appears to be a new and decidedly "kinky" sexual practice. Given the "otherness" that they think they see and determining that it must accordingly be foreign in origin, one of them asks, "Is that a London thing you're doing?" (38). As I have limited this study to twentieth-century British women authors, the same question might pertain here. No, this is not a "London thing" I am doing. I do not wish to suggest that there is anything particularly "British" about lesbian panic, nor do I wish to suggest that the paradigm I elaborate is in any way peculiar to women writers or even to the twentieth century. Rather, I have limited my range so as to be able to look at the evolution of this trope in a single legal system and cultural milieu over a limited span of time—the approximately seventy-five years between Virginia Woolf and Jeanette Winterson. In this way, I have reduced the possibility of "flattening out" the many variables that a more comprehensive selection would involve. I also feel that the literature of this particular national and historical period is particularly rich in examples of gender and sexuality variance, and that its potential remains yet to be tapped.

I cannot, in this study, possibly hope to contain every example of lesbian panic in literature, or in Anglophone literature, or in women's fiction, or even in my own specific field of twentieth-century British women's fiction. I think of this not as a limit, however, but as an opening. I feel certain that examples of lesbian panic are there to be found in the literature and other cultural artifacts of every nation and every language and every period written by authors of every sexual and gender persuasion; one of the few prerequisites for lesbian panic, it seems to me, is a situation in which a growing consciousness on the part of women of their own bodies and desires—what Virginia Woolf calls "this very queer knowledge"—collides with the mores of a society in which "liking girls" is proscribed and vilified. Thus I regard this work not as a final word on the topic but as an opening, an invitation to further dialogue on an issue that, historically speaking, has long been invisible in plain sight.

ACKNOWLEDGMENTS

NO WORK THAT REQUIRES a tremendous degree of effort, such as this one, can come to fruition without the cooperation and assistance of many others. This book has gone through many permutating shapes and purposes in its five years of existence prior to publication. It was, at first, what seemed to be chaotic mental synapse that struck me one summer day in 1991 while reading under the California sun; chaotic because it threatened to disrupt all my notions about the dissertation I was planning to write on twentieth-century British women writers and their use of irony. Soon thereafter, the initial concept evolved into a conference paper, delivered at the 1992 Modern Language Association convention in New York City. As this paper developed, not only did the idea overwhelm my original dissertation, it *became* the dissertation. This volume, then, is only the most recent configuration of this "book of changes." Throughout its period of evolution, I have accumulated many debts of gratitude.

First of all, I thank the best of all possible dissertation co-chairs, Anne K. Mellor and Michael North of the Department of English, University of California, Los Angeles. Throughout this work's graduate school phase, both of them showed, each in her or his respective manner, just the right combination of patience and impatience with me—and always knew which of the opposing dynamics was the appropriate one to apply at any given time. Both, too, were incredibly generous in matters of time, advice, and personal concern, particularly during some very bleak moments. I thank, too, Kathryn Norberg, Jayne Lewis, King-Kok Cheung, and Kathleen Komar, who all participated at various points in my qualifying examinations and on the dissertation committee. I am grateful as well to the UCLA Center for the Study of Women and its committee members for awarding an earlier version of this text the Mary Wollstonecraft Dissertation Prize, and to Penny Kanner, who most magnanimously established and endowed this prize.

Special thanks are also due to members of the academic community who have freely given advice and encouragement over time. Lillian Faderman, initially in her pedagogical capacity while visiting professor at the University of California, Los Angeles, and later as *Between Men/Between Women* series editor for Columbia University Press, has never flagged in her support. Terry Castle was another early supporter who has seen this work through many of its various stages; I thank her for her extraordinary professional and personal kindnesses and advice. Eve Kosofsky Sedgwick has been an inspiration; I thank her for her graciousness and good wishes when I discussed this project with her. Other members of the profession, particularly Regina Barreca, Eileen Barrett, David Bergman, Patricia Cramer, Karla Jay, Margaret Higonnet, Charles Mahoney, Jean Marsden, and Judith Roof, have given advice and support in their respective ways. I particularly thank Professor Roof for prepublication access to the manuscript of her most recent book, *Come as You Are: Sexuality and Narrative*. Fay Weldon's ever-amusing comments on my discussion of her work have been most welcome. Ann Miller, Associate Executive Editor for the *Between Men/Between Women* series, has shown heroic patience, understanding, and compassion through all my professional and personal vicissitudes and peregrinations in the course of the production of this text. Manuscript editor Susan Heath has done an admirable job of assisting me in clarifying passages whose meanings were probably known only to myself and in sorting out all the postdissertation clutter that remained, revenantlike, even after my own revisions. Susan Pensak, as always, has done a tremendous job of seeing this book through the final stages of production.

I also extend my thanks to those who taught me when I was an undergraduate at California State University, Dominguez Hills, and have since become valued friends and colleagues. Violet Jordain, my first mentor, and Lois Feuer have always been lifesavers but never more so than during the final, daunting months of my writing the dissertation. Lila Geller, Michael

Shaffer, Marilyn Sutton, and Sharon Klein (presently of California State University, Northridge) have constantly given their ongoing support to my academic progress.

It would be wrong to say that the period during which this work took shape was not, at times, fraught with personal distress. I got by, to paraphrase an old song, with more than a little help from my friends and relatives. To Robert Arambel, Colleen Jaurretche, Aline Marguet, Sheila Rhodes, and Marlene Villarreal, the friends who *did* save my life, a group whom I affectionately dub my "psychic friends network," I extend my gratitude and love. I want to acknowledge my sisters Joan DeVillier and Mary Louise Monahan and my niece Linda DeVillier for encouraging me as well.

Finally, to my sister Kate Lanehart I owe a tremendous debt of thanks for a lifetime of generosity, love, and kindness far above and beyond the call of sororal duty. She has never let me down. I dedicate this book to her.

Lesbian Panic

INTRODUCTION

Toward an Axiom of Lesbian Panic

What is woman? Panic, general alarm for an active defense. Frankly, it is a problem that the lesbians do not have.

—Monique Wittig, "The Straight Mind"

Nothing happened. Nothing! Nothing!

—Virginia Woolf, *To the Lighthouse*

lost gone away no never nothing ever happened

—Maureen Duffy, *The Microcosm*

LET US CONSIDER A FAMILIAR SCENARIO: A young woman, courted by an aggressive and impetuous young man, is more far more deeply attached to her daring and androgynous female companion. One evening in a garden, the passion between the two women reaches a climactic point. They kiss; but their moment of *jouissance* is disrupted by the appearance of the young man, who ridicules them in their socially awkward juxtaposition. Upset by this incident, the young woman abandons both her suitors and marries a relatively undemanding and uninteresting admirer. Afterward, her life becomes one of external privilege and respectability, which serves to mask the sexual repression, depression, and pointlessness of her quotidian existence.

Or another: A popular and flamboyant teacher, middle-aged and never married, attracts a coterie of schoolgirls. One girl, frustrated by being less than first in her teacher's affections, attempts to draw closer to her, at least metaphysically, by engaging in an affair with the older woman's male lover. When this liaison comes to a crisis, the student publicly exposes and denounces the teacher's seditious political beliefs. The disgraced teacher is dismissed from her position; the student retreats to the celibate homosociality of the convent.

Or still another: Two divorced mothers share a flat. This arrangement not only provides a certain economy in terms of housing expense and a system of mutual child care that allows them to conduct their various affairs with men, it also serves as the foundation of the close friendship between them as they face the challenges of life as "free women." But one woman's lover, a psychiatrist, warns her that her living arrangements with the other woman are not "good for her," implying that their relationship is unconsciously lesbian. Accordingly, she moves out of her friend's home and rents an expensive flat of her own. Her lover subsequently abandons her, and, in her solitude, she suffers a nervous breakdown.

And, finally, another: A highly respectable, sixtyish widow, in possession of a lavish house, a family, and a doting male admirer, becomes obsessed with finding two girlhood friends whom she has not seen in fifty years. When, through elaborate machinations, she is reunited with them, she desires the constant companionship of one of them, a successful and unmarried businesswoman whose private life is surrounded by secretiveness. After a pleasant outing, she pleads with her friend to retire and come live with her; her friend demurs. She asks if her friend is a lesbian, and, without directly answering the question, the friend angrily leaves. Subsequently, the widow is found unconscious from a head injury, the result of striking her head against the wall in her frustration and shame.

If these scenarios sound familiar, they indeed are. They stand as crucial turning points in four widely read novels by some of the more celebrated female authors of the early and middle twentieth century; namely, Virginia Woolf's *Mrs. Dalloway* (1925), Muriel Spark's *The Prime of Miss Jean Brodie* (1961), Doris Lessing's *The Golden Notebook* (1962), and Elizabeth Bowen's *The Little Girls* (1964), respectively. Yet despite the familiarity of these narrative incidents and the considerable amount of critical attention given these writers and their texts, they have heretofore remained undefined as what, I posit, they in fact are: narrative manifestations of lesbian panic. In terms of narrative, lesbian panic is, quite simply, the disruptive action or reaction that occurs when a character—or, conceivably, an author—is either unable or unwilling to confront or reveal her own lesbianism or lesbian desire. Typically, a female character, fearing discovery of her covert or unarticulated lesbian desires—whether by the object of her desires, by other characters, or even by herself—and motivated by any of the factors previously described, lashes out directly or indirectly at another woman, resulting in emotional or physical harm to herself or others. This destructive reaction may be as sensational as suicide or homicide, or as subtle and vague as a generalized neurasthenic malaise. In any instance, the character is led by her sense of panic to commit irrational or illogical acts that inevitably work to the disadvantage or harm of herself or others.

While this study is not, strictly speaking, a purely psychoanalytical approach to the narratives examined, a clinical description of the symptoms of "panic," a condition classified within the larger category of anxiety disorders, is useful in shaping the definition of the phenomenon that occurs so frequently in the narratives under consideration here:

> [A] *panic attack* is defined as a period of intense fear or discomfort in which the person experiences . . . shortness of breath or smothering sensations; dizziness, unsteady feelings, or faintness; palpitations or accelerated heart rate; trembling or shaking; sweating; choking; nausea or abdominal distress; depersonalization or derealization; numbness or tingling sensations; flushes (hot flashes) or chills; chest pain or discomfort; fear of dying; and fear of going crazy or doing something uncontrolled.
>
> (Norton, Walker, and Ross 8–9)

The physical symptoms, while described to some extent in novelistic episodes of lesbian panic, are of secondary significance in comparison with the mental ones: depersonalization, fear of death (often in collusion with an apparent death wish), and, more particularly, the "fear of going crazy or doing something uncontrolled"—or even the actualization of the latter—are among the most common manifestations of lesbian panic in the novel.

Still, as I am not a psychologist but a literary critic, my purpose is not to apply a clinical diagnosis to the motivations of characters in texts; rather, I use this as paradigm, quasi-metaphorically as a means to discover the "unspeakable" or palimpsestic subtext that lies beneath the surface of apparently heterosexually oriented narratives. In doing so, I follow Sedgwick's example in her application of "homosexual panic" to male-authored novels. She does not employ the term in its recent and more common (and unfortunate) connotations of the legal defense strategy far too often utilized to "justify" the generally male perpetrators of violent hate crimes against gay men; rather, Sedgwick draws upon a "relatively rare psychiatric diagnosis" in which the term "homosexual panic" is apt inasmuch as "it refers to the supposed uncertainty about his own sexual identity of the perpetrator of the antigay violence" (*Epistemology* 20). I would modify this phrase slightly to define the key factor in what I here term lesbian panic; namely, that the uncertainty of the female protagonist (or antagonist) about *her* own sexual identity is at the heart of every fictional episode analyzed in this volume. While the parameters of lesbian panic can be seen to permutate over time and in accord to setting and other narrative circumstance, the anxiety arising from the characters' uncertainty in sexual matters remains a constant.[1]

Despite the tendency of lesbian panic to cover itself—much as the afflicted protagonists described go to great feats of illogic and deception to cover their forbidden desires—that lesbian panic is a recurring narrative scenario, not only in these texts but in many others, *should*, paradoxically, be apparent. Indeed, it strikes me as *so* self-apparent that I have chosen, following Sedgwick's example, to term this concept an "axiom" (*Epistemology* 1–63). But at the same time, once again paradoxically, this axiom does not quite fit the definition of a "truth universally acknowledged," for there has heretofore been a continuing critical reluctance, if not refusal, to see lesbians and lesbianism outside those contemporary and generally demotic narratives clearly labeled "lesbian literature." This has, until very recently, obscured what is very much in plain sight. As a result of this tendency, which Terry Castle aptly cites as the "ghosting of the lesbian" (5), we find novelistic incidents such as those already cited discussed only obliquely in literary criticism—when they are discussed at all. For example, in the scenario from Bowen's *The Little Girls*, a richly suggestive and momentarily explicit dialogue transpires between Dinah, the central character, and Clare ("Mumbo"), her businesswoman friend, after Clare declines an offer to live with Dinah, and Dinah, speaking tangentially about the male neighbor with whom she maintains an affectionate relationship, hypothesizes that "boredom is part of love":

> "That I deny!"
> "Well, of affection."
> "That I doubt."
> "Then you've no affections.—Mumbo, are you a Lesbian?"
> "Anything else, would you like to know?"
> "I only wondered."
> "You 'only wondered' whether Sheikie had killed anyone."
> "She said, 'not exactly.' "
> "Shall we leave this at that?"
> "Are you annoyed?"
> "Why? . . . As you remarked at that same time, 'People like to be taken an interest in.' That is true of all of us. . . . All the same, you

> know, one can injure feeling. You are wrong in saying that I have no affections."
>
> "I don't care what you are!"
>
> "That is the worst thing you have said yet."
>
> "But I care for you! . . . And you care for me—or so I had thought? I wanted you. I wanted you to be there—here, I mean. Whatever you think of yourself, you are very strong. . . . Stay with me for a little, can't you?"
>
> (197)

This passage, which begs explication for its rhetoric of "unspeakable" seduction, is nothing less than a homoerotic overture made by one woman to another. It immediately precedes Clare's rejection of Dinah's repeated invitation to stay the night and Dinah's self-inflicted physical injury. But while it functions as the key to the denouement (in which resolution can only come about with Clare's return to the bedridden invalid Dinah), it is nonetheless elided in criticism of Bowen's novel. One of the more explicit commentaries informs us that, "taking umbrage at one of Dinah's remarks, Clare gives her an objective characterization of herself" (Austin 63); no more, no less.

As an alternative to such elision through euphemism, literary critics have also dealt with the problem of discussing through association those incidents that I am defining as lesbian panic. Thus in one discussion of Anita Brookner's *A Friend from England* (1987), the reader is informed that the protagonist, Rachel Kennedy, is "a female version . . . of John Marcher in Henry James's 'The Beast in the Jungle.'" (Sadler 135). Although this particular critique offers no further elaboration of its allusion to James's short story, this observation is, for the duly perceptive, far from trivial. Rather, it becomes the first term of a critical syllogism, the second term of which can be found in *Epistemology of the Closet*, in which "The Beast in the Jungle" serves as the foundational text for Sedgwick's elaboration of her paradigm of "homosexual panic" (182–212). Accordingly, I would argue that in this specific case the third term would provide a name for the elaborate and irrational machinations of Brookner's character in her obsession with the insipid daughter of a parvenu family; that name is lesbian panic. But in a more general sense this previously unarticulated third term must stand as a bulwark of an even greater critical concern; that is, that the panic evoked by presence of the lesbian or even the perception of lesbianism has long functioned as a pervasive pattern in literature representing women's lives and consciousness. It is time, then, that we call it by name and perceive it for what it is.

The model I propose bears, of course, a resemblance to Sedgwick's concept of homosexual panic. It is not, indeed cannot be, a systematic transferal across sexual boundaries because of the substantial historical differences in the social regulation of male and female sexual expression. Sedgwick, following Gayle Rubin and Luce Irigaray, sees male-dominated social order as based on "homosocial desire" (*Between Men* 1) and the exchange of women. This system of exchange is, in its most mundane configurations, accomplished through erotic triangulation, whereby men enact their desire for one another through the medium of the shared woman. In this manner, male desire is sublimated and controlled in the name of maintaining power relations between men. A breakdown in this system—that is, the threatened enactment of male homosexuality—sets the stage for homosexual panic, the irrational and often violent response of one man to the real or imagined sexual attentions of another.[2]

What is at stake for a man in Sedgwick's model is his status in the male power structure; to enact a sexual preference for another man is to forfeit one's subject position in the exchange of women and, by extension, to forfeit one's subjectivity. Yet this model does little to explain the dynamics of lesbian panic, for, under this system, the threatened loss of subjectivity that impels a man to homosexual panic is the normative condition of women, the objects of exchange. As objects, women cannot construct a parallel system of exchange of men beyond the occasional erotic triangle, other than in narratives that do not aspire to verisimilitude.[3] Within a text, such triangulation may allow for a tacit, unarticulated mode of female homoerotic desire or give rise to some stirring of lesbian consciousness.[4] But while it would follow that lesbianism would perforce involve the formation of female sexual subjectivity, the realization of their desire is not, for most female fictional characters, a liberatory move. Typically, what is at stake for a woman under such conditions is nothing less than economic survival, as the object of exchange is inevitably dependent on the exchanger for her continued perceived worth; indeed, for a "commodity," in Irigaray's term, to lack exchange value is tantamount to meaninglessness. In many historical texts, moreover, lesbianism frequently lacks a name, much less an acknowledged or acceptable identity. Accordingly, the fear of the loss of identity and value as object of exchange, often combined with the fear of responsibility for one's own sexuality, is a characteristic response; it is from precisely such fears that lesbian panic arises.

The conditions of lesbian panic have long been inscribed in narratives by and about women. Most of the influential texts forming the "Female Tradition" delineated by Virginia Woolf, Ellen Moers, Elaine Showalter, and others generally contain some variation of these conditions and almost inevitably end with the heroine's marriage.[5] As Rachel Blau DuPlessis observes, such narrative conventions promote the "cultural and narrative ideology" (xi) of heterosexuality of which they are products:

> As a narrative pattern, the romance plot muffles the main female character, represses quest, valorizes heterosexual as opposed to homosexual ties, incorporates individuals within couples as a sign of their person and narrative success. The romance plot separates love and quest, values sexual asymmetry . . . is based on extremes of sexual difference, and evokes an aura around the couple itself. In short, the romance plot, broadly speaking, is a trope for the sex-gender system as a whole. . . . [T]he conventional outcomes [are] strongly identified with certain roles for women.
>
> (5–6)

Indeed, those narratives that do not end with marriage (e.g., those "failed" romance plots of seduction and betrayal) end with the female protagonist's death, thus indicating the limited options available to women under this "sex-gender system."

Because the narrative closure in such texts relies on the female protagonist being subsumed into institutional heterosexuality (or being annihilated), lesbianism may be said to have no legitimate or fixed place in the narrative conventions that have historically informed female-authored texts since the great upsurge in women's writing in the eighteenth century. Yet paradoxically, because the lesbian—or even the abstract concept of lesbianism—is at odds with the prescribed outcomes of such traditional plots, female homoerotic desire, or the threat of it, is assured a place, albeit a dubious or ambiguous one, in women's narratives. If we accept as a given that fictional modes rely upon a basis of conflict and resolution, then, as D. A. Miller has observed, "the state of quiescence assumed by a novel before the beginning and supposedly recovered by it at the end" is "nonnarratable," and only "instances of disequilibrium, suspense, and general insufficiency" can provide "incitements" to narrative (ix).[6] Judith Roof, employing Freud's paradigm of "normal" (i.e., hetero) sexuality as a central narrative shaping cultural ideologies, is more to the point on the specific function of disruptive "perversions" in the shaping of stories:

> Freud situates the perversions as the spot where the story falls apart, a spot that is also a part of the story, serving its function as inhibition or dissociation only in relation to the narrative's ultimate end, "the discharge of sexual substances.." . . [Perversions] threaten to substitute themselves for this normal end pleasure. . . . Supplanting the proper conclusion, perversions cut the story short, in a sense preventing a story at all by tarrying in its preparations. But this premature abridgment only has significance in relation to the "normal" . . . Perversion, then, acquires its meaning as perversion precisely from its threat to truncate the story; it distorts the narrative, preventing the desirable confluence of sexual aim and object and male and female, precluding the discharge of sexual substances, and hindering reproduction.
>
> (*Come as You Are* xx–xxi)

The very presence of the "perverse" and "perverted" lesbian, which can surely provide any and all of the factors both Miller and Roof delineate, obviously creates not only the conflictual tension necessary to propel the narrative but also requires her eventual disempowerment and banishment from the plot. This forced disappearance is necessary lest she disrupt the marriage plot, which is, after all, little more than a polite, even feminized description of Freud's narrative of the "discharge of sexual substances." Accordingly, Roof argues, the presence of the lesbian functions as a pretext for the reassertion of the heterosexual plot. This sort of resolution, I suggest, is frequently accomplished through the medium of lesbian panic.

An early and not very subtle example of the lesbian as a factor of narratability and disequilibrium in the context of the romance plot can be found in Maria Edgeworth's *Belinda* (1801).[7] Edgeworth's central plot line is a simple one: Belinda Portman, a marriageable young woman, is introduced into worldly society for the explicit purpose of acquiring a suitable husband. In the course of doing so, Belinda finds herself unwittingly in the midst of various erotic triangulations, configurations that are variously comprised of both men and women or women only, including one that makes the heroine the term of exchange between a mother and her daughter. While all these emotional entanglements serve on some level to try the heroine's virtue and threaten, at least indirectly, to tarnish her public reputation, the greatest danger to her marriage market valuation is that posed by Harriot Freke, a woman who habitually dresses in male attire, participates in duels, prowls the streets of London at night in search of excitement and trouble, and leads other women astray to join in her adventures. Mrs. Freke has, moreover, served as a catalyst for the spiritual (if not public) "ruin" of Belinda's sponsor, Lady Delacour, who, it would seem, had once been much enamored of this singular woman. Belinda resists Mrs. Freke's attempt to "carry [her] off in triumph" (225), but subsequently, upon seeing Mrs. Freke and her latest conquest Miss Moreton cavorting in public, she exhibits what the post-Freudian reader would identify as hysteria, clinging to her male companions for protection in fear that Mrs. Freke will abduct her to avenge the earlier rejection. Mrs. Freke is subsequently removed from the plot with violent and heavy-handed symbolism: as she engages in a voyeuristic espial on her erstwhile companion Lady Delacour, her leg is mangled by a man-trap set at the foot of a cherry tree. So injured, she vanishes, unable to persist in her caprices. Subsequently, and conceivably consequently, Lady Delacour repents her earlier conduct and Belinda marries the reformed rake Clarence Hervey, who is, ironically, first introduced in the text as a cohort of Mrs. Freke.

As awkward as *Belinda* may be in its narrative execution and its frequently bewildering character motivations, it nonetheless stands as an outstanding example of the "rules" of the courtship plot: the dangerous and even seductive "masculine" woman makes the plot interesting—arguably Mrs. Freke is the most interesting and least conflicted character in this work—but she must be sacrificed lest she stand between the heroine and the economic security and social respectability of the marriage bed.

That these "rules" are firmly in place some four decades later is clearly and far more subtly evinced by Charlotte Brontë's *Jane Eyre*, a novel that has since become a metanarrative of women's writing. The orphan Jane Eyre finds the first real happiness of her life in the all-female environment of the Lowood School, and, with the opportunity to become a teacher there upon the completion of her own studies, she would, conceivably, be quite happy to spend the rest of her days there. Were this to occur, however, there would be no Rochester, no courtship plot, indeed, no *Jane Eyre* as we know it. Accordingly, the possibility of any homoerotic idyll is disrupted first when Jane's beloved Helen Burns, asleep in her companion's arms, succumbs to a typhus epidemic, and second by the seemingly sudden marriage of Miss Temple, the teacher capable of expanding her charge's "considerable organ of Veneration" (40). As the loss of these two loves gives her no reason to remain at Lowood, the heroine embarks on the romantic quest that leads her to Thornfield Hall and its master. When later in the novel the potential of homosocial life with the Rivers sisters recurs (along with the profferment of a celibate marriage from their brother), Jane "hears" the voice of heterosexual romance beckoning her return to Rochester.[8]

Significantly, aside from Belinda Portman's transient fit of phobia and Jane Eyre's "psychic" experience, neither heroine engages in the irrationality characteristic of lesbian panic nor does she respond to the threat of the lesbianism with physical violence. These protagonists merely enact the predominant cultural epistemologies of heterosexuality as the conventions of their genre require without questioning its presumed superiority over any alternative narrative. Typically in late eighteenth- and early nineteenth-century texts, the "threat" is given no name other than the nebulous label of impropriety. Nina Auerbach notes that in this period "few . . . were certain of what [lesbianism] was" (390); the romantic heroine, for whom innocence is a generic prerequisite, could not, accordingly, betray any direct knowledge of forbidden sexuality.[9] The locus of lesbian panic in these texts, then, is not in the psyche of the heroine, as it is in the twentieth-century narratives I shall discuss. Rather, what is in evidence here is a curious form of authorial lesbian panic: the woman writer creates a compelling and "dangerous" (and thus interesting) female character only to destroy her so that the narrative ideologies of institutional heterosexuality may be fulfilled. Yet because the novel is, as Bakhtin suggests, a dialogic form, while the embodiment of lesbian desire may vanish from the narrative, her discourse remains. In this manner, Harriot Freke's quasi-Wollstonecraftian exhortation to sexual liberation for women and Helen Burn's stoical Johnsonian resistance to the dangers of the imagination—discourses inevitably at odds with the epistemology of the romance plot—remain as suggestions of alternative narratives, written, ironically, by the very hand that erased their speakers.

Belinda and *Jane Eyre* are, of course, products of a culture that predates not only Freud but also medical sexology. While the homoerotic attachments that abound in either text can be construed as sexually "innocent," particularly by those who hold that homosexuality as we presently define it did not exist prior to the formulations of later nineteenth- and early twentieth-century medical sexologists, by the end of the nineteenth century the pathologized stigma of lesbianism would almost automatically attach itself to such representations of emotional attachments between women.[10] Bonnie Zimmerman has demonstrated (126–44) that the degree and frequency of affectional bonds between women is significantly decreased over time in the writings of George Eliot, for example, as the discourses of sexology gain currency in British intellectual circles.[11]

The naming and defining of lesbianism, while effectively obviating the discourse of "romantic friendship" between women, also created new narrative possibilities, as evinced by various fin-de-siècle fictions of the Decadent or "New Woman" modes. But while such texts allow for a representation of lesbianism as such, they do not override the need for the narrative strategy of lesbian panic. Rather, they exacerbate that need through the sensationalistic presentation of the lesbian figure as particularly dangerous, amoral, or evil.[12] As the lesbian must therefore be destroyed for the sake of men and women alike, her violent removal from the plot, recalling that of Harriot Freke, becomes even more deeply inscribed as a narrative pattern. Almost as soon as this pattern is in place as a literary trope, shifts in social consciousness relative to a growing demand for women's suffrage and professions for women nevertheless instigate the formulation of new plots in women's fictions. Many modernist women writers and their successors, as DuPlessis observes, "invented or deployed [narrative strategies] . . . explicitly to delegitimate romance plots and related narratives":

> These strategies involve reparenting in invented families, fraternal-sororal ties temporarily reducing romance, and emotional attachment to women in bisexual love plots, female bonding, and lesbianism. . . . As well, the writers undertake a reassessment of the mechanisms of social insertion of woman through the family house, the private sphere, and patriarchal hierarchies, inventing narratives that offer, in the multiple individual and the collective protagonist, an alternative to individual quests and couple formation.
>
> (xi)

But while such attempts to delegitimate the romance plot might render lesbianism or other forms of love between women attractive alternatives to predominant narrative ideology, they do not perforce legitimate lesbianism as a result. The exchange of women, as much modern and contemporary literature indicates, has stalwartly resisted its own dismantling, and the woman who would forfeit her own exchange value does so at the risk of social and economic marginalization. Thus, while lesbianism has become both narratable and representable in twentieth-century fictional discourse, the ongoing pathologizing and marginalization of lesbianism virtually necessitate lesbian panic as a narrative adjunct.

The scenarios presented at the beginning of this chapter underscore this point. In *Mrs. Dalloway*, for instance, Woolf literally backgrounds the romance plot, displacing it from its usual predominance by reducing it to a recurrent memory that is inextricably entwined with the memory of lesbian panic. While a cause-and-effect relationship is thus created between the past disruption of homoerotic desire in the garden and the emotional stagnation of Clarissa Dalloway's life in the present, the apparent unresolvability of the central protagonist's sexual dilemma is underscored by the juxtaposition of her narrative with those of her two younger alter egos. For Septimus Warren Smith, suicide offers a surcease from the homosexual panic that manifests itself as madness. Simultaneously Doris Kilman, a woman who, however futilely, would attempt to create for herself a homoerotic narrative outside "the family house, the private sphere, and patriarchal hierarchies," becomes the monstrous embodiment of the embitterment that ensues from the social ostracism her refusal to participate in the exchange of women provokes.

Conversely, in *The Prime of Miss Jean Brodie* and *The Golden Notebook*, Spark and Lessing respectively create narratives in which the female protagonist seeks to define herself as a heterosexual woman outside the structures of institutional heterosexuality. In their quests to become autonomous sexual beings, both Jean Brodie and Anna Wulf simultaneously—and, for the most part, incongruously—position themselves outside formal hierarchical structures of exchange yet attempt not only to retain but even inflate their exchange value as "special" women. Indeed, as part of their self-envisioned exceptionalism, they participate in a modified exchange of men with the other women in their lives. Accordingly, breakdowns in the relationships between the women characters, combined with male reluctance to accept object status, create the conditions for lesbian panic in both narratives, and, as a result, both novels find closure in rather desperate remedies. Not only are both Jean Brodie and Sandy ultimately desexualized by their consequent circumstances in Spark's novel, they are also effectively rendered non-narratable since the condition of an aged, broken woman is, for the most part, as quiescent as that of a contemplative nun. In *The Golden Notebook*, by contrast, Anna and her friend Molly choose some degree of reassimilation into the structures of institutional heterosexuality, as marriage counselor and wife respectively, conceivably as an acceptable (and non-narratable) alternative to madness and chaos.

Of the four novels I mention at the beginning of this chapter, however, Bowen's *The Little Girls* most drastically reconfigures the relationship of lesbian panic to heterosexual plots. Following Woolf, Bowen focuses her narrative on the life of a central older protagonist who is left to ponder the meaning of the past. In Bowen's novel, however, the two alter egos are the protagonist's contemporaries, former classmates in a girls' school some fifty years earlier. Simultaneously, the romance plots in which these women were involved during their years of separation are backgrounded to the point where they are merely an unrepresented given, a blank space between the two dichotomized narratives that matter: that of undefined longings and ruptures in the past and that of an awkward disruptive attempt in later life to explain and heal the lingering hurt. In this manner the original function of lesbian panic as a disruption of the romance plot is transformed and reversed; in *The Little Girls*, lesbian panic is the central narrative, while the narrative of romance, courtship, and marriage is reduced to a subordinate disruption.

Examined chronologically, the novels of Woolf, Spark, Lessing, and Bowen delineate the decline of the romance plot as a viable narrative during the late modernist period. As women writers became increasingly concerned with representing events other than courtship and marriage in women's lives, so did the need arise to create new "stories" reflecting new social and sexual ideologies.[13] Particularly since the 1970s, with the advent of much feminist and lesbian discourse, the prospect of lesbianism as a narrative alternative has informed many female-authored fictions to greater or lesser degree, as has the counterdiscourse of homophobia and heterosexism. Consequently, lesbian panic has not only become a more frequent phenomenon in contemporary fiction, it has also has taken on a variety of configurations, whether in novels that adhere to the fading "Great Tradition" or in those that partake in a peculiarly female-authored form of postmodernism.

An example of the former may be found in Anita Brookner's *A Friend from England*. Here, both the author and her novel quite consciously evoke the ambiance of silences and secrets that permeates the narratives of now-traditional novelists such as Henry James and Virginia Woolf. But the ultimate futility of protagonist Rachel Kennedy's obsessional quest to retain the lovely but utterly insipid Heather Livingstone as an infantilized entity in an idealized and static family romance serves to illustrate the impossibility of arranging late twentieth-century life or narrative plots according to nineteenth-century or even modernist paradigms. Conversely, as the postmodern narrative breaks down traditional "rules" that govern the structures and closures of narrative, so does it possess the potential for representing lives and actions that defy traditional sexual roles and mores—as does lesbianism.

Yet this linkage of lesbianism and postmodernism is far from unproblematic, particularly in an epistemological sense. As Laura Doan notes, "disagreement abounds . . . over what constitutes a 'lesbian' and what is understood by the term *postmodern*" (ix). Indeed, the epistemological terror inherent in the very lack of fixed meaning attached to the word "lesbian" is at the root of much of the lesbian panic in the novels I discuss. The difficulty—if not the impossibility—of defining who or what is "lesbian" undermines the surety and clarity that the structures and role assignments of institutional heterosexuality assume to provide.[14] Accordingly, while female homoerotic tension fulminates in these novels, the word "lesbian" itself is nowhere in sight, unless it appears as an accusation one woman character utilizes as a projection against another, generally to deflect any suspicion of her own desires.

To link this free-floating signifier with another, then, is doubly problematic. Yet, while recognizing the manifold difficulty of linking the two terms, postmodernism, as Judith Roof notes, "provides a legitimating metanarrative for a lesbian identity politics" (48). By extension, I would add, it provides a means by which all those various entities that might be deemed "lesbian" may be narrated explicitly and without the recourse to unspeakability and unnameability that marks the texts I have discussed so far.[15] And while I am loath to assume the hubristic authority of defining "postmodernity" with any finality or certainty, I believe that certain parameters or characteristics may be attributed to what I am deeming postmodern narratives of lesbian panic that coincide with their ability to present their subject matter in an explicit manner.

The novels by Brigid Brophy, Maureen Duffy, Beryl Bainbridge, Emma Tennant, Fay Weldon, and Jeanette Winterson that I will examine in the final chapter all evince, to some extent, the "range of aesthetic practices" that, according to Patricia Waugh, are characteristic of early 1980s definitions of the postmodern, particularly "playful irony, parody, parataxis, self-consciousness, [and] fragmentation," rather than the "pervasive cynicism" the designation has since come to signify (5). Simultaneously, they partake in the "playgiarism" Carol McGuirk finds a hallmark of much postmodern British women's writings: a "strong . . . element of parodic allusion [to canonical "classics"] in plot, characterization, and style" (947). In their refusal to assume the rhetorical stance of justified female victimage in their explorations of lesbian panic, these texts are applications of Waugh's "first lesson of postmodernism": that "it is impossible to step out of that which one contests . . . one is always implicated in the values one chooses to challenge" (33). Accordingly, by foregrounding lesbian panic in their narratives while employing these strategic challenges to past tradition—and, indeed, to "authority" in all its various meanings—these texts have delineated the means by which this phenomenon may be forthrightly, even brutally, represented.

But as a lesbian critic I must ask if this latest stage in narrative evolution, so to speak, is enough. This study documents the movement from lesbian panic as an unconscious mechanism in eighteenth- and nineteenth-century courtship plots through modernist stratagems of silence and innuendo to the frank and often violent explication of repressed female homoerotic desire peculiar to postmodernism. But even if it is now possible to narrate lesbian panic directly, are we yet able to define lesbianism itself, much less narrate it?

In her metafictive *De Bewondering*, Dutch critic and novelist Anja Meulenbelt, speaking through the persona of her lesbian novelist protagonist, makes a sardonic observation on the manifold problems of categorization, sexuality, and narrative: "Novels are not lesbian . . . Novels have no sexual preference. People have sexual preferences. Women are lesbians, some women, all women as far as I'm concerned" (114).[16] Her ironic and predatory spin on Jill Johnston's Lesbian Nation manifesto notwithstanding, Meulenbelt aptly delineates the conditions that attain in any discussion of lesbian panic as a narrative strategy. Although our narrative ideologies are almost inevitably informed by the conditions of heterocentric society, a novel, in and of itself, is neither queer nor straight; rather, it is a dialogic form that, ideally, encompasses a multiplicity of voices and perspectives and thus resists easy classification in terms of such binary oppositions. But while no novel, not even those devoted primarily or exclusively to the representation of lesbian "lifestyles" may be accurately denoted as "lesbian," the possibility that lesbianism can appear anywhere, even in narratives in which the cultural hegemony of heterosexuality, institutional or otherwise, is accepted as a given, will continue to create the potential for lesbian panic. Any woman *might* be a lesbian—or at least be perceived as one—including oneself. Hence, for fictional women characters, as well as the "real life" counterparts of whom they are the mimetic reflection, the pervasiveness of this threat, will, on some level, continue to obviate closeness and collaboration between women, just as it will continue to supply narratability or a story to be told—as long, that is, as heterosexuality remains a privileged category and women continue to evaluate themselves accordingly.

Clearly, lesbian panic is amply narratable; but can the same be said for lesbianism itself? As we try to invent new stories that need not rely on the ideologies of heterosexuality for their strategies and closure, can we find a way to tell a story that neither posits lesbianism as a fearsome danger nor merely reduces it to a simulacrum of heterosexual romance? I would like to believe that recent explicit narratives of lesbian panic, such those authored by Bainbridge and Weldon, serve to deconstruct the narrative of lesbian panic so that we might, eventually, just get over it. At the same time, we must create narrative strategies that carve out a space in fiction for lesbianism as a thing in and of itself, without the flattening effect of "normalizing" it or likening it to something that it is not. More than a decade ago, Catharine R. Stimpson envisioned, after Roland Barthes, the possibility of the lesbian novel of "zero degree deviancy." Yet, given that heterosexuality remains institutionally privileged, it seems unlikely that this ideal can be achieved in any purely mimetic narrative. The recent trend toward magic realism in lesbian fiction, particularly by such authors as Jeanette Winterson, Rebecca Brown, Monique Wittig, Nicole Brossard, Eileen Myles, and others, would seem to indicate as much. But until new narrative strategies become commonplace and as long as the romance plot lingers like a revenant, lesbian panic will remain a recurring phenomenon in female-authored fiction.

CHAPTER ONE

"This Very Queer Knowledge": Virginia Woolf's Narratives of Female Homoerotic Desire

Surely it was time someone invented a new plot, or that the author came out from the bushes.

—Virginia Woolf, *Between the Acts*

IN 1929, AT THE MID-POINT of her literary career, Virginia Woolf, formulating her theory of androgyny in *A Room of One's Own*, asked, "Why do I feel that there are severances and oppositions in the mind, as there are strains from obvious causes on the body?" (97). The causes of these "severances and oppositions," she believed, arose from centuries of social practice that had effectively divided humanity into distinct and separate groupings of male and female, groupings with separate spheres, functions, and roles and, accordingly, vastly separated modes of behavior and thought. Such dichotomies, which inevitably limit an individual's perceptions of the whole in any ethos, must also, Woolf speculates, inhibit and distort the art a dichotomized mind produces: "Perhaps a mind that is purely masculine cannot create, any more than a mind that is purely feminine, I thought" (98).

To break down these barriers, to achieve the mental (if not physical) androgyny Woolf urges, would require no less than the breaking down not only of traditional Victorian constructions of gender, those performed attributes that, according to Judith Butler, "constitut[e] the identity [they are] purported to be" (25) but also of the constructions of sexuality supported by such notions of gender. Carolyn G. Heilbrun notes that because of individual fear (and, by extension, the relative comfort of the path of least resistance) highly restrictive divisions of sex, gender, and sexuality are not easily discarded: "Androgyny appears to threaten men and women even more profoundly in their sexual than in their social roles. There has been a fear, not only of homosexuality or the appearance of homosexuality, but of impotence and frigidity as the consequence of less rigid patterns of sexual behavior" (xi-xii). Accordingly, for Woolf, homosexuality, the fear of homosexuality, and the panic that arises from this fear are integral factors in her artistic endeavors to create individuals who are able to transcend the highly codified gender restrictions of the generations that preceded hers. Ironically, she reveals that both impotence and that female sexual disinterest called frigidity are more apt to result from the restrictive codes of sexual behavior that supposedly preserve social order than from the loosening of those dicta.

Numerous studies have been devoted to Woolf's role in liberating the novel from its rigid nineteenth-century conventions and recreating it as a medium for the aesthetic sensibilities of modernism.[1] Relatively little attention, however, has been given to the extent to which this transformation is, in Woolf's hands, inextricably linked with an exploration of nontraditional gender and sexuality and her quest for a way to articulate these ideas. Few novelists prior to the gay and lesbian liberation movement of the early 1970s have been so extensively involved in exploring lesbian possibilities in narrative form as has Virginia Woolf. Few have examined so closely the dynamics of economics, social class and privilege, medical science, and codes of silence and inhibition that have historically prevented women from acting upon their erotic impulses, particularly with other women. Accordingly, in seeking a new novelistic form—novels, according to a character in *The Voyage Out*, about silence—Woolf analyzes in exacting detail the causes and effects of lesbian panic. And it is through this process that Woolf is able to arrive, at the end of her career, at the representation of the lesbian who, despite her marginality, is nonetheless central to the [re]ordering of society.

In *The Voyage Out*, as a boat carries a band of British tourists up the river into the heart of a South American jungle forest, Terence Hewet sits on deck and reads these enigmatic lines from Walt Whitman's *Leaves of Grass*:

> Whoever you are holding me now in your hand,
> Without one thing all will be useless.
>
> (267)[2]

Whitman's personified book, which reveals and celebrates the secret pleasures of homosexual love only to the percipient reader, warns its peruser, "holding me now in your hand," that without this special knowledge, this "one thing," all efforts to unlock its meaning will be in vain. Terence Hewet, an aspiring novelist who wants "to write a novel about Silence . . . the things people don't say" (216), reads these lines as he prepares to propose marriage to Rachel Vinrace, the protagonist of Woolf's own novel about "the things people don't say." Ironically, in a narrative that superficially resembles a traditional courtship plot, Terence, whom Woolf positions as the facilitator of Rachel's incorporation into institutional heterosexuality, lacks Whitman's "one thing" and accordingly finds himself bereft of the closure such a plot promises.

Whitman's cautionary note, positioned at the beginning of one of the most enigmatic portions of *The Voyage Out*, also serves as caveat to Woolf's reader. If apprehended by a reader blind to the variety of homoerotic possibilities Rachel Vinrace encounters in her abbreviated process of maturation, the text will defy the conventional critical wisdom and present itself as a hopelessly incoherent—if beautiful—literary failure. For such has been the critical heritage of Woolf's first novel, which has long stood as a problematic text to her critics. Because of its position in her oeuvre, however, it demands critical attention. While early, predominantly male critics have routinely praised it as "one of the finest first works by any author" (Fleishman 21), they have also routinely tempered their uncertain admiration for the novel—"whatever its aesthetic merit" (McDowell 73)—with apologies for the impossibility of "mak[ing] its purpose clearer or shed[ding] light on its obscurities" (Guiget 197). In order to discuss this compelling and mysterious work at all, therefore, such critics have generally attempted either to explore the novel's "interesting" use of language and allusions to classical and Renaissance sources or to see it as a traditional novel of courtship, a relic of Woolf's Victorian heritage, inexplicably aborted and subverted at the last moment. The seeming irrationality of the latter possibility can be rationalized as a result of the faulty judgment of a budding genius afflicted with tragic madness. Conversely, feminist critics have subsequently endeavored to perform the task Guiget deemed impossible; yet their attempts to clarify authorial purpose or textual obscurity have focused on discussions of heterosexual awakening, patriarchal oppression of the female characters, or the displacement of the mother-daughter relationship; or they have analyzed the novel as exemplar of the female bildungsroman.

After all these attempts at clarification, *The Voyage Out* remains nonetheless problematic: What is the purpose of a courtship plot in which the heroine dies—willingly or even willfully—before the marriage can ever occur; and what is the purpose of a bildungsroman in which the heroine has so little chance to develop to any very meaningful end, save the rejection of marriage? I would suggest that the greatest shortcoming of these interpretations is a lack of Whitman's "one thing," resulting in an assumption that Woolf privileges heterosexuality—and heterosexual perception—in this text.[3] Conversely, discernment of the lesbian subtext and the episodes of panic that arise therefrom provides a key to the dreadful knowledge Rachel Vinrace derives from her voyage of development; this knowledge informs the denouement through which Woolf first attempts to kill the Angel in the House by destroying the narrative structures that perpetuate her existence.

In undoing the courtship plot, Woolf nevertheless employs many of its traditional features. As in earlier models of lesbian panic, the threat of lesbian desire in *The Voyage Out* is embodied not in the prospective bride/heroine but rather in a secondary female character. Yet unlike Harriot Freke in Maria Edgeworth's *Belinda* or Helen Burns in Charlotte Brontë's *Jane Eyre*, characters whose threatening presence is both intermittent and cut short by mishap, Helen Ambrose is present throughout the narrative, appearing before Rachel and ultimately surviving her. That Helen is initially the primary focus of narration in the beginning chapters and subsequently relinquishes center stage to Rachel has been deemed a structural problem in this work; the enigmatic quality of her presentation, however, compels attention to her motives and desires.

Helen first appears in a state of emotional distress, weeping, ostensibly, at the thought of leaving behind her children while she embarks on a voyage many months in duration.[4] Why her presence on this journey takes priority over her maternal duties is nonetheless unclear, and while her grief is ascribed to this separation, little subsequent reference is made to the children or to her concern for them. Here, as elsewhere in the text, Helen is characterized not by any tangible and absolute qualities but rather by the absence or indefiniteness thereof. Her emotional responses are inconsistent with her actions and thus suggest that the outward signs she presents conceal rather than reveal her motives and feelings. Similarly, her appearance of "normative" British womanhood in marriage and maternity masks the lack of conventionality that places her in contradistinction with other women of her class and status. While most of the minor female characters disport themselves with trivial gossip and concerns, Helen, who passes her time aboard ship reading G. E. Moore's *Principia Ethica*, prefers the company and conversation of intellectual men; and while Clarissa Dalloway can proclaim that she feels for her husband "what my mother and women of her generation felt for Christ" (52), Helen is apparently content in a companionate marriage.[5] Given her ability to negotiate social norms through outward appearance while retaining a sense of individuality, Helen would seem to be able to present the niece entrusted to her tutelage with an acceptable alternative version of the ends of the courtship plot. Yet Helen's own sexual dysphoria, manifested in emotional vacillation, destabilizes her quasimaternal authority over Rachel and climaxes in an otherwise inexplicable display of panic.

As part of her greater structure of elaborate self-masking, Helen's disdain for women's conversation, her preference for male companionship, and her marriage to Ridley Ambrose all give the appearance of male-centeredness and heterosexuality while actually signifying neither. Her contempt for petty femininity is matched by the contempt she feels toward the hypermasculinity of her "big and burly" brother-in-law, Willoughby Vinrace (24). Her interactions with men are primarily intellectual and lacking in flattery and flirtation. Likewise, while her scholar husband relies almost childishly upon her for his comfort and privacy, their relationship, while devoid of any demonstrable sexual passion, is marked by affectionate friendship. Given his long periods of isolation while writing, moreover, Ridley is often absent to Helen even in his presence; indeed, their marriage had achieved a "stage of community" that allowed them "to become unconscious of each other's bodily presence . . . and in general seem to experience all the comfort of solitude without its loneliness" (195). Her contacts with men, then, allow Helen to achieve a sort of privacy and life of the mind similar to that which Rachel wishes to gain through submersion in music. But while the relatively naive Rachel's attempts result in a reinforcement of her unsocialized conditions, Helen's more sophisticated withdrawal provides a façade of matronly privilege and propriety that allows her hidden proclivities to pass undetected, not only in society but in the perceptions of many readers.

Lyndie Brimstone speculates that the lesbianism present in Woolf's texts has, by and large, gone unnoticed because many of her fictional characters are, "like Vita Sackville-West, Violet Trefusis, Vera Brittain and Woolf herself, all seemingly 'normal' women who enjoyed lesbian attachments 'between the lines' of their respectable marriages" (94).[6] Textual evidence of

Helen's lesbianism, accordingly, is concealed quite literally "between the lines" of *The Voyage Out* by means of tacit allusion or indirect representation. An indication of the otherwise unarticulated conditions of the Ambrose marriage may be discerned in one of the rare instances in which Ridley participates in a social gathering. At a tea with various other members of the English party in Santa Marina, Mrs. Thornbury, the quintessential devoted wife and mother, "sweetly" if incongruously responds to one of Ridley's philosophical observations by exclaiming, "You men! Where would you be if it weren't for women!" Ridley, who finds the idle prattle of the company "unsympathetic," "grimly" replies, "Read the *Symposium*" (199). The reference to Plato's discourse on male homosexual love is, understandably, lost on this matron, yet it underscores Ridley's understanding of, if not his covert desire for participation in, an all-male world free from such "feminine" attentions. His response draws the attention of the garrulous Mrs. Flushing, who, although ignorant of the particulars of the text, wonders where she can obtain a translation. But although a subsequent reading of Sappho's "Ode to Aphrodite" will, according to Louise De Salvo, stir "hidden Sapphist tendencies in Mrs. Flushing" (1980 134), Ridley replies that she "will have to learn Greek" (199), indicating his apprehension that her ignorance of "Greek love" as well as the Greek language serves as an obstacle to her understanding.

Even more revealing are the silences that surround many of Helen's conversations, particularly those with the homosexual St. John Hirst. Like Ridley Ambrose, Hirst finds most women intolerably mindless and the social intercourse of men and women revolting. Accordingly, he is relieved and gratified to discover the company of Helen, who is, significantly, "the only woman I've ever met who seems to have the faintest conception of what I mean," one to whom he "could talk quite plainly . . . as one does to a man—about the relations between the sexes" (162). Helen's worldliness and lack of dependence on men renders her *like* a man in Hirst's estimate; at the same time, her apparent lack of sexual interest in men frees Hirst from the burden of paying her the sexual attentions he is loath to give any woman. Encouraged by Helen's knowing response, Hirst quickly engages her in a forthright discussion about all the matters perplexing him, yet the contents of their conversation are so unspeakable that they must be kept not only from the other guests in the crowded ballroom in which they sit but also from the reader. Accordingly, the whole of their "long" conversation is condensed into one paragraph of indirect discourse that remains oblique to those who fail to read "between the lines":

> Certainly a barrier which usually stands fast had fallen, and it was possible to speak of matters which are generally only alluded to between men and women when doctors are present, or the shadow of death. In five minutes he was telling her the history of his life. It was long, for it was full of extremely elaborate incidents, which led on to a discussion of the principles on which morality is founded, and thus to several very interesting matters, which even in this ballroom had to be discussed in a whisper, lest one of the pouter pigeon ladies or resplendent merchants should overhear them, and proceed to demand that they should leave the place. When they had come to an end, or, to speak more accurately, when Helen intimated by a slight slackening of her attention that they had sat there long enough, Hirst rose, exclaiming, "So there's no reason whatever for all this mystery!"
>
> (162–63)

But while there may be "no reason" between Hirst and Helen for "all this mystery," obviously reasons remain for mystery between author and audience. Given the volume of directly rendered conversation consisting of little more than idle chit-chat throughout the text, this compression can hardly be attributed to stylistic concerns. Rather, we can only surmise that the "very interesting matters" they share, topics that, if heard, would evoke the opprobrium of the "pouter pigeon ladies" and "resplendent merchants," involve that love that truly dared not speak its name in Edwardian England.[7]

In a strange interlude following this conversation, a vision of life without such repression is realized as social barriers and gender roles drop momentarily. Although the ballroom musicians pack their instruments and leave, the crowd, still eager to dance, calls upon Rachel to play the piano. Given this opportunity to indulge in her greatest pleasure, she eschews the usual popular numbers, "hymn tunes, played very fast, with bits out of Wagner and Beethoven" (165) and performs an eclectic repertory including a Mozart sonata, "old English hunting songs, carols, and hymn tunes," music for which the usual dance steps will not suffice. Accordingly, once the traditional dance music is discarded, so are gender-based dance traditions. Terence performs "the voluptuous dreamy dance of an Indian maiden," while Helen suggestively "seizes" the spinster Miss Allan, and together the two women whirl round the dance floor (166). Yet this lapse, as it were, in Helen's façade is an isolated incident, and as she is rarely alone with a woman, her desires remain concealed.

When initially faced with the prospect of months of close companionship with Rachel, Helen attempts an emotional subterfuge. She represses herself emotionally and retreats into the outward display of scorn she reserves for women, claiming that "women of her own age usually bor[ed] her, [and] she supposed that girls would be worse" (20). But Woolf reveals elsewhere that Helen "did not like to feel herself the victim of unclassified emotions" (277), and that when under emotional duress, it is "only by scorning all she met that she [keeps] herself from tears" (9). She therefore initially distances herself from her niece by scorning the younger woman's social ineptness, and only after Rachel begins to enjoy the attentions of Clarissa Dalloway does Helen, provoked by jealousy, take an active interest in her well-being. Helen's emotional discomfort in her relationship with Rachel continues to wax and wane throughout the novel. But because her emotional state cannot be attributed to its actual cause, it is represented only indirectly through seemingly inexplicable gestures, sighs, sudden mood swings, and, most tellingly, her constant oscillation between attitudes of affectionate mentoring and distant disinterest and disapprobation.

That Rachel is the daughter of Helen's long-dead sister-in-law Theresa makes the dynamics of their relationship all the more problematic. Theresa, Ridley's sister, "had been the one woman Helen called friend," and in an erotically charged passage in the first draft of the novel, Helen, "flushing" and "with Rachel pressed to her," articulates the complexity of her feelings: "I've never told you, but you know I love you, my darling . . . Sometimes, you're so like Theresa, and I loved her" (*Melymbrosia*, 209). Helen's entangled desires thus encroach numerous taboos; not only does Rachel reawaken her aunt's love for Ridley's sister, but, as Helen has assumed the role of a maternal surrogate for Rachel, her desires become quasi-incestuous, echoing the previous attachment. Moreover, through this surrogation, Helen's object of desire is bifurcated, while she herself assumes a bifurcated subject position in the sublimation of her desires. Her suspicion of Willoughby's "nameless atrocities with regard to his daughter, as indeed she had always suspected him of bullying his wife" (24), while possibly accurate, may reflect her anger at his disruption of female-female love and her projection of her own sense of guilt as well as her projection of her own sense of guilt. As Rachel moves away from Helen's influence toward the romantic attentions of Terence Hewet, Helen's jealousy gradually turns to panic, and because this panic is unarticulable, on the part of both the author and the character, it becomes all the more potent and explosive.

This ever-increasing tension reaches its climax at a crucial moment of the courtship plot, in what Mitchell A. Leaska has termed the "strangest [passage] . . . of any in Virginia Woolf's fiction" (30). At the first disembarkation of the boat after Rachel and Terence have agreed to marry, the couple, who have yet to announce their betrothal, wander ahead of the other into the wilderness landscape. Suddenly, a pursuer rushes upon them:

> A hand dropped abrupt as iron on Rachel's shoulder; it might have been a bolt from heaven. She fell beneath it, and the grass whipped across her eyes and filled her mouth and ears. Through the waving stems she saw a figure, large and shapeless against the sky. Helen was upon her. Rolled this way and that, now seeing only forests of green, and now the high blue heaven, she was speechless and almost without sense. At last she lay still, all the grasses shaken round her and before her by her panting. Over her loomed two great heads, the heads of a man and woman, of Terence and Helen.
>
> Both were flushed, both laughing, and the lips were moving; they came together and kissed in the air above her. Broken fragments of speech came down to her on the ground. She thought she heard them speak of love and marriage. Raising herself and sitting up, she too realised Helen's soft body, the strong and hospitable arms, and happiness swelling and breaking in one vast wave.
>
> (283–84)

The savage and erotic violence of Helen's actions, which would seem nothing so much as an enactment of lesbian rape, stands in sharp contrast to the worldly and aloof demeanor she has heretofore displayed. Yet this most obvious interpretation is confounded by Terence's reaction. In "looming" along with Helen over the fallen girl, he is positioned as a co-predator in a mimetic realization of Rachel's ongoing rape phobias; yet in exchanging laughter and a kiss with Helen he presents simultaneous possibilities of both infidelity and the establishment of a triad, both of which would implicate Helen as Rachel's rival rather than Terence as Helen's rival. Subsequently, as Terence apparently informs Helen of the engagement, the older woman's embrace of the younger becomes a motherly benediction in a *rite du passage* ; yet the orgasmic images with which Woolf inscribes this embrace connote that what Rachel "realises" is nothing less than the intent of Helen's lesbian desire.

That Woolf's characters resume their everyday, upper-middle-class propriety and sociability immediately thereafter and never speak of this incident only increases the passage's disturbing inexplicability. If, as Leaska observes, this incident has "received the least comment" (30) from Woolf's critics, then the reasons for this lacuna are apparent. Pamela Caughie, one of the few critics addressing this challenge, examines *The Voyage Out* in terms of the problems it poses to conventional narrative expectations. Arguing that the "disturbing quality of the scene is its point, not some obscurity to be cleared up or dismissed," she posits that the "lack of satisfaction" the scene offers to the reader's "desire for consummation and confirmation" functions as a means of "keep[ing] the disturbing force of sexuality vibrating through the novel" (204). The disruptive inexplicability of the passage does indeed contribute to the tension that is prerequisite in D. A. Miller's paradigm of narratability. I would add to Caughie's argument that not only does this incident confound typical narrative expectations in its lack of sexual resolution, it also, perhaps more significantly, frustrates most conventional attempts to draw any distinction between heterosexuality and homosexuality. Yet it would follow from Caughie's argument that the confusion that results is an end in itself. An examination of Woolf's earlier drafts, however, would indicate that this is not the case; rather, they give evidence of an ongoing struggle on the author's part to articulate, in a mode acceptable to her audience, "the things people don't talk about."[8]

In a holograph version dated 1912, Helen's desire for Rachel is unambiguous, as is her rivalry with Terence. The "uneasy" Helen, who has been carefully observing the "significant" interactions of the pair as they wander into the forest, advises the rest of the party that she will "fetch" them as if they were delinquent children:

> Helen was off, sweeping over the ground at a considerable pace & leaving a trail of whitened grass behind her. The figures continuing to retreat, she broke into a run, shouting Rachel's name in the midst of great panting. Rachel heard at last; looked round, saw the figure of her aunt a hundred yards away, and at once took to her heels. Terence stopped and waited for her. But she swept past him, cantering over the waving ground like one of the deer themselves, pulling handfuls of grass and casting them at Rachel's back, abusing her roundly as she did so with the remnants of her breath. Rachel turned incautiously to look, caught her foot in a twist of grass and fell headlong. Helen was upon her. Too breathless to scold, she spent her rage in rolling the helpless body hither and thither, holding both wrists in one firm grasp, and stuffing eyes, ears, nose, and mouth with the feathery seeds of the grass. Finally she laid her flat on the ground, her arms out on

> either side of her, her hat off, her hair down. "Own yourself beaten!" she gasped. "Beg my pardon!" Lying thus flat, Rachel saw Helen's head pendent over her, very large against the sky. A second head loomed above it, "Help! Terence!" she cried. "No!" he exclaimed, when Helen was for driving him away. "I've a right to protect her. We're going to be married."
>
> For the next two seconds they rolled indiscriminately in a bundle, imparting handfuls of grass together with attempted kisses. Separating at last, and trying to tidy her hair, Helen managed to exclaim between her pants, "Yesterday! I guessed it!"
>
> (Leaska 35–36)

The distinctions between heterosexual and homosexual desire absent in the published version are more clearly drawn in this earlier attempt. Terence assumes the traditional, socially prescribed role of defender, with the "right to protect" the woman he has claimed as his own. Despite this clarification, the passage is possibly more disturbing in its own manner than that which supersedes it, for it would seem that the incomprehensibility of the latter is primarily a means of obscuring desires too unseemly and unspeakable to be articulated forthrightly. Helen, in plunging into pursuit, steps out of any subject position that, according to the lights of the early twentieth century, could conceivably be termed "female" and positions herself as a "male" opponent to Terence's "right." In addition, the sheer sadism evident in Helen's actions and words (particularly that Rachel owns herself "beaten") not only indicate a truly sinister aspect of the lesbian "threat" she poses to the courtship plot but also replicate the conditions of heterosexuality that she scornfully disdains and Rachel obsessively fears. Finally, this passage offers its own ambiguities. Helen's response to Terence's announcement of his prerogative, her engaging Rachel in erotic play that might simply be deemed kissing "under other conditions," is simultaneously a challenge to male authority and an expression of affectionate, even maternal, goodwill in the context of a celebratory occasion. Subsequently, the scene moves incongruously toward an attempted resolution in Helen's congratulatory remark, which is actually little more than a compliment to her own proleptic intuition.

Melymbrosia, the earliest complete draft of the novel extant, provides an insight into the original function of this scene, one in which the dynamics of subject-object relationship between the two women shift significantly. Helen, although warned by Hirst, suggestively, of the dangers of snakes in the "rich thick grass," is nonetheless "in a reckless mood" (208). Reluctantly,

Hirst accompanies Helen, who uncharacteristically exclaims at the beauty and the "benevolence and goodness" of the world as she ventures into the jungle. Suddenly, Rachel appears:

> Helen felt Rachel springing beside her.
>
> She went ahead, and called back over her shoulder to Helen, "It's like wading out to sea!"
>
> She left behind her a trail of whitened grass, like a track in water. Without thinking of her forty years, Helen cried "Spring on! I'm after you!" whereupon Rachel took longer leaps and at last ran. Helen pursued her. She plucked tufts of feathery blades and cast them at her. They outdistanced the others. Suddenly Rachel stopped and opened her arms so that Helen rushed into them and tumbled her over on to the ground. "Oh Helen Helen!" she could hear Rachel gasping as she rolled her, "Don't! For God's sake! Stop! I'll tell you a secret! I'm going to be married!"
>
> Helen paused with one hand upon Rachel's throat holding her head down among the grasses.
>
> "You think I didn't know that!" she cried.
>
> For some seconds she did nothing but roll Rachel over and over, knocking her down when she tried to get up; stuffing grass into her mouth; finally laying her absolutely flat upon the ground, her arms out on either side of her, her hat off, her hair down.
>
> "Own yourself beaten" she panted. "Beg my pardon, and say you worship me!"
>
> Rachel saw Helen's head hanging over her, very large against the sky.
>
> "I love Terence better!" she exclaimed.
>
> "Terence" Helen exclaimed.
>
> She sat clasping her knees and looking down upon Rachel who still lay with her head on the grass staring in to [sic] the sky.
>
> "Are you happy?" she asked.
>
> "Infinitely!" Rachel breathed, and turning round was clasped in Helen's arms.
>
> "I had to tell you" she murmured.
>
> "And if you hadn't, I knew" said Helen.
>
> "He's unlike any one I've ever seen" said Rachel. "He understands." Lost in her knowledge of Terence, which she could not impart, she said no more.
>
> (208–09)

In this passage, the erotic interplay between the two women is not only considerably less violent—the threat of physical restriction and punishment is certainly subdued in comparison to that which appears in subsequent revisions and can be deemed playful—but it is also mutual. Indeed, Rachel, the pursuer in this case, invites Helen's participation. The presence of the homosexual Hirst, who is completely absent in later versions, together with Terence's absence, removes every trace of heterosexuality from the scene, giving it the ambiance of a lesbian utopia in an Edenic setting. That a "snake" should appear to disrupt this brief paradise is figuratively fulfilled in Rachel's recollection of her own betrothal, which jolts her into a protest against the action she has instigated and becomes the direct causation of Helen's apparently jealous use of physical force. Yet once Helen expresses verbally her jealousy and her desire for the younger woman's love, Rachel offers an almost apologetic explanation for her happiness, her engagement to man who "understands," although precisely what Terence understands is unclear and has been effectively erased in Woolf's process of revision.

Louise De Salvo, who has painstakingly examined the many phases in the production of this text, observes that "Woolf's tendency, as she got closer to publication, was to blunt the clarity" (Introduction xiv). Given the legal restrictions and social inhibitions of the time, such self-censorship is surely understandable. Alex Zwerdling, who notes that the literary circumspection of Woolf and other members of the Bloomsbury group on sexual matters stands in sharp contradistinction to the "extraordinary" liaisons marking their personal lives, posits that "this deliberate inhibition of free expression seems odd until one remembers the fate of bolder experiments" (168). A notable example is D. H. Lawrence's idyllic representation of a lesbian encounter in *The Rainbow*—published, like *The Voyage Out*, in 1915—which was ruled obscene by a British court despite the appendage of Lawrence's ostensibly moralistic title "Shame" to the chapter in question. Nevertheless, as Woolf obscures the precise relationship between the women, both in the particular scene and the text in general, she evokes the more sinister possibilities of alternatives to institutional heterosexuality, especially those of sadomasochism, amazonism, and a general breakdown of social and gender hierarchy. Such possibilities are, significantly, nothing less than the outcome predicted by late nineteenth-century medical sexologists should lesbianism be allowed to flourish unchecked.[9]

The fear of fin-de-siècle European society, encouraged by medical sexology, that lesbianism and its inherent refusal to submit to the "evolved" social institutions of marriage and motherhood would ultimately result in a return to "bestial primitivism" (Dijkstra 335–36), is implicit in the setting of Helen's scene of lesbian panic. In the South American jungle, away from the safeguards of upper middle-class British culture, Helen is unrestricted in exploring and enacting the "bestial" tendencies that would otherwise remain repressed. In this sense, the text becomes a journey to a female "heart of darkness." But whereas Joseph Conrad's male protagonist discovers only "the horror" of male power and corruption instead of an idealized homosocial bond with Kurtz, both Helen and Rachel encounter the fearful depths of repressed female sexuality.[10] The visit of the British tourists to a native village immediately after the encounter between Helen and Rachel serves to underscore this social dread. In one of Woolf's rare representations of racial "others," naked native women sit passively and disinterestedly on the ground, nursing their infants and regarding their guests "with the motionless inexpressive gaze of those removed from each other far, far beyond the plunge of speech" (284). Ironically, this spectacle causes neither Helen nor Rachel shame or repugnance about their covert homoerotic desires; if anything, it presents the "natural" condition of motherhood as "devolved" and static. Indeed, the village scene marks the beginning of Rachel's resistance to her own engagement, as the native women leave her with a sense of "insignificance" and "pain" in her being "in love" (285).

Woolf's revision of the lesbian encounter in the realm of "nature" from the pastoral to the pathological and, ultimately, to the incoherent, however, shifts the function of these contiguous scenes from that of a premarital homoerotic rite of female initiation to that of lesbian panic. As the ostensible rationale for Helen's reactions become more obscure, so does her alarm at the courtship plot she sees unfolding become more intense and palpable. In the final, published version, her pursuit of Rachel and Terence as they seek solitude in the forest, becomes an impotent, futile attempt to interfere with the seemingly inevitable heterosexual consummation, now configured as "natural" in the "primitive" setting.[11] Yet even if it were in Helen's power to disrupt the courtship plot in more than a symbolic manner, the point becomes moot, as Woolf provides Rachel with an escape from immurement in the institution of matrimony; and if Rachel does not unambiguously embrace her means of escape, she certainly does not resist its force.

Rachel accedes to the seduction of death at the end of a narrative marked by her continual resistance to a variety of proffered sexual experiences. That a courtship plot that contains many of the "archetypal" elements of the quest narrative should be abruptly curtailed by the death of the bride/seeker most assuredly thwarts most highly conditioned narrative expectations. Given the intertextual allusions Woolf provides, it is fair to say that this novel begins in the spirit of *Persuasion* or *Pride and Prejudice*, with a young woman's "coming out" into the world of adulthood (i.e., courtship and marriage), only to conclude in the atmosphere of *Wuthering Heights*, in which the only viable and acceptable consummation is that of the Liebestod. To understand *The Voyage Out* as a quest narrative, however, is to assume a search on Rachel's part; whether she actively seeks anything beyond her hermetic space in which she can dwell in art and music is certainly debatable. Contrastively, that she finds much that she does not actively seek, in the world of men and women whose very identities, actions, and thoughts are controlled and preordained by socially constructed gender roles, is most evident.

Woolf first presents Rachel as a completely unsocialized young woman, raised in relative isolation by her father's two unmarried sisters. Exposed to little learning or culture save that which she fancies—Cowper, Bach, and Emily Brontë—she has scarce knowledge of sexuality and desire. Thus, "at the age of twenty-four she scarcely knew that men desired women and was terrified by a kiss" when Richard Dalloway makes his overture to her aboard the ship. Her ensuing sexual awakening, to which she responds with alternating moods of fascinated exhilaration and utter revulsion, is only the first in a series of shocks as the depth and variety of human sexuality is revealed to her. In the person of Clarissa Dalloway at sea and among guests in the hotel in Santa Marina, she is introduced to the world of the British middle-class matron, whose sexual energies are employed solely for the sake of the Empire and for whom marriage and motherhood have become patriotic duties. Within the microcosm of the latter setting, Rachel witnesses the enactment of the traditional courtship plot. Susan Warrington, thirty years old, single, and attendant upon an ailing, elderly aunt, meets Arthur Venning, an eligible and relatively young barrister, who is fetishistically attracted to "a buckle [she] wore one night at sea" (139). On a stroll with their fellow tourists, Susan and Arthur, in the course of a conversation ridden with the clichés of popular romance, discover their mutual disdain of erudition, declare their love, plight their troth, and proceed to lie on the ground in each other's arms—a short distance from the rest of the tourists. Rachel, who accidentally stumbles upon them, responds simply and tellingly: "I don't like that" (140). Her audience, significantly, is her "understanding" fiancé-to-be, who responds, sympathetically if ambiguously, "I can remember not liking it either," then interrupts himself to speculate whether Arthur will prove a faithful husband—a projection, perhaps, of the conditions of his own intended married state. Although Rachel's consequent reaction is to feel so "sorry for them . . . [that] I could almost burst into tears" (140–41), she soon discovers the social rewards for participation in such "unlikeable" actions as Susan, who heretofore "had no self" (134), becomes the focus of her fellow travelers' attention.

Conceivably, Helen, in her roles of matron and mentor, should be able to allay Rachel's anxieties about sexuality and marriage. Yet Helen is herself in a destabilized sexual position, and her "pragmatic" advice does little more than reveal her own distaste for the heterosexual act: "You oughtn't to be so frightened. . . . It's the most natural thing in the world. . . . The pity is to get things out of proportion. It's like noticing the noises people make when they eat, or men spitting; or, in short, any small thing that gets on one's nerves" (91). But if this "maternal" advice has the subliminal intent of dissuading Rachel from heterosexual experience, it does not follow that she will be more open to its opposite.

Within this microcosm of British society displaced in a tropical setting, the possibilities proffered to this young woman include a number of a vaguely homoerotic variety as well.[12] In one visit to the hotel, preliminary to the jungle expedition, Rachel endures two panic-ridden encounters with women, both of which reveal the extent to which ignorance, feigned or otherwise, in such "unspeakable" (and thus unspoken) interchanges safeguard both parties from blame.[13] In the first, the sexually opportunistic Evelyn Murgatroyd, thwarted in the execution of her heterosexual adventures, seizes Rachel, who "had no wish to go or to stay," and leads her upstairs to her room, "two stairs at a time" (246). The domineering Evelyn alternately emotes over the brutality of men and attempts to enlist Rachel in her proposed schemes for the promotion of social causes and women's rights; all the while, Rachel, scarcely listening, sits "vacant and unhappy" (248). This impasse is broken when Evelyn sits beside Rachel on the floor and, asserting the importance of being human and "real," places her hand on Rachel's knee. Rachel displays no reaction yet feels "that Evelyn was too close to her, and that there was something exciting in this closeness, although it was also disagreeable" (249). Evelyn, for her part, continues to rant uninterruptedly about her beliefs, the illegitimacy of her birth, and the meaning of "being in love" (250), until, wanting "intimacy," she discerns that "Rachel was not thinking about her. . . . Evelyn was tormented . . . always being rebuffed" (251). Silence overtakes both women, and Rachel grows visibly uneasy. At this point Evelyn, who has clearly played the aggressor in this exchange, switches subject positions and feigns victimage; as her erstwhile captive creeps toward the door, she cries out, "What is it you want? . . . You make me feel as if you were always thinking of something you don't say. . . . Do say it!" (251). Rachel, in turn, rather incoherently expresses her hopes that Evelyn will marry one of her many suitors and leaves to wander, without direction, through the hotel.

In this mutual rhetoric of silence, neither woman verbally expresses her desires or anxieties directly, allowing both to feel innocent of blame—if nonetheless distressed—in the aftermath. Evelyn sets a tone of seduction by speaking continuously on a wide variety of topics, all of which have sex or sexuality as a common thread. Simultaneously, she avoids any direct reference to desire between women, allowing her hand on Rachel's knee, a gesture that could just as easily signify close friendship, to communicate this possibility. Rachel, in turn, maintains complete passivity. In this manner, she avoids the responsibility inherent in either acceptance or rejection—until Evelyn, growing impatient, provokes discomfort and the potential for panic. At this Rachel leaves, in order to forestall any emotionally or socially disastrous consequences. Moreover, as if to absolve herself from culpable participation in forbidden activities, she invokes in her departure the now-decontextualized concept of institutional heterosexuality in order to erase what has and what has not transpired.

Rachel's unreflecting flight nevertheless fails to save her from the dangers posed by other women. Wandering into a courtyard, she is transfixed by the almost surrealistic spectacle of an elderly native woman decapitating a chicken with "vindictive energy and triumph," a metaphorical representation of her own imagined victimage at the hands of her elders. While Rachel gazes with fascination at "the blood and ugly wriggling," she is approached by Miss Allan, a teacher of literature, who in the same breath comments wryly on the carnage and invites the young woman to her room. As in the previous episode, Rachel complies without resistance, "for it seemed possible that each new person might remove the mystery which burdened her" (252); yet what ensues is no less "mysterious" than her contretemps with Evelyn. Miss Allan "liked young women, for she had taught many of them" (253), yet she is hard-pressed to "entertain" the recalcitrantly unresponsive Rachel. In a symbolically charged attempt to break this social stalemate, Miss Allan offers her guest a piece of ginger, which she can only extract from its jar by means of a button-hook. Before the gift can be retrieved, however, Rachel demurs, certain that she would not like it. To this refusal, presented in much the same language as Rachel's reaction to Susan and Arthur's coupling, Miss Allan launches into a disjointed and didactic, if nonetheless suggestive, disquisition on experience that needs little explication:

> You've never tried? . . . Then I consider that it is your duty to try now. Why, you may add a new pleasure to life, and as you are still young— . . . I make it a rule to try everything. . . . Don't you think it would be very annoying if you tasted ginger for the first time on your deathbed, and found you never liked anything so much? I should be so exceedingly annoyed that I think I should get well on that account alone.
>
> (254)

Rachel accepts the ginger, only to be so distressed she must "spit it out." Miss Allen wonders if Rachel is sure she has "really tasted it," but Rachel answers by throwing the offending sweet out the window. Unshaken, Miss Allan rules it, with pedagogical authority, "an experience anyway" (254).

Although Rachel is as resistant to the enjoyment of ginger as she is to other, more dangerous pleasures, she remains in the teacher's room, filled with an ineffable longing:

> Surely there must be balm for all anguish in her words, could one induce her to have recourse to them. But Miss Allan . . . showed no signs of breaking the reticence which had snowed her under for years. An uncomfortable sensation kept Rachel silent; on the one hand, she wished to whirl high and strike a spark out of the cool pink flesh; on the other she perceived there was nothing to be done but to drift past each other in silence.
>
> (255)

Rachel envisions the realization of surcease from her distress in terms that are remarkably and simultaneously physical, erotic, and violent. But Rachel can no more articulate her anguish than she or Miss Allan can define the cause of the older woman's reticence, and thus no spark can ever be struck. Instead, Miss Allan offers aphorisms about age and the difficulties of life, as well as droll stories about a talismanic bottle of crême de menthe she has continued to exchange with a woman friend for twenty-six years, about a female colleague who overcame the "unsatisfactory" nature of her life by breeding guinea-pigs, and about "a yellow guinea-pig [that] has had a black baby" (256). Like Evelyn, she discourses endlessly on ambiguously sexual themes, all of which are constructed in a manner that appears innocent of erotic intent. Simultaneously, in an elaborate display of passive-aggressive behavior, she removes her coat, skirt, and blouse and, citing her need to arrange her hair and change clothing, she enlists Rachel's help in dressing for dinner with the seemingly rational explanation that "I should be particularly glad of your assistance, because there is a tiresome set of hooks which I can fasten for myself, but it takes from ten to fifteen minutes; whereas with your help—" (256). Rachel says nothing, but cooperates, while Miss Allan continues her discussion of guinea pigs, for Miss Allan "was not an impulsive woman, and her life had schooled her to restrain her tongue" (257). They descend to dinner, where the plan for the fateful jungle expedition is put in motion.

That Woolf should juxtapose these two scenes, in which two vastly dissimilar women employ parallel strategies to stimulate homoerotic interest while impeding its actualization, indicates that desire between women, far from being an extreme or isolated phenomenon, is, in reality, quite commonplace. The apparently self-defeating mechanisms of this suggestive rhetoric are an end in themselves. Because no clearly defined sexual action can occur under the circumstances, the participants are allowed the frisson arising from potential danger without the guilt or responsibility its realization would entail. Thus Rachel, immediately after fleeing from one encounter she finds both "exciting" and "disagreeable," does not hesitate to allow herself to be coerced into experiencing a second.

Because Rachel's sexual reactions are mitigated to a very great extent by dread and resistance, any attempt to define sexual preference in her case must ultimately be frustrated. What can be ascertained, through a *via negativa*, is her lack of differentiation between male- and female-inspired sexual dread. Her response to Evelyn is merely an encapsulation of the "physical pain of emotion," succeeded first by "strange exultation" and then by a feeling of being "merely uncomfortable," which she undergoes in the wake of Richard Dalloway's kiss (76, 77). This vision of "something . . . which is hidden in ordinary life" culminates in a nightmare fraught with sexual symbolism:

> She was walking down a long tunnel, which grew so narrow by degrees that she could touch the damp bricks on either side. At length the tunnel opened and became a vault; she found herself trapped in it . . . with a deformed man. . . . His face was pitted and like the face of an animal. The wall behind him oozed with damp. . . .
>
> She felt herself pursued. . . . A voice moaned for her; eyes desired her. All night long barbarian men . . . stopped to snuffle at her door.
>
> (77)

For Rachel, the physical "violation" of the kiss resonates as rape, and male sexuality is signified as bestial and grotesque. The unsubtle vaginal symbolism of this dream, though, can only indicate that this pursuit arouses desire as well as dread.

The threat of female sexuality produces remarkably similar results in her subconscious. In the aftermath of her encounter with Helen, Rachel grows increasingly querulous in her relationship with Terence; returning from the jungle to the structures of British society in Santa Marina, she sickens and dies. In a fevered deathbed hallucination, Helen and the bedside nurse replace the "barbarian men" of the earlier dream:

> [She] found herself walking through a tunnel under the Thames, where there were little deformed women sitting in archways playing cards, while the bricks of which the wall was made oozed with damp, which collected into drops and slid down the wall. But the little women became Helen and Nurse McInnis after a time, standing in the window together whispering, whispering incessantly.
>
> (331)

The most singular difference between the two dreams is in the pursuers' mode of vocal expression. Whereas the men "moan" and "snuffle," the women whisper, as befits the actual and rhetorical silences that surround their desires.

Shirley Neuman posits that the orgasmic description of Rachel's "happiness" in Helen's embrace, occurring at the moment of the announcement of her engagement, suggests on Rachel's part "not only an unwillingness to face the sexual implications of marriage but an unresolved ambiguity about her sexual choice"; that "in making the socially acceptable female choice—marriage," she has ultimately "ventured too far" (63).[14] If so, as Rachel is given no viable mode in which she could potentially articulate or resolve this ambiguity, death would seem the only acceptable alternative to marriage for her, much as it did for the numerous "unmarriageable" female protagonists of eighteenth-century and Victorian novels. To attribute Rachel's death to lesbian panic would overdetermine not only Woolf's intent but also the multiplicity of conflicting forces affecting Rachel's psyche; surely what Alex Zwerdling terms a "revulsion from heterosexuality" (170)—or, at the very least, the panic arising from the prospect of being permanently subsumed into institutional heterosexuality—is an active agent in her retreat from life and its possibilities. Yet, in her very unwillingness or inability to attempt a resolution of her sexual dilemma, Rachel becomes an unviable, indeed, a non-narratable character.

Rachel Blau DuPlessis argues that "Rachel's death may accordingly be interpreted as the death of a person who evaded constitutive components of her *Bildung*," and "that Woolf meted out death as Rachel's punishment for her being insufficiently critical and vocal" (51). In this case, Mrs. Thornbury's pious self-reassurance in the wake of Rachel's death, that "surely order did prevail" (360) possesses an ironic truth. In form, if not in content, *The Voyage Out* remains a traditional novel; the restoration of order prerequisite for closure in the form can prevail only through the removal of the embodied sign of contradiction. Yet, as Duplessis points out, its ending is "the aggressive act of the author against the hegemonic power of the narrative conventions with which the novel is, in fact, engaged—love and quest" (50). By aborting the mechanisms of the courtship plot, Woolf begins the process by which she undermines the narrative and social ideologies that configure desire between women as the ultimate agent of disorder.

This process did not move forward without hesitation, without one more attempt to anatomize, subvert, yet possibly redeem the courtship plot. If the unsocialized Rachel Vinrace was "inadequately critical and vocal" to survive, Woolf nevertheless refashioned her in the more sophisticated character of Katharine Hilbery, the heroine of her second novel, *Night and Day*, which may be seen as the comic version of *The Voyage Out*.[15] Like Rachel, Katharine has little interest in conventional heterosexual pursuits of romance and marriage, preferring instead the privacy in which to engage in her personal, abstract passion; whereas Rachel would lose herself in music, Katharine has no greater desire than to explore the pristine exactness of algebraic equations—a passion that, as Suzanne Raitt notes, she is "unable to work . . . into the everyday texture" of life (Introduction xxiv). That Katharine has the wherewithal to indulge in this unlikely course of pleasure at all—much less to free herself of a passionless engagement formed out of conformity to social norms and subsequently join herself with a man for whom she feels an intellectual attraction—is due in great part to her environment. Unlike Rachel, she is positioned in a familial network of lively and supportive, albeit highly eccentric, women and, as a result, is hardly bereft of guidance or consolation.

Katharine's ultimate rationalistic engagement to Ralph Denham, who is as deeply involved in his literary endeavors as she is in mathematics, would seem the actualization of the metaphysical, rather than physical, relationship between man and woman that Rachel Vinrace vainly sought. Yet this apparently ideal situation is complicated by the presence of third parties. Katharine's original fiancé, the dilettante William Rodney (who bears more than a passing resemblance to St. John Hirst), can readily exchange her lack of affection for the genuine interest of her cousin Cassandra; Ralph's relationship with suffragist Mary Datchet, however, offers perhaps the most significant of plot complications in this convoluted narrative.

Jane Marcus observes in *Virginia Woolf and the Languages of the Patriarchy* that "one has the odd feeling that the only really satisfactory ending to the novel would be in Katharine Hilbery's marriage, not to Ralph but to Mary Datchet. Desire is present in the novel's one erotic moment when Mary touches Katharine's skirt" (23). Indeed, there are several such moments; as Shirley Nelson Garner notes, "in a novel where there is scarcely any touching, [Mary] continually touches Katharine" (328). Most tellingly, each of these physical encounters (57–61, 274–78, 359, 450) occur within the context of conversations between the two women concerning Ralph, their shared love interest; in most instances Mary reassures Katharine that she will abnegate her own claims to Ralph's affections. The relationship between the two women, conjoined with the previous triangulation comprising William Rodney, Katharine, and Ralph, is virtually a paradigmatic example of Terry Castle's lesbian reconfiguration of the "Sedgwickian model" of male homosocial bonding through the mediation of a female third party—a configuration that in itself undergirds many narrative instances of male homosexual panic or safeguards against its eruption.[16]

Castle posits that "in the most radical transformation of female bonding—i.e., from homosocial to *lesbian* bonding—the two female terms indeed merge and the male term drops out" (73). But this does not occur in *Night and Day*. Mary, quite emphatically, drops out, surrendering herself to a spinsterhood devoted to the political struggle for women's rights—a project overseen in the text, most ironically, by a man—and, in the end, becoming a distant, disembodied guardian angel to the newly betrothed couple. Upon becoming engaged, the thoughts of both Ralph and Katharine turn to Mary, yet neither dares see her, lest they "risk the destruction" of the "globe which we spend our lives in trying to shape, round, whole, and entire from the confusion of chaos" (503). Rather, they gaze at her window and pay tribute to "something impersonal and serene in the spirit of the woman within, working out her plans far into the night—her plans for the good of a world that none of them were ever to know" (506). Thus Mary becomes, in Castle's term, "ghosted" (4), the fate of many fictional characters who pose a lesbian threat to the courtship plot.[17]

Mary's translation into feminist sainthood not only allows the courtship plot to come to its preordained if nonetheless eccentric conclusion, with the central couple freed from the guilt they might feel over the pain they have both caused this paragon, it also eliminates the need, either before or after the fact, for lesbian panic in the narrative. Unlike the dangerously embodied Helen Ambrose, who survives the literally ghosted bride-to-be, the "continually touch[ing]" Mary is reduced to a benevolent metaphysical force. The potentially lesbian moments are enshrouded in the same stratagems of silence that obscured Rachel's interactions with Evelyn Murgatroyd and Miss Allan in *The Voyage Out*. Katharine may attempt "to conceal [a] momentary flush of pleasure" as Mary approaches her (60), and Mary may suggestively "[finger] the fur on the skirt of [Katharine's] old dress" (278), but no verbal acknowledgment of these sensations or actions is forthcoming from either woman. Indeed, with "no wish to speak," both "for some time" sit "silent, side by side" (278). Thus, as the intentions and conduct of both women remain unquestioned, no one is shamed, no one panics, no one dies; and the relationship between the two women becomes, ostensibly, little more than a most congenial resolution of the eternal triangle, one of the most usual conflicts of the romantic comedy.

In this sense, narrative expectations are fulfilled; yet, as Marcus has suggested, the conclusion seems somehow amiss. The highly original, indeed odd, configurations of the conventional "props" of novelistic romance in *Night and Day* would tend to destabilize if not completely undermine the telos of the courtship plot and institutional heterosexuality. Instead, the very unlikeliness of all the potentially subversive features of this novel, superimposed as they are on traditional resolutions, obscures what this novel would, optimally, reveal and thwarts critical analysis. Accordingly, it is hardly surprising that, as Marcus laments, "critics have not been kind to *Night and Day*" (18), either at the time of its publication or subsequently.[18]

The narrative pitfalls inherent in *The Voyage Out* and *Night and Day* demonstrate the difficulties Woolf could not overcome in narrating female homoerotic desire within traditional novelistic modes, particularly the necessity of its destruction. For Woolf, discarding the convention's traditional novelistic form became the means by which she was able to circumvent the intrusion of the Victorian sexual mores that allowed female characters few alternatives to closure in marriage or death. Early in 1920, after great disappointment arising from the unfavorable critical reception of *Night and Day*, Woolf recorded the genesis of an "idea of a new form for a new novel":

> Suppose one thing should open out of another . . . doesn't that give the looseness and lightness I want; doesn't that get closer and yet keep form and speed, and enclose everything, everything? My doubt is how far it will enclose the human heart—Am I sufficiently mistress of my dialogue to net it there? For I figure that the approach will be entirely different this time: no scaffolding; scarcely a brick to be seen; all crepuscular, but the heart, the passion, humour, everything as bright as fire. Then I'll find room for so much—a gaiety—an inconsequence—a light spirited stepping at my sweet will. Whether I'm sufficiently mistress of things—that's the doubt . . . but I see immense possibilities in the form I hit upon more or less by chance. . . . [I]s one pliant and rich enough to provide a wall for the book from oneself without its becoming, as in Joyce and Richardson, narrowing and restricting? My hope is that I've learnt my business sufficiently now. . . . Anyhow, I must still grope and experiment but . . . I had a gleam of light. Indeed, I think from the ease with which I'm developing the unwritten novel there must be a path for me there.
>
> (*Diary* II, 13–14).

The stream-of-consciousness technique already employed by James Joyce and Dorothy Richardson, among others, offered Woolf the possibility of rendering and enclosing "everything, everything"—sensations, desires, fantasies—that had had no place in the cumbersome "scaffolding" of the courtship plot. By 1920 she had herself ventured into this mode in several impressionistic short pieces that allowed the representation of perception with minimal plot and closure. Despite Woolf's misgivings about the "narrowing and restrictive" effect of the technique in the hands of Joyce and Richardson—which she attributed to "the damned egotistical self" (14)—the ability of these authors to narrate a wide variety of "forbidden" sexual desires and behaviors in this mode without the burden of a closure imposed by moralistically based aesthetics or ideologies, could not have been lost on her.[19]

But before Woolf would use this "new form" to create a "new novel" of female homoerotic desire, she would venture into a world from which "women who wrote [novels] were excluded by their sex" ("Women and Fiction" 79)—the male homosocial world of academia, law, and the military. Given the unknowability of men's lives to most women of Woolf's age, her attempt to recreate and explain the life and death of a lost brother was, of necessity, a fiction riddled with gaps and elisions. *Jacob's Room*, the product of Woolf's breakthrough, is, as Lyndall Gordon puts it, a "collage of broken impressions that makes up the portrait of a young man" and, more important, "a startling rejection of the 'and then . . .' narrative of *Night and Day*" (168)—a rejection that subsequently facilitated her anatomization of both female and male homosexual panic in *Mrs. Dalloway*.

In her presentation of the events of one not-very-eventful day in the life of an apparently privileged London society lady, Woolf effectively deconstructs both the ideology of the courtship plot and the dynamics that have heretofore conjoined lesbian (or, for that matter, male homosexual) panic to the conventions of romantic love through radical and systematic fragmentation. Through a rejection of chronological plot (similar to that she employed in *Jacob's Room*), Woolf reconfigures the fractured and scattered events of Clarissa Dalloway's past. In doing so, she makes the events of some three decades before—particularly those leading to and resulting from a collision between the demands of heterosexual courtship and the lure of lesbian desire—part of the continuous present of the protagonist's memory. Consequently, she underscores the pervasive influence of these events on Mrs. Dalloway's subsequent thoughts, actions, and decisions, as well as her physical and psychological health.[20] Through this fragmentation of chronology Woolf represents the self-repression and occlusion, in the consciousnesses of Mrs. Dalloway and her ancillaries Septimus Warren Smith and Doris Kilman, of past events that have functioned as the motivations for and foundations of their respective present states. In so delineating this interaction of the present and past, Woolf effectively analyzes the dynamics of lesbian and male homosexual panic, a comprehensive narrative factor that becomes clear through a reconstruction of the original sequence of events with particular attention to Woolf's highly connotative language.

As the middle-aged Clarissa Dalloway, the wife of a successful politician, expends the limited energies of her day on apparently trivial preparations for the evening's party, she recalls, through a series of associative prompts, her adolescence at her familial home, where, as an attractive and desirable young woman, she was wooed by three lovers, two male and one female. Little is required to elicit these memories; in the first instance, at the very outset of the novel, the squeaking of doors that "would be taken off their hinges" for the party and the fineness of the morning weather evoke for her the "little squeak of hinges, [when] . . . she had burst open the French windows and plunged at Bourton into the open air" (3). Because the association is so indirect and the image evoked in response so vivid, one could surmise that the shock, pain, and subsequent ongoing loss connected with the memory of Bourton is ever-present, just beneath the surface of her consciousness. Initially, Mrs. Dalloway's recollection of the setting of youthful romance is confused and distorted as she contemplates apparently inaccurate but nonetheless suggestive statements that she attributes to the most aggressive of her suitors, Peter Walsh: " 'Musing among the vegetables?'—was that it?—'I prefer men to cauliflowers?'—was that it?" (3). As the day wears on and Mrs. Dalloway's memories become more acute, however, modifications of the phrases are revealed as the hallmarks of the encounter by the fountain that propelled her into a choice between duty and love, between expectation and desire, between heterosexual privilege and homosexual marginality, choices that more than amply serve as the catalyst for lesbian panic.

Clarissa Dalloway's morning outing to purchase flowers for the party takes place, in a very literal sense, in rather ordinary London streets; simultaneously, it is a journey through a landscape in which, according to an observer, "everything seemed very queer" (26), both denotatively and, it would seem, connotatively.[21] As her protagonist progresses on this microcosmic quest for the ostensibly trivial (and yet, as the fragments of memory imply, for an explanation of her present state of being), Woolf introduces, either through the medium of Clarissa's consciousness or by means of omniscient narration, a variety of characters—including Doris Kilman, Septimus Warren Smith, Clarissa's daughter Elizabeth, Lady Bexborough, Lady Bruton, and even the florist Miss Pym—each of whom deviates to some extent from the heterosexual norm. Her assessments of and mental associations with certain of these characters—Lady Bexborough's being "interested in politics like a man" (10), Elizabeth's "being in love" with Miss Kilman (11), Miss Kilman as a "brutal monster" (12), Lady Bruton "cut in impassive stone" (30)—stir conflicted if yet obscure emotional responses within her and contribute to the almost sinister tone of discomfort lurking beneath her outward pose of cheerful mannerliness. Once she has returned from her journey and exposed these tenuous ideas and images to somewhat begrudging scrutiny, however, the direct cause of her constant, indefinite, and only partially concealed distress is revealed.

While in the florist shop, Clarissa enjoys, for a fleeting moment, a feeling of closeness, indeed pleasure, with one woman that enables her to overcome for the nonce the animosity she feels for another—Doris Kilman, the embittered and repressed teacher to whom her daughter has grown too close:

> And as she began to go with Miss Pym from jar to jar, choosing, nonsense, nonsense, she said to herself, more and more gently, as if this beauty, this scent, this colour, and Miss Pym liking her, trusting her, were a wave which she let flow over her and surmount that hatred, that monster, surmount it all; and it lifted her up and up when—oh! a pistol shot in the street outside! (13)

A "violent explosion" (14), nothing more, in reality, than the backfire of a passing motor car, interrupts this brief idyll, leaving Miss Pym incongruously apologetic and Clarissa, for an interim, literally absent from the text. This incident serves as the means by which the narrative point of view shifts, for the first time in the novel, from the limits of Clarissa's consciousness to a form of omniscience and allows for the introduction of characters unknown to the protagonist. But while it may seem inconsequential to the narrative otherwise, this episode, by presenting female homosocial/homoerotic pleasure in a floral setting, interrupted by the suggestion of lethal violence and underscored by a jealousy arising from the triangulation of affections, simultaneously recalls (for Clarissa) and foreshadows (through the nonchronological arrangement of plot) another seemingly insignificant moment that, in effect, has shaped the entire course of her subsequent life.

Exhausted by her errand, Clarissa Dalloway ascends, "like a nun," to her attic room, the ascetic space that has become her retreat, at her husband's own insistence, since her "illness" (31), an unspecified yet symbolically pointed malfunction of the heart. Realizing that only her husband has been invited to lunch with Lady Bruton, she enters her cell-like enclosure stung by the social rejection of another woman and thwarted in a desired homosocial connection attainable only through the medium of formal society functions, the only medium in which a Mrs. Dalloway might be assumed to possess some expertise.[22] Within this space of refuge from the demands of marital heterosexuality—for both she and her husband are complicit in this arrangement—her dismay over this rejection, which takes on what will become a familiar pattern of hetero/homoerotic triangulation, gives way to a meditation on her "failure" as a wife:

> She had read late at night of the retreat from Moscow. . . . And really she preferred to read of the retreat from Moscow. He knew it. So the room was an attic; the bed narrow; and lying there reading, for she slept badly, she could not dispel a virginity preserved through childbirth, which clung to her like a sheet. Lovely in girlhood, suddenly

> there came a moment—for example on the river beneath the woods at Clieveden—when, through some contraction of this cold spirit, she had failed him. And then at Constantinople, and again and again. She could see what she lacked. . . . It was something central which permeated; something warm which broke up surfaces and rippled the cold contact of man and woman.
>
> (31)

While this passage is certainly decorous in its circumspection, it is difficult to imagine that its meaning could be misconstrued. Clearly, Clarissa recognizes her own lack of heterosexual desire, her inability to derive or give pleasure in the marital act, a "lack" labeled by medical science as "frigidity."[23] It is also obvious that her sexual reticence is not a response to sexual cruelty, for Richard Dalloway is presented as a considerate man, making her "failure" all the more acute. Indeed, the implied analogy between her retreat from marital duties and Baron Marbot's retreat from Moscow during the Napoleonic Wars suggests the extent to which Clarissa envisions the expectations of heterosexuality as a battle in which defeat is inevitable.[24]

Simultaneously, she realizes that the "contraction of this cold spirit" is not necessarily a given for her, that the "something warm" is not restricted to the "contact of man and woman"; it is potentially present in "women together" as well:

> For *that* she could dimly perceive. She resented it, had a scruple picked up Heaven knows where, or, as she felt, sent by Nature (who is invariably wise); yet she could not resist sometimes yielding to the charm of a woman, not a girl, of a woman confessing, as to her they often did, some scrape, some folly. And whether it was pity, or their beauty, or that she was older, or some accident—like a faint scent, or a violin next door (so strange is the power of sounds at certain moments), she did undoubtedly then feel what men felt. Only for a moment; but it was enough. It was enough. It was a sudden revelation, a tinge like a blush which one tried to check and then, as it spread, one yielded to its expansion, and rushed to the farthest verge and there quivered and felt the world come closer, swollen with some astonishing significance, some pressure of rapture, which split its thin skin and gushed and poured with an extraordinary alleviation over the cracks and sores! Then, for that moment, she had seen an illumination; a match burning in a crocus; an inner meaning almost expressed. But the close withdrew; the hard softened. It was over—the

> moment. Against such moments (with women too) there contrasted (as she laid her hat down) the bed and Baron Marbot and the candle half-burnt.
>
> (31–32)

This oft-cited passage, perhaps the most erotically charged in all of Woolf's writing, bears close scrutiny for its ability to present in glowing poetic imagery an argument against the social and scientific dicta that have led to the "frigidity" of Clarissa Dalloway and others of her ilk.[25] Once Clarissa acknowledges her capacity for erotic pleasure in interactions with other women, her mood immediately turns to resentment directed at the pronouncements of the medical sexologists, the self-proclaimed arbiters of "Nature (who is invariably wise)," who inflict "scruples" of self-blame and self-doubt on those who fall outside their definition of "natural." Yet even for Clarissa Dalloway, who has obviously long repressed such erotic urges in her attempts to fulfill and maintain her roles as society lady and politician's wife, the strength of the desire, even if restricted to her private ruminations, overwhelms the strictures of medical discourse. She acknowledges her participation in nonspecific but nonetheless pleasurable contacts with other women, similar in its kind not only to her interrupted interlude with Miss Pym but also with those engaged in almost as a matter of course by the various female characters in *The Voyage Out*. Subsequently she yields to a vivid meditation of female homoerotic pleasure, culminating in an orgasmic exclamation of *jouissance*, before returning to the drab reality of her sterile room.

Even so, this interior monologue, defining her chronic unease and disability, releases the ever-present memory that she has heretofore struggled to repress, that of "this falling in love with women," of "her relation in the old days with Sally Seton. Had not that, after all, been love?" (32). In a somewhat more prosaic mode than that of her earlier meditation, she recalls the unconventional young woman who smoked cigars, spoke freely in the presence of men, pawned her jewelry to finance a sudden visit to Clarissa, imparted her knowledge about sex, picked flowers, and, having forgotten her bath sponge, "ran along the passage naked" at Bourton: "the charm was overpowering, to her at least, so that she could remember standing in her bedroom . . . holding the hot-water can in her hands and saying aloud, 'She is beneath this roof. . . . She is beneath this roof!' " (34). In the presence this romantic figure, with whom she idealistically planned a future of socialist activism free from the constraints of marriage, Clarissa was able to feel "cold with excitement" and "a kind of ecstasy" comparable, ironically, to Othello's: "if it were now to die 'twere now to be most happy" (34, 35). This affair of the heart reaches its culmination in "the most exquisite moment of her life," when, separating themselves from a party of strolling dinner guests in the garden, they pass "a stone urn with flowers in it":[26]

> Sally stopped; picked a flower; kissed her on the lips. The whole world might have turned upside down! The others disappeared; there she was alone with Sally. And she felt that she had been given a present, wrapped up, and told just to keep it, not to look at it—a diamond, something infinitely precious, wrapped up, which, as they walked (up and down, up and down), she uncovered, or the radiance burnt through, the revelation, the religious feeling!—when old Joseph and Peter faced them:
>
> "Star-gazing?" said Peter.
>
> It was like running one's face against a granite wall in the darkness! It was shocking; it was horrible!
>
> Not for herself. She felt only how Sally was being mauled already, maltreated; she felt his hostility; his jealousy; his determination to break into their companionship. All this she saw as one sees a landscape in a flash of lightning—and Sally (never had she admired her so much!) gallantly taking her way unvanquished. . . .
>
> "Oh this horror!" she said to herself, as if she had known all along that something would interrupt, would embitter her moment of happiness.
>
> (35–36)

What is most immediately perceptible about this passage is the intensity and extremity of the emotions represented, particularly as it is a recollection of an event more than thirty years in the past. Yet if Clarissa's emotional responses, whether in the past or in response to memory (for here again past and present are conflated), seem exaggerated in proportion to the actions that actually transpired, it must be understood that this is the crucial moment in which the course of her life was set.[27] Briefly, she experiences not only lesbian pleasure but the potential for fulfillment that seems a metaphysical "revelation" of hidden truth. Yet before she is able to grasp the possibilities of this obscure knowledge, the discourse of shame, in the person of the mocking Peter Walsh, is reinscribed in her consciousness: a union between two women is improper, unnatural, derided.[28] Peter's intrusion in effect reasserts male sexual superiority and control, and reestablishes the male-centered social order that the two women, particularly Sally, threaten to subvert. For Clarissa, who envisions their apprehension, as it were, by the forces of masculinity as the prelude to persecution, an incident that is in a very literal sense little more than an ill-timed verbal exchange becomes, metaphorically, a physical assault.

In the aftermath, the embittered Clarissa succumbs to an elaborate form of lesbian panic. Her "something infinitely precious" has been discovered by others and, to her mind at least, rendered shameful. Unable to forgive, she thoroughly dismisses Peter, the most aggressive and possessive of her suitors. So unforgiving is she that some thirty-five years later, when Peter returns on the day of her party from a long sojourn in India, she avenges herself by subjecting him to a reconfigured triangulation with her daughter, "my Elizabeth" (48), which aggravates and gnaws at his own repressed memories throughout the course of the day and the novel.[29] Although this elimination of the third party of this particular triangle would seem to clear the way for an uninterrupted relationship with Sally, Peter's intrusion has succeeded in establishing the "scruple" that would remain through the years. Clarissa quarrels with Sally as well, and the woman she had so loved virtually vanishes from her life. To fill the gap that ensues, she hastily marries sexually undemanding Richard Dalloway, a man who had heretofore been the butt of her friends' jokes, and thus chooses respectability and repression as her mode of living.

In a section that comprises something less than the initial quarter of the novel, Woolf presents the underlying condition that informs Clarissa Dalloway's life, the causes and effects of her self-closeting. Given her social status and position, it could easily be posited that she had little alternative. Yet the remainder of the novel is given over to the contemplation of other possibilities, personified by the two other major homosexual characters. In comparing *Mrs. Dalloway* with more demotic forms of historical gay and lesbian fiction, Patricia Cramer notes that Woolf's novel "presents the three characteristic endings in coming out narratives written before 1969 [i.e., pre-Stonewall] in the fates of its three homosexual characters: the ending in marriage and suppression of homosexual feelings (Clarissa); loneliness and ostracism (Miss Kilman); and suicide (Septimus)" (180). Thus *Mrs. Dalloway* becomes a compendium of homosexual narrative possibilities and an analysis of their dynamics. Although the outcomes are in all cases bleak and fraught with some degree of panic, Woolf nevertheless not only leaves open the question of whether such fates are, in fact, inevitable but also, through the intensely vivid image of an unrealized lesbian union that effectively concludes the opening portion of the narrative, suggests the hope that the actualization of such a love is not as impossible as it seems.[30]

In her plotting of *Mrs. Dalloway*, Woolf might be said to have put the courtship plot in its place—in the distant past and as the result, rather than the cause, of lesbian panic. Moreover, as DuPlessis points out, Woolf subverts the relationship structures crucial to the courtship plot so that the heterosexually bonded lovers who are typically the focus of the action and interest are replaced by the "psychic twinship between a man and a woman who never meet," the "unsexual, nonromantic central couple" formed by Clarissa and Septimus Warren Smith (57). The "union" of these two linked yet disparate figures is "consummated" only in Clarissa's conscious acknowledgment of and identification with the grotesque death of the young man who had "plunged holding his treasure" (184)—unlike Clarissa who forfeited the "present" given her in the garden long ago. Numerous critics have explicated the images, phrases, and thoughts, even the repressed homosexuality and oppression at the hands of medical science (and, by extension, medical sexology)—personified by Sir William Bradshaw who treats them both for their respective "failures"—that connect this pair.[31] Yet in terms of social and economic class, age, and sex, so vast a gulf looms between the two as to render them polar opposites; alive, Septimus would not be permitted to intrude upon Mrs. Dalloway's party.[32] These characters' responses to their own repressed sexualities, moreover, are predicated by the historical differences in social and cultural behaviors for men and women, in the unequal legal treatment accorded male and female homosexuality, and the traditional "separate spheres" of war and domesticity. Thus, in their shared phenomenon of homosexual panic and their respective outcomes, the simultaneous similarities and dissimilarities of the pair illustrate, perhaps more acutely than in any other literary work, the analogous yet distinctly different forces at work in Sedgwick's paradigm and that developed in this study.[33]

In the character of Septimus Warren Smith, Woolf presents the tragic by-product of the male bonding idealized in Western culture through the glorification of war and "manly virtue," a homosociality that fears and forbids the expression of same-sex desire. Sedgwick provides an analysis of the "self-contradictory and anathema-riddled quicksands" that surround this institutional dictate:

> The result of men's accession to the double bind is, first, the acute *manipulability*, through fear of one's own "homosexuality," of accul-

> turated men; and second, a reservoir of potential for *violence* caused by the self-ignorance that this regime constitutively enforces. The historical emphasis on enforcement of homophobic rules in the armed services in, for example, England and the United States supports this analysis. In these institutions, where both men's manipulability and their potential for violence are at the highest possible premium, the *pre*scription of the most intimate male bonding and the *pro*scription of the (remarkably cognate) "homosexuality" are both stronger than in civilian society—are, in fact, close to absolute.
>
> (*Epistemology* 186)

Given these circumstances, "widespread, endemic male homosexual panic" is virtually inevitable (186). Septimus's origins as a member of the working class seeking to better his standing and expectations through acculturation into middle-class standards renders him particularly prone to the "manipulability" Sedgwick describes.

His self-ignorance (or, more precisely, the repression of his self-knowledge) when, through a "muddled up" admixture of "vanity, ambition, idealism, passion, loneliness, courage, laziness" and an anxiety "to improve himself," he attempts to enact heterosexuality by paying court to the woman who taught Shakespeare in the night school he attends, a woman who "lit in him such a fire as burns . . . *without heat*, flickering a . . . flame ever ethereal and insubstantial" (84–85). This infatuation, quite expectedly, comes to nought; Miss Pole, with remarkable pedagogical sangfroid, rebuffs his awkward love poems, "ignoring the subject . . . [and] correct[ing] in red ink" (85). Subsequently, Septimus, who had so far been "a border case, neither one thing nor the other" (84), turns to male mentoring, one of the "compulsory relationships," according to Sedgwick, that "force men into . . . the middle distance of male homosocial desire" (186), for direction. Concerned for his protégé's health—for "he looked weakly"—Mr. Brewer, the managing clerk for Septimus's employer and a man who is habitually "paternal with his young men," takes the youth under his wings, "advises football" for the development of virility, and paves the way for a successful future in the firm—until war intervenes (85).

As "one of the first to volunteer" (86), Septimus steps from the "middle distance of male homosocial desire" directly into the "self-contradictory quicksands." Participation in the violence of combat produces in him "the change which Mr. Brewer desired": "he developed manliness; he was promoted"; at the same time, he crosses the line between homosocial to homoerotic desire: "he drew the attention, indeed the affection of his officer, Evans by name" (86). Woolf suggestively represents the relationship between the two men through an image that is simultaneously replete with innocence and bestiality, a paradoxical admixture strangely appropriate for socially extolled men at war, yet sympathetically evocative of an idealized male homosexuality:

> It was a case of two dogs playing on a hearth-rug; one worrying a paper screw, snarling, snapping, giving a pinch, now and then, at the old dog's ear; the other lying somnolent, blinking at the fire, raising a paw, turning and growling good-temperedly. They had to be together, share with each other, fight with each other.
>
> (86)

This bliss in the midst of carnage is as short-lived as was Clarissa's with Sally. As the war draws to a close, Evans (a man "undemonstrative in the company of women") is killed in action, and Septimus, with no way to mourn a beloved companion, precipitately marries Rezia, the daughter of Italian innkeeper with whom he is lodged, becoming "engaged one evening when the panic was on him—that he could not feel" (86). Although he returns home with his bride to a hero's welcome and an enviable job promotion from his old firm, Septimus is afflicted with a madness that cannot be completely attributed to shell shock, a madness that results in his preoccupation with prurience, the belief that he is "pocked and marked with vice" (91), and the self-accusation that he had "committed an appalling crime and been condemned to death by human nature" (96).[34] Shakespeare, once his vehicle for attempted heterosexuality, becomes for him the authority by which to proclaim that "Love between man and woman was repulsive. . . . The business of copulation was filth" (89).

Both Clarissa and Septimus marry in panic and in haste, in order to find some form of shelter or concealment from unspeakable desires. Because of socially inscribed roles, however, the relative successes of their having "schemed," having "pilfered," as Clarissa calls it (185), are drastically dissimilar. While by the 1920s Miss Kilman might tell Elizabeth that "every profession is open to the women of your generation" (136), such was hardly the case for Elizabeth's mother. As a young, upper middle-class woman in fin-de-siècle British culture, Clarissa had been reared without any expectation of her achieving any significant accomplishments or, for that matter, assuming any significant responsibilities. Rather, the greatest expectation—indeed, an imperative—imposed upon her was simply that she marry well and be decorative. Having accomplished that, her "failure" would at least appear a success. Given her privileged status, even her apparent "frigidity" would hardly seem amiss, for virtuous women of the day were thought, as a matter of course, to feel no sexual desire or pleasure.[35] For Septimus, however, the duties demanded and expected of a married man—potency and paternity—prove impossible and push him further into panic and psychosis.

Woolf introduces Clarissa's "psychic twin" early in the novel, in the "gap" in Clarissa's consciousness following the backfire that disrupts her reverie with Miss Pym. Septimus, in his penultimate state of madness, wanders and raves in Regent's Park. The long-suffering Rezia, in tears, prepares to escort her husband to his appointment with Sir William Bradshaw, a specialist in such cases whom she hopes will accomplish the cure that the negligent and ineffectual general practitioner Dr. Holmes could not. Naive and "without friends in England" (16), she is unable to comprehend either the disintegration of her marriage, her husband's tremendous unhappiness, or his refusal simply to be a husband: "He was happy without her. Nothing could make her happy without him! Nothing! He was selfish. So men are. For he was not ill. Dr. Holmes said there was nothing wrong with him" (23). In this initial episode, his ravings, including the sudden public outburst "I will kill myself" (16), yield no indication of causality. Yet, as Mitchell A. Leaska observes, two "contradictory tendencies" are evident: a pervasive fear of persecution expressed through "self-accusatory feelings [and] panic," alternating with the presumption of his own Messianic "super-morality which makes him superior to other mortals," which, in combination with each other, suggest a guilt originating in "something he has done which he feels to be a violation of his society's code of morality" (105).[36] In the course of his next appearance, coinciding with Peter Walsh's interlude in the park, the patterns of Septimus's mental associations become clearer. His ventures in the park are a quest for Evans, who, he imagines, answers his singing "from behind the tree" (70). The linking of Evans and trees, moreover, is part of a greater associative network in which trees are related to panic and Evans is related to Greece, the traditionally held originary site of male homosexual love (Leaska 107). Subsequently, canine imagery, through which Woolf elsewhere represents the relationship between the two men, becomes part of the hallucinations and the dynamics of his homosexual panic become clear. As he mutters "No crime; love," in response to the "voices" who command him to tell the "supreme secret" to the Prime Minister and the Cabinet, "a Skye terrier snuf[s] his trousers," causing

Septimus "an agony of fear": "It was turning into a man! He could not watch it happen! It was horrible, terrible to see a dog become a man!" (67–68).

Rezia, despite every good intention, is the unwitting catalyst of his demise. Lonely, confused, and unaware of the source of her husband's agitation, she urges him to normalcy and fatherhood—"she must have children" (89). But such demands only serve to increase his despair, as he imagines his "crimes" mocking him "over the rail of the bed in the early hours of the morning at the prostrate body which lay realising its degradation; how he had married his wife without loving her; had lied to her" (91). Her best efforts to cure him merely deliver him into the hands of the men of science who would indeed label him a criminal and an invert; but because she interferes in his medical examination, claiming "he has done nothing wrong whatever" (96), Sir William Bradshaw judges Septimus little more than a malingerer who "lives for himself alone" (98) and who is in need of "a long rest in bed" (96). In a moment of insight, Septimus wonders, "But if he confessed? . . . Would they let him off then, his torturers?" (98); but when the opportunity to do so comes, he is unable to remember his "crime." His appointment with Sir William draws to a meaningless close, and he is sent home to await his commitment to one of "Holmes's homes" (97).

In a brief respite from madness before he is to be taken away, Septimus makes one last and seemingly sane performative act of marriage and gender, an act corresponding to Judith Butler's argument that gender "constitut[es] the identity it is purported to be," that "there is no gender identity behind the expressions of gender; that identity is performatively constituted by the very 'expressions' that are said to be the results" (25). Internalizing the Shakespearean message to "fear no more" that has heretofore lingered in Clarissa's consciousness, Septimus enacts husbandly affection, playing with Rezia while she makes a hat and asking after the landlady's married daughter, a woman whose pregnancy Rezia has envied. His jokes cheer her, and she perceives his behavior not as performative but, rather, as reality: "How it rejoiced her that! Not for weeks had they laughed like this together, poking fun privately like married people. . . . Never had she felt so happy! Never in her life!" (143). To Rezia, the mere enactment of "normalcy" and expected gender roles seems a result, a miraculous cure, in and of itself. Yet Septimus's performance is merely that, for even as he diverts her, he internally questions the reality of objects in the room and fears to look at his wife's face "in case it were deformed," lest he discover something "frightening or disgusting in her" (142). It is, moreover, a performance that cannot be sustained. Once Rezia takes the hat downstairs to present to her pregnant neighbor,

Evans intrudes once more upon Septimus's consciousness. Dr. Holmes arrives to remove the patient, and, despite the insistence of Rezia (who believes her husband out of danger) that the doctor leave, Septimus escapes his "tormentors," flinging himself "vigorously, violently down on to Mrs. Filmer's area railings" (149). Holmes, as befits his authoritative social position, is allowed a ferociously and bitterly ironic last word on the matter: "No one," he explains, "was in the least to blame" (150).

In her introduction to the 1928 Modern Library edition of *Mrs. Dalloway*, an essay that is, among other things, an exemplar of authorial diffidence and disingenuity, Woolf reveals a "scrap," "of little importance or none perhaps": "[I]n the first version Septimus, who later is intended to be her double, had no existence; and that Mrs. Dalloway was originally to kill herself, or perhaps merely to die at the end of the party." She adds, with irony and mock sincerity, that "such scraps are offered humbly to the reader in the hope that like other odds and ends they may come in useful" (vi). Indeed, the "usefulness" of this information has led many critics to look no further than DuPlessis's model of the "unsexual, nonromantic central couple" in envisioning the fundamental configuration of the novel. Such an assumption, however, overlooks the third party of what is, in fact, a triangle, the constantly repeated and reconfigured structure upon which this novel is built. At almost the same moment as Clarissa's "psychic twin" impales himself on his landlady's rusted railings, Elizabeth Dalloway sets out on a bus ride that is no less than a journey of self-exploration and autonomy after a hasty and rather awkward farewell to her mother's other double, Doris Kilman.

For the first two-thirds of the novel, Miss Kilman does not appear directly, despite her brief but looming presence in the opening pages, as a disruptive thought preying upon Clarissa's consciousness. As such, she is, to use Terry Castle's model, the lesbian ghost, in this case a vampire-like incubus, "one of those spectres with which one battles in the night; one of those spectres who stand astride us and suck up half our life-blood, dominators and tyrants" (12). Simultaneously, she represents the return of the repressed through a grotesque mirror imaging of the younger Clarissa Parry, the woman Clarissa might have been had she not become Mrs. Dalloway. Years before at Bourton Clarissa had sat with Sally "hour after hour, talking in her bedroom at the top of the house, talking about life, how they were to reform the world. They meant to found a society to abolish private property, and actually had a letter written, though not sent out. The ideas were Sally's, of course—but very soon she was just as excited" (33). Even in this idealized dream of a socialist and presumably lesbian utopia, similar to Evelyn Murgatroyd's in *The Voyage Out* or that utopia never brought to fruition in Woolf's short story "A Society," Clarissa plays a passive role, much as she later does when faced with Richard Dalloway's Tory ideologies. But while Clarissa has become a woman with little in the way of social conscience or conviction, this dream not only stands as a reminder of the lost moment, it also mocks the privileged and materialistic Clarissa in the person of Miss Kilman, who, in her poverty and bitterness, represents the harsh realization of the once-sweet ideal.

Significantly, Elizabeth is, in the novel's present, the same age as her mother was during her passionate involvement with Sally in the past. Thus, the first image of Miss Kilman, Elizabeth's Christian socialist tutor, in Clarissa's consciousness is that of the seducer of younger woman.[37] Unlike Sally, however, she is not a romantic figure but rather a type of the child molester who, somewhat incongruously, utilizes traditional Christianity—in contrast to Clarissa's "atheist's religion of doing good for the sake of goodness" (78)—to secure her quarry. A contemplation of her own ladylike "passion" for shoes and gloves leads Clarissa first to the enigma of Elizabeth, who "cared not a straw for either of them" (11), then to a fretful concern that her daughter "might be falling in love" with Miss Kilman and participating in her Anglican devotions, an associative sequence indicating that the mother is as concerned with the feminine aesthetics lacking in the relationship and its metaphysical inclinations as she is with its substance:

> Anyhow they were inseparable, and Elizabeth, her own daughter, went to Communion; and how she dressed, how she treated people who came to lunch she did not care a bit, it being to her experience that the religious ecstasy made people callous (so did causes); dulled their feelings for Miss Kilman would do anything for the Russians, starved herself for the Austrians, but in private inflicted positive torture, so insensitive was she, dressed in a green mackintosh coat. Year in and year out she wore that coat; she perspired; she was never in the room five minutes without making you feel her superiority your inferiority; how poor she was; how rich you were; how she lived in a slum without a cushion or a bed or a rug or whatever it might be, all her soul rusted with that grievance sticking in it, her dismissal from school during the War—poor embittered unfortunate creature!
>
> (12–13)

This extraordinary passage, comprised of two very prolix sentences, leads us circuitously through the whole of Clarissa's highly complex response to

Miss Kilman, a character she keeps ever at a distance through the exclusive use of her formal name. She moves quickly from the central relationship between the teacher and the student (which, with herself as the third party, forms yet another triangle), the potential sexual improprieties of which seem to disturb her little, to the Christianity that seems to encompass both a disdain for feminine beauty and a profound asociality, and thus a disdain for the most salient features of the society matron's quotidian mode of existence. Her assessment of the "callousness" of Miss Kilman's political activism, perhaps a projection of her own apathy, turns again, inevitably, to aesthetics and fashion and the image of the teacher's green mackintosh, an article of clothing associated not only with poverty in its constant use but also with the physicality of a woman who sweats and makes her presence felt, unlike the ethereal and disembodied Mrs. Dalloway. Subsequently, she engages in a hyperbolic and unconsciously guilty assessment of the other woman's economic marginality in contrast to her own wealth, only to end, ironically, with an expression of pity. For Clarissa Dalloway does, on some level, recognize not only the differences between appearances and reality (differences which she herself has manipulated for years) but also her reverse image in Doris Kilman: "For it was not her one hated but the idea of her, which undoubtedly had gathered in to itself a great deal that was not Miss Kilman; . . . for no doubt with another throw of the dice, had the black been uppermost and not the white, she would have loved Miss Kilman! But not in this world. No" (12). Clarissa, if only subliminally, recognizes her own forfeiture of the love of women, having chosen instead the wealth and security that, because they are the rewards of male patronage, are not the lot of the lesbian. The panic Miss Kilman arouses is actually the memory of Clarissa's long-ago lesbian panic. In another world, she or Sally Seton could have loved—indeed, could have been—Doris Kilman, but not in a world in which the love of women might mean the renunciation of beautiful shoes and gloves.

The moment of recognition is fleeting, however. Her offense at Doris Kilman's lack of gentility and the sexual threat she presents not only to Elizabeth but, it would seem, to Clarissa as well, takes on the imagery of rape and bestial primitivity in Clarissa's mind:

> It rasped her . . . to have stirring about in her this brutal monster! to hear twigs cracking and feel hooves planted down in the depths of that leaf-encumbered forest, the soul; never to be content quite, or quite secure, for at any moment the brute would be stirring, this

> hatred, which especially since her illness, had power to make her feel scraped, hurt in her spine; gave her physical pain, and made all pleasure in beauty, in friendship, in being well, in being loved and making her home delightful rock, quiver, and bend as if indeed there were a monster grubbing at the roots, as if the whole panoply of content were nothing but self love! this hatred!
>
> (12)

The "brutal monster" in the forest of the soul, an image that suggestively echoes Henry James's "The Beast in the Jungle," is at first another image of Miss Kilman, an abrupt departure from her being the object of pity only a moment before. The brute expands to encompass all of Clarissa's sexual fears, frustrations, and repressions, becoming a causal factor in her "illness" and leaving her in a state metaphorically approximating that of sexual violation. Then, once more, she returns to her concerns for security and beauty, only to find the monster of sexual repression—now also including her desire for material comfort, the self-love by which she has betrayed herself—destroying the foundations of her house and, by Freudian extension, her very being. Only when she enters the tranquillity of Miss Pym's shop, with its more idyllic reminders of things past, is she soothed and freed from her torment, while Miss Kilman, who has yet to be actually seen outside of Clarissa's consciousness, disappears until relatively late in the novel.

In the afternoon of Mrs. Dalloway's day, Miss Kilman is once more a presence, even if, at first, still out of sight. When Richard Dalloway returns from his lunch engagement with Lady Bruton, bearing roses in hand but unable to tell Clarissa that he loves her, his wife is in a state of distress, equally vexed at the thoughts of "having to invite all the dull women in London to her parties" and of "Elizabeth closeted all this time with Doris Kilman" (117). In this rare interchange between these marriage partners, the differences in the couple's perceptions of the teacher and their subtle but palpable oppositionality in this matter become clear. To Clarissa's announcement that "that woman Kilman" (118) is with their daughter, Dalloway, after some idle chat about other matters, absentmindedly inquires after "our dear Miss Kilman," only to be informed tersely that "Kilman arrives just as we've done lunch. . . . Elizabeth turns pink. They shut themselves up. I suppose they're praying" (119). Clarissa's summary of events and Dalloway's mental response ("he didn't like it; but these things pass over if you let them" [119]) indicate that religion and illicit sexuality, however incompatible they may be to one another, are equated in the minds of both parents: both, moreover, quite apparently feel ill-equipped to challenge this double threat. Thus, Richard Dalloway can do little to assuage his wife's anxiety other than bring a pillow and blanket and bid her to rest, a cure similar in kind to that which Sir William offers Septimus.

This rest and the ensuing eschatological contemplation of things past are interrupted by Elizabeth at the door—and Miss Kilman "outside the door . . . listening to whatever they said" (123). At this juncture the narrative perspective shifts, for the first time, from Clarissa's consciousness to that of Doris Kilman. While Clarissa's earlier mental representations of the woman cannot be called other than grotesque distortions, Miss Kilman's perceptions and obsessions clearly—and aggressively—mirror those of Clarissa:

> Yes, Miss Kilman stood on the landing, and wore a mackintosh; but had her reasons. First, it was cheap; second, she was over forty; and did not, after all, dress to please. She was poor, moreover, degradingly poor. Otherwise she would not be taking jobs from people like the Dalloways; from rich people, who liked to be kind. . . . [Mrs. Dalloway] came from the most worthless of all classes—the rich, with a smattering of culture. They had expensive things everywhere; pictures, carpets, lots of servants. She considered that she had a perfect right to anything that the Dalloways did for her.
>
> She had been cheated. Yes, the word was no exaggeration, for surely a girl has a right to some kind of happiness? And she had never been happy, what with being so clumsy and so poor. And then, just as she might have had a chance at Miss Dolby's school, the War came; and she had never been able to tell lies. Miss Dolby thought she would be happier with people who shared her views about the Germans. She had to go. . . . Then Our Lord had come to her (and here she always bowed her head). She had seen the light two years and three months ago. Now she did not envy women like Clarissa Dalloway; she pitied them.
>
> She pitied and despised them from the bottom of her heart, as she stood on the soft carpet, looking at the old engraving of a little girl with a muff.
>
> (123–24)

Just as Clarissa Dalloway seeks to justify her wealth, frivolity, and self-centeredness through aesthetic disapprobation of her nemesis's poverty and unfashionability, so does Doris Kilman promote, through her political and religious ideologies, her lack of worldly goods and social contacts as a sign of her moral superiority over a woman whom she deems incapable of diligence, serious purpose, or self-sacrifice. As such, Doris Kilman is the negative reflection of Clarissa Dalloway, the figurative throw of the dice in which, to use Clarissa's image, the black is uppermost and not the white. Ideology, moreover, serves Miss Kilman as the means by which to perpetuate her bitterness, the means by which she can reassure herself that in a system of higher good than that of Mrs. Dalloway's "good for the sake of goodness," she has been cheated through no fault of her own. While there is, in fact, much truth in this assessment, the comforts of ideology do not inspire her to a Christian ideal of brotherly (or, for that matter, sisterly) love, for her works of charity are almost inevitably for strangers; rather, those comforts give her permission to hate and allow her, to paraphrase Slavoj Zizek, to enjoy her symptoms of marginality, to indulge the "hot and turbulent feelings which boiled and surged in her" (124), and utilize them as a weapon against those she deems morally inferior. Her ideologies, like her gluttony, function after all as surrogates for the sexual and aesthetic gratification, the "right to some kind of happiness," both she and her society deny her.

In this manner, Doris Kilman, who has relatively few antecedents save the sinister governess Miss Lane in Charles Dickens's *Little Dorrit*, becomes a prototype of the manipulative and embittered lesbian of subsequent literature. While Clarissa Dalloway, with her love of flowers, beauty, and luxury, may be seen as a ladylike and repressed descendent of the decadent lesbians prevalent in fin-de-siècle art and literature, Miss Kilman, with her "unlovable body" (129) and her ideological self-righteousness, anticipates the sinister and demonic lesbian figures common in much mid-twentieth century literature. She also anticipates the almost stereotypical "political lesbian" who appears frequently—often cast heroically—in popular lesbian fictions of the 1970s and later.[38] With her intelligence, her "knowledge of modern history . . . thorough in the extreme" (125), and her virtual exclusion from the male-dominated world of academia, moreover, she shares many attributes with the highly sympathetic Olivia and Chloe in *A Room of One's Own*. Thus, as a basically virtuous but altogether unpleasant lesbian scholar in the context of *Mrs. Dalloway*, she is perforce a problematic character, for any sympathy she elicits is adulterated by her alienating demeanor.

This bifurcated quality in Miss Kilman is evinced in both her brief confrontation with Clarissa Dalloway and her subsequent outing for tea with Elizabeth. As Miss Kilman prepares to depart with Elizabeth, Mrs. Dalloway emerges from her room, setting the stage for psychological combat. Elizabeth, who "could not bear to see them together," flees on a fragile excuse, and Miss Kilman, glaring and glowering, seeks a "religious victory" over her opponent, who, in turn, contemplates the hypocrisy of her rival for love of and control over "the beautiful girl" (125). Yet as these negatively mirroring interlocutors face each other, the "monster armoured for primeval warfare," sorely out of her element, disintegrates in her opposite's gaze to become "merely Miss Kilman, in a mackintosh, whom Heaven knows Clarissa would have liked to help" (126). But because Clarissa has forsaken the love of women for the sake of economic security and because Doris Kilman in her religion and, ironically, poverty, lacks either the permission or the wherewithal to establish a relationship with another woman, they have both relinquished the ability to "help" each other; so Clarissa merely says good-bye—and laughs. Accordingly, they engage in a reversed form of lesbianism in which hatred becomes for both a pleasurable substitute for love; and Clarissa's laugh and parting injunction "Remember the party!"—a signal of mockery for Miss Kilman as much as it is a reminder for Elizabeth—repeatedly pierces and tortures the consciousness of the vanquished woman.

The choice of a department store, the social monument to materialism and consumerism, as the locus for a tête-à-tête between Miss Kilman and Elizabeth is informed as much by the former's sadomasochism as it is by her need to purchase that most feminine of garments, a petticoat.[39] En route, she glories in the fact that "she had got Elizabeth" (129), yet all the while mutters to herself that she must control her own "fleshly desires" (128). Miss Kilman, unlike Clarissa and Septimus, makes no effort to deny or disguise her homoerotic inclinations through attempted assimilation into heterosexuality, institutional or otherwise. But while she clearly acknowledges both her desires and their sources, her position as a teacher (who is, moreover, dependent upon the Dalloways for her income) inevitably obviates any liaison with her charge, while her poverty, bitterness, and unattractiveness all work to minimize the possibility of any other relationship. Consequently, she transfers her sexual cravings to another mode of physical gratification: "Except for Elizabeth, her food was all that she lived for; her comforts; her dinner, her tea, her hot-water bottle at night" (129)—and Elizabeth and food take on for her virtually the same valences.

Accordingly, as they enter the department store restaurant, Miss Kilman is in a state of "abstraction" (129) as the objects of both of her main desires are so near at hand. Indeed, Miss Kilman eats "with intensity," coveting the pink cake consumed by a child at an adjoining table and sensually yet grotesquely devouring a chocolate éclair, all the while reciting her litany of grievances against society, personified, in her mind by Clarissa Dalloway. This manipulation of triangulated affections combined with gluttony climaxes in a moment of subdued but nonetheless devastating lesbian panic:

> She was about to split asunder, she felt. The agony was so terrific. If she could grasp her, if she could clasp her, if she could make her hers absolutely and forever and then die; that was all she wanted. But to sit here, unable to think of anything to say; to see Elizabeth turning against her; to be felt repulsive even by her—it was too much; she could not stand it. The thick fingers curled inward.
>
> (132)

Prosaically if ironically echoing Clarissa's Shakespearean sentiment, "if it were now to die 'twere now to be most happy," Miss Kilman, encumbered by the grievances she has collected for so long, equating love with possession and consumption, and recognizing her own embittered unloveliness, loses her moment and once more turns her sorrow and frustration inward. She can only lament aloud that "people don't ask me to parties," despite her awareness that "this egotism was her undoing." As a result, her student, daunted by the display of ferocious self-pity, flees like "some dumb creature," while Miss Kilman, echoing Clarissa's parting imperative, pleadingly cries after her, "Don't quite forget me" (132).

Doris Kilman's lesbian panic, unlike the respective panics of Clarissa and Septimus, is never expressed in a singular dramatic action, such as dishonest marriage or suicide. Rather, it takes the more subtle but equally pervasive form of a lingering psychological malaise, a chronic unhappiness that prevents its bearer not only from forming any useful or nurturing attachments with others but also from changing the conditions from which the panic arises. Left alone "at the marble table among the éclairs" (133), Doris Kilman "lurches" in distress from the department store and into the shelter of Westminster Abbey, where she can be "not a woman, a soul" (134). Having once more elected the comforts of ideology as a safeguard against her physicality—"her largeness, robustness, and power" (134)—she partakes in a metaphysical self-immolation and disappears from the text.

Once both Septimus and Miss Kilman have enacted their panic-driven self-sacrifices (almost simultaneously in the novel's chronological schemata), the central triangular configuration of the narrative begins to dissolve. In the process, however, Clarissa Dalloway, in the midst of her party, intuitively gains self-knowledge from her two "secret sharers." Seeing the picture of the little girl with the muff, which had earlier triggered Miss Kilman's meditation of spite, Clarissa recalls her nemesis to her consciousness "with a rush": "Kilman was her enemy. That was satisfying; that was real. Ah, how she hated her—hot, hypocritical, corrupt; with all that power; Elizabeth's seducer; the woman who had crept in to steal and defile (Richard would say, What nonsense!). She hated her: she loved her. It was enemies one wanted, not friends" (175). While the image of Doris Kilman as molester, is, as Richard Dalloway's interpolated voice suggests, for the most part a projection (for, as Elizabeth's flight from the restaurant demonstrates, she is not that easily or readily seduced), it nonetheless serves a vital purpose for Clarissa. Although time and social conditions have placed her far beyond the point of realistically contracting a lesbian relationship with any woman, she is nonetheless able to derive a gothically tinged frisson from the very tangible homosocial animosity and rivalry they share through their respective relationships with Elizabeth. She recognizes, too, that passionate hatred is a negative mirroring of passionate love and is, in its way, equally erotic. This "arrangement," as it were, is undoubtedly far from any ideal; but for Clarissa it is "satisfying," it is "real"; it is, moreover, the form of lesbianism, however perverse, still within her grasp.

Conversely, she identifies with the mental anguish and death of Septimus Warren Smith. While wondering "why had he done it?," she envisions his death in terms related to her own past, equating his "treasure" and the "thing there was that mattered" with her own moment of passion at Bourton, repeating, once again, Othello's lines of doomed love. She understands, too, "life [has been] made intolerable" (185) for Septimus and her alike by Sir William Bradshaw, the "great doctor . . . obscurely evil, without sex or lust" (184). She deduces from this their shared and forbidden desires, their kinship.[40] Yet, considering the relative comforts, privilege, and status that the forfeiture of her own "treasure," have bought, she is overcome with shame:

> Then . . . there was the terror; . . . if Richard had not been there . . . she must have perished. But that young man had killed himself.
>
> Somehow it was her disaster—her disgrace. It was her punishment to see . . . here a man, there a woman, in this profound darkness, and she forced to stand here in her evening dress. She had schemed; she had pilfered. She was never wholly admirable.
>
> (185)

Septimus's suicide thus forces Clarissa to examine her heretofore unexamined life and judge whether or not it is, or has been, worth living. If it were

Woolf's original intention that Clarissa should die, through suicide or heart failure, her "punishment" for scheming and pilfering has been commuted, so to speak, to a life of "forced" parties and triviality, a life now marked by an understanding of her own motivations.

By unlinking self-knowledge and death, Woolf eschews a tragic ending. Rather, she allows her protagonist a reconciliation with the past through a moment of psychological healing, tempered by an acknowledgment of that which she has lost. As the triangle of Clarissa, Septimus, and Doris Kilman fades, having served its purpose, it is replaced by the original configuration of Clarissa, Peter Walsh, and Sally Seton, all of whom are reunited at the party.

Peter, whom Septimus earlier in the day mistook for Evans returned from the dead, shares with Clarissa in his own life of loss—his lack of a career or stable relationship—the living death that results from the absence of self-knowledge and the forfeiture, through excessive emotionality, of one's "treasure." He shares, moreover, certain traits with Septimus. Peter, "not altogether manly" (156), is typical of the male hysteric who must constantly enact hypermasculinity in order to maintain his heterosexual identity in male-dominated society. Judith Butler posits that gender, which Peter enacts to a far greater degree than Septimus, "is the repeated stylization of the body, a set of repeated acts within a highly rigid regulatory frame that congeal over time to produce the appearance of substance, of a natural sort of being" (33). Peter's thoroughly unsubtle and constant manipulations of his pocketknife are merely the symbolic manifestation of a gender performance more directly executed through his chronic, often fantasized womanizing. But while Septimus is unable to sustain the performance for any length of time and thus elects to die, Peter, like Clarissa, is congealed in a life of empty and ultimately feckless repetitions of masculine tropes, of being never wholly admirable.

Ironically, Sally Seton has, like Clarissa, exchanged "something infinitely precious" for status and security. Arriving at the party as an uninvited guest, Sally reveals herself as Lady Rosseter, the wife of a wealthy Midlands industrialist and the mother of "five enormous boys" (171). Seeing her once beloved friend for the first time in many years, Clarissa sadly discovers that Sally, too, is marked by loss:

> She hadn't looked like that, Sally Seton, when Clarissa grasped the hot water can, to think of her under this roof, under this roof! Not like that! . . .

> One might put down the hot water can quite composedly. The lustre had gone out of her.
>
> (171)

Whether the closeted and thus unexamined life is worth living is a question too complex, as Woolf rightly knew, for a simple answer. Yet in at last examining her life and weighing what was gained and what was lost, Clarissa Dalloway is allowed a second fleeting reconfiguration of the lost moment. As the guests depart, Peter and Sally, who have spent much of the evening in reminiscences of Bourton, linger. Given the ongoing attachment between the two, it is evident that Peter's loss of Clarissa is, in fact, Sally's loss as well, for it is conceivable that the original triangular relationship could have continued through time and marriage.[41] Seeing Richard Dalloway with Elizabeth, Sally, who had mocked him in the old days and thought him unworthy of Clarissa, relents, concluding that the quality of brain is less important than that of the heart. Peter, for his part, is filled with "this terror . . . this ecstasy": "It is Clarissa, he said. For there she was" (194). Coming from the perspective of Peter, who remains, after all these years, passionately in love with Clarissa, this ending, as Emily Jensen suggests (176), places him in Clarissa's position in the garden at Bourton, his epiphanic moment threatened by the presence of Sally as interloper. As such, it is, metaphysically at least, a moment of making amends for the past. But it is also a shared moment between the three, all of whom have remained trapped at the earlier moment, unwilling or unable to define either what transpired or the price each has paid for his or her reaction and thus unable to progress emotionally. Accordingly, it is a moment of self-reflection and mourning for the loss that ensued from lesbian panic long ago—which is sadly the optimum, in terms of resolution and closure, to which these three, with the passage of time, can aspire.

Mrs. Dalloway presents a microcosmic view of a society in which homosexual panic, both in its male and female varieties, is not only pervasive but debilitating both to the afflicted individuals and to the community of which they are members. If any character can be said to escape the effects of homosexual panic relatively unscathed, however, it is Elizabeth Dalloway. Only on the verge of adulthood, she remains an adolescent who "really care[s] for her dog most of all" (11) and apparently has "no preferences" (135) in terms of sexuality any more than she does in choosing buses to ride as she escapes her teacher. Despite her rather ambiguous devotion to Miss Kilman, the older woman seems little more to her than an interesting alternative to a mother primarily concerned with beauty and decorum, and her flight is that of a youth from yet one more oppressive and manipulative adult "always talking about her own sufferings" (136). What is clear nonetheless is Elizabeth's knowledge that she, unlike her mother, has the ability to choose the life she will lead, as a doctor or a farmer—if not as a society lady, for she need not marry.

Carolyn G. Heilbrun (165) has noted that the "Chinese eyes" that set Elizabeth Dalloway apart from all of her mother's kinswomen are also characteristic of Lily Briscoe in Woolf's subsequent novel *To the Lighthouse.* The implied relationship between the two is apt, for Lily represents the further development of a woman who has the possibility of rejecting the institutional heterosexuality that had heretofore been compulsory. As an aspiring artist and lesbian—and she is no less in the process of becoming one than the other—Lily must negotiate the well-meaning but ill-advised urgings to marriage of the presiding matron, Mrs. Ramsay, and the potential for panic that lies in her unrealizable homoerotic desire for this very woman.

To the Lighthouse, the fifth of Woolf's nine novels, stands at the chronological center of her oeuvre. Similarly, it stands as a watershed text in which she brings to completion her struggle against what Joseph Allen Boone has called the "wedlock plot."[42] In this text, as Boone observes, "by means of . . . narrative devices that violate conventions of fictional realism, Woolf simultaneously dismantles the Victorian marital ideal embodied in the . . . union of complementary opposition" (201). Lily's bildung is set against—indeed, in opposition to—the crepuscular marriage of Mr. and Mrs. Ramsay, a couple so identified with the traditional marriage of separate spheres and binary oppositions along sex and gender lines that they are differentiated from one another not by given names but by their respective sex-related marital honorifics. "The Window," the first section of the novel resembles *Mrs. Dalloway* in its depiction of the quotidian events of an apparently representative day in the marriage of the Ramsays as they vacation with their children and guests at their summer home. Once again employing an almost telepathic stream of consciousness, Woolf delineates the dynamics and limits of dichotomized masculine and feminine gender roles and their toll on this couple. After years together, they are permanently infantilized adults, desperately dependent upon one another for identity and meaning, and yet blocked by the limits of their perceived duties from communicating meaningfully with one another or with their children.

Lily Briscoe, the Ramsays' "spinster" houseguest, provides the counterpoint to this exhaustion of the marriage plot. In a hierarchical schemata, she is perforce deferential to her hostess, the matriarchal Mrs. Ramsay, who not only employs the manipulative power of the powerless that her role grants her but who urges the source of her own powerlessness—the marriage plot—on others.[43] Unquestioning of her own state, Mrs. Ramsay declares of her female visitors, "they all must marry, since in the whole world whatever laurels might be tossed to her . . . an unmarried woman has missed the best of life" (49). Along with this "friendly" advice, Lily is subjected to the taunts of Charles Tansley, another houseguest, that she has no alternative to the preordained narrative of a woman's life: "Women can't paint, women can't write" (48). Complicating these tensions is Lily's emotional involvement with Mrs. Ramsay. Because it is love that truly dare not speak its name in this repressive context, Lily expresses her desires through an almost filial devotion; but to please Mrs. Ramsay would mean the rejection of artistic aspirations and submission to the injunction "all must marry."[44] Accordingly, the development of Lily's subplot is based on her refusal to surrender to either the dominant plot or an alternative narrative of panic. In this manner, Lily is allowed to moved beyond deadlocks of self-negation forced upon the homosexual characters in *Mrs. Dalloway.*

Lily's "trial" is placed, narratively if not chronologically, in the middle (section IX) of the first part. The episode is not so much an event in the course of the day as it is Lily's recollection, spurred by Tansley's invective, of her highly ambiguous feelings about Mrs. Ramsay as an individual. After recounting the considerable difference in status between them and numerous incidents of the older woman manipulating others and "presiding with immutable calm over destinies which she completely failed to understand" (50), Lily recalls an interlude with Mrs. Ramsay in which Lily attempts to define the "essence" of the other woman but, in effect, defines what is within herself:

> Was it wisdom? Was it knowledge? Was it, once more, the deception of beauty . . . or did she lock up within her some secret . . . ? Sitting on the floor with her arms round Mrs. Ramsay's knees, close as she could get, smiling to think that Mrs. Ramsay would never know the reason of that pressure, she imagined how in the chambers of the mind and heart of the woman who was, physically, touching her, were stood, like the treasures in the tombs of kings, tablets bearing sacred inscriptions, which if one could spell them out, would teach one everything, but they would never be offered openly, never made pub-

> lic. What art was there, known to love or cunning, by which one pressed through into those secret chambers? What device for becoming, like waters poured into one jar, inextricably the same, one with the object adored? Could the body achieve, or the mind, subtly mingling in the intricate passages of the brain? or the heart? Could loving, as people called it, make her and Mrs. Ramsay one? for it was not knowledge but unity that she desired, not inscriptions on tablets, nothing that could be written in any language known to men, but intimacy itself, which is knowledge, she had thought, leaning her head on Mrs. Ramsay's knee.
>
> Nothing happened. Nothing! Nothing! as she leant her head against Mrs. Ramsay's knee. . . . Mrs. Ramsay rose. Lily rose. Mrs. Ramsay went. For days there hung about her, as after a dream some subtle change is felt in the person one has dreamt of, more vividly than anything she said, the sound of murmuring.
>
> (50–51)

This erotically charged passage, while recalling those in *Mrs. Dalloway*, differs from them in its rhetoric and form. Rendered, prior to its exclamatory climax, predominantly by questions, it reflects the uncertainty of Lily's desires and her purpose in pursuing them. She approaches Mrs. Ramsay, at first psychically, in order to discover something "lock[ed] up within her," something ineffable that, Lily believes, will explain to her the "meaning of life" she repeatedly queries. This approach, however, is enmeshed in self-deception, for, as Lily herself has seen, Mrs. Ramsay is not particularly knowledgeable and possibly not very wise; the only knowledge or wisdom she possesses is of an intuitive sort and thus cannot be imparted to another.[45] Lily begins to undeceive herself with her acknowledgment, obliquely articulated, of the secret "reason of that pressure," the erotic intensity of their physical contact; but the secret is immediately veiled once more as Lily creates a "loftier" purpose for her stratagem—the quasi-archaeological quest for the artifacts of a lost, ancient, and presumably female culture—which, in its passive aggression, recalls those of Miss Allan and other women in *The Voyage Out*. The unlikely image of Mrs. Ramsay as a collected object never put on display does not endure; it gives way, by means of the suggestion of "love and cunning," to images of like joined with like in physical and psychic union in a "language not known to man."

But this highly metaphorical representation of lesbian desire ends not in orgasmic rapture, as does the "match burning in a crocus" passage in *Mrs.*

Dalloway; rather, it ends in frustration—and denial. "Nothing happened," in the sense that Mrs. Ramsay will, in fact, "never know the reason"; nothing beyond Lily's covert erotic pleasure in this acceptable homosocial display of affection will ever transpire between them. Decorum notwithstanding, it is questionable whether Mrs. Ramsay would comprehend "the reason" even if Lily *could* express it directly. As Nina Auerbach has noted in another context, women of Mrs. Ramsay's generation did not, generally speaking, read the sexologists (Woolf emphasizes that Mrs. Ramsay does not, as a practice, read books) and thus were unlikely to be "certain of what [lesbianism] was" (390). Simultaneously, the assertion that "nothing happened" *could* function as a mode of denial and panic, a self-erasure of the realization of homoerotic desires. If Lily were to panic, this is precisely the point in the narrative at which she could retreat into a safe posture, perhaps even gratify Mrs. Ramsay's matchmaking whims and renounce her art, and thus remain within a respectable proximity to "the object adored"—or create an alternate narrative of physical or psychological self-destruction.

But Lily does not panic; and something, in fact, *does* happen. The "subtle change" that, in Lily's perception, hangs around Mrs. Ramsay—a nonverbal "murmuring"—is the recognition of desires that remain, for Lily, unarticulable in "any language known to man," but are present all the same. By recognizing her desires without panic, Lily is able to plot her own narrative as artist rather than accept that which Mrs. Ramsay would impose on her; and because she evades the living death of denial and self-abnegation, she is able to retain a love for Mrs. Ramsay, in spite of the older woman's very obvious shortcomings.

As artist and lesbian, Lily's two-fold task of development reflects Woolf's continued concern with the relationship between the two roles, a connection that is manifest in its rudimentary stages in *The Voyage Out* with the sexually undefined Rachel as unfulfilled musician and the repressed Miss Allan as literary anthologizer. This dual personification culminates in *Between the Acts* with the openly lesbian Miss La Trobe as dramaturge.[46] The creative artist and the lesbian are linked, in Woolf's philosophy, with the androgynous mind; if either is to flourish, they must transcend the limitations of the nineteenth-century gender roles inscribed and reinforced by marriage, as both a cultural institution and a narrative mode.[46] It is appropriate then, that "The Window" represents not only the advent of Lily's quest but also the decline of Mrs. Ramsay, both as author and protagonist of the "wedlock plot." Throughout the first section Mrs. Ramsay attempts to perpetuate her own role by imposing it on the succeeding generation of women. To this end, she not only attempts, unsuccessfully, to join Lily and the aged bachelor William Bankes but also oversees and ordains the engagements of her own daughter Prue and her minion Minta Doyle. Thus, as one without any other authority or art, she seeks both to justify her own life and achieve a tangential form of immortality. At the end of the dinner that serves as a celebration of these betrothals and, metaphorically, as her self-apotheosis, Mrs. Ramsay muses that all her guests "would . . . however long they lived, come back to this night . . . [and] how, wound about in their hearts, however long they lived she would be woven" (113).

But her prophecies are ironic; although "The Window" concludes with the declaration that Mrs. Ramsay "had triumphed again" (124), the following section, "Time Passes," marks the destruction of the marriage plot, indeed of the Ramsays' world. Mrs. Ramsay dies "rather suddenly" (128)—in a subordinate clause of a parenthetical passage—while the summer house, the symbol of her matriarchy, falls into dereliction and the gendered narratives she had put in motion founder.[48] Prue dies in childbirth, a sacrificial victim of the marriage plot, while the union of Minta and her husband Paul disintegrates in adultery—only to become a relationship open to alternative sexual liaisons and held together by friendship, an arrangement Mrs. Ramsay could neither envision nor endorse. Simultaneously Andrew Ramsay, destined to carry on his father's male role, dies a casualty of the "masculine" pursuit of war. It is incumbent upon those remaining, then, to formulate new modes of relationship, ones that are based on the recognition of a shared humanity rather than gender dichotomies.

"The Lighthouse," the final section of the novel, marks the reunion of the survivors more than a decade after the summer represented in "The Window." While Mr. Ramsay prepares to undertake the long-promised but never realized journey to the lighthouse with his youngest son and daughter, Lily sets about her never-completed task of executing her artistic vision. To do so, she must first resist the urge to fall prey to a form of what can readily be called "heterosexual panic." With his characteristic "insatiable hunger for sympathy" (151), the widowed Mr. Ramsay approaches Lily, disrupting her attempts to paint. Mrs. Ramsay had set an example of passive sacrifice and sexual surrender in response to such demands: "[she was] a rosy-flowered fruit tree laid with leaves and dancing boughs into which the beak of brass, the arid scimitar of . . . the egotistical man, plunged and smote, demanding sympathy" (38). But Lily, refusing to replicate Mrs. Ramsay's role and sexuality, reacts in resistance to his "indecent" display of grief: "His immense self-pity, his demand for sympathy poured and spread itself in pools at her feet, and all she did . . . was to draw her skirts a little closer round her ankles, lest she should get wet" (152). By envisioning Mr. Ramsay's wants in terms of a rape and insemination she must combat, Lily has not overthrown the gender distinctions the Ramsays and their society imposed; rather, she has only chosen a highly feminized resistance, as opposed to feminine passivity, in the face of a masculinized demand for sympathy, a quality that should, ideally, be ungendered. Yet in her desire for escape she has an epiphanic and metonymic vision: Mr. Ramsay's boots, "walking . . . of their own accord, expressive in his absence of pathos, surliness, ill-temper, charm" (153). She cannot give him gendered sympathy he wishes, but she can praise the aesthetic quality of the now-ungendered boots, allowing him to respond in turn with a conversation on the non-emotive and neutral topic of the benefits of well-made boots. Having engaged her on purely human—and, in Woolf's view, androgynous—terms, he kneels in his gratitude to tie her shoes and thus demonstrate his technique of knot-tying. In "this completely inappropriate moment," she is able to feel sympathy for this "figure of infinite pathos" (154) about to impart on his own voyage of self-discovery. Ironically, in their mutual transcendence of gender roles, "he no longer needed it. He had become a very distinguished, elderly man, who had no need of her" (154). The one no longer required to demand, the other no longer required to surrender or resist, they are able to proceed with their respective quests.

As Lily begins to paint, she creates a narrative, that of the Ramsays' courtship. As she creates the details of the couple's early days, she assumes control of the narrative structure through which her culture once sought to define and regulate her life and her sexuality. In her hands the courtship plot becomes not a law of nature but merely a fiction, an artifice that can be manipulated and changed, inscribed and revised as the author deems necessary or desirable. Thus, it is a plot in which she need not play a part. She can, then, have her "vision."

Lily Briscoe's success as an artist is a purely personal one. Her painting would not be an object of acclaim; rather, "it would be hung in the attics . . . it would be destroyed. But what did that matter?" (208). Likewise, her acknowledgment and affirmation of her lesbianism is purely interiorized, for Woolf does not, at last, represent her in a relationship with another woman. Yet this "vision," too, in the context of the novel, is enough. By negotiating the traps of gender, Lily has, in the end, acquired the *potential* to create artistically and to love another woman should she so choose, for she is, significantly, the first of Woolf's lesbian characters to progress beyond lesbian panic.

After *To the Lighthouse*, neither lesbian panic nor the process of lesbian self-actualization plays a major role in Woolf's fiction. Rather, she turned to a comic mode of celebration in *Orlando*, her playful pseudobiography of her lover Vita Sackville-West, in which she renders lesbianism palimpsestically behind a narrative of transsexuality and androgyny.[49] Subsequently, as the spread of fascism threatened the very fabric of society and civility, Woolf grew less concerned with the development of the individual character as a focus for her novels and more concerned with the concept of community in which the individual functions as part of the greater whole. *The Waves* and *The Years*, accordingly, feature lesbian and homosexual characters as integrated and, to some extent, "normalized" members of society, as Alex Zwerdling notes:

> Woolf's [later] fiction frequently depicts homosexual and lesbian attachments with sympathy and yet without special pleading. . . . [T]heir feelings are taken seriously and treated with the same basic dignity as those of the more sexually conventional characters. Presenting such people as in some sense ordinary meant challenging both Victorian and post-Victorian sexual prejudices, and Woolf tries to show that the more generous spirits are capable of casting off those destructive properties.
>
> (170–71)

Given the magnitude of the evolution of Woolf's representations from the characters surrounded by silences and panic in *The Voyage Out*, the achievement of this narrative inclusion is a significant accomplishment for one author, particularly in a period notable for its legal proscription of homoerotic subject matter. Yet Woolf, in her valedictory work, makes one last examination of homosexual panic as a symptom of the impulse to war, contrasted with the image of the lesbian playwright as the commemorator and preserver of history and culture.

Written as the Nazi invasion of Europe progressed and an invasion of England seemed at hand, *Between the Acts* represents the pageant of English history as it is played out at a rural village festival at the Oliver family home. Set in June 1939, it crystallizes the central moment of the six-month interim between the German invasion of Czechoslovakia and the British declaration of war. In the character of Giles Oliver, scion of the British landed gentry, Woolf personifies the problem of the domestic "dictator" whom, as she suggested in *Three Guineas*, the Englishwoman might need to fight "in our own country before we ask her to help us crush him abroad" (53).[50] He is, as Alex Zwerdling observes, a "good indigenous example" (308) of what Woolf described in *A Room of One's Own* as the "pure . . . self-assertive virility" (154) already established in Italy by Mussolini.

Bristling with anxiety at the thought of the armed conflict to come, Giles exerts his "manliness" through marital infidelity and socially sanctioned aggression toward William Dodge, the homosexual friend of his guest Mrs. Manresa. Viewing the "horror" of William knowingly inspecting an antique coffee cup, Giles ceases the opportunity to "hang his rage" on William, "conveniently":

> A toady, a lickspittle; not a down-right plain man of his senses; but a teaser and twitcher; a fingerer of sensations; picking and choosing; dillying and dallying; not a man to have straightforward love for a woman . . . but simply a — At this word, which he could not speak in public, he pursed his lips; and the signet-ring on his little finger looked redder, for the flesh next it whitened as he gripped the arm of his chair.
>
> (60)

But surrounded by women who, because they do not share Giles's masculine power or prerogatives, do not share his hatred of the "mind-divided little snake in the grass" William (73), Giles enacts his aggression in a thoroughly puerile manner. Escaping the pageant, he engages in the "child's game" of stone-kicking, castigating with each kick Mrs. Manresa, William Dodge, and, among other objects of scorn, his own cowardice. Spying a snake unable to swallow the toad trapped in its mouth, Giles terminates his game to destroy this "monstrous inversion"—a phrase that pointedly evokes the sexologists' term for homosexuality, as does the configuration of a "birth the wrong way around" (99)—by stamping both creatures to death. The nexus of hypermasculine cruelty and sexual gratification are clear: "The white canvas on his tennis shoes was bloodstained and sticky. But it was action. Action relieved him" (99). When asked later by a pageant-goer if English society of the present were not more civilized than that of past represented in Miss La Trobe's tableaux, Giles inarticulately sputters, "*We?* . . . *We?*" (111, emphasis original), as if to indicate his inability or unwillingness to be assimilated into the social order, particularly an order that includes the homosexual close at hand. Yet, as Giles glares sidelong at William, the transference inherent in his animosity is revealed: "It was a bit of luck—that he could despise him, not himself" (111). Thus Woolf draws a deft analogy between the "foreign" forces of fascism that derive power from the hatred and suppression of marginalized groups and individuals within their own nations and the socially sanctioned hatred of homosexuality characteristic of Britain's patriarchy, the group she also holds responsible for the ongoing subjection of English women.[51]

In dramatic contrast to the homegrown tyranny of Giles Oliver—and the self-deprecating internalized homophobia of William Dodge—Miss La Trobe, the last and most complete of Woolf's lesbian artist figures, represents the preservation of what her creator regards as the finest aspects of British culture and history. Having lived openly, if not particularly happily, with an actress, this "rather shabby Sappho" (95), in Jane Marcus's phrase, is an "outcast [whom] Nature had set apart from her kind" (247), a woman not "presumably pure English" (57). Yet the purpose of this outsider's pageant is nothing less than "to communicate the literary history of England to an English audience" (Lee 211), to exhort them, in the face of war and the threat of invasion, to recognize and retain what is enduring and salutary about their culture. In invoking this culture, however, her task is not to establish a sense of national unity both similar to and in opposition with the nationalism promoted by fascism but rather to adduce "the capacity of the human spirit to overflow boundaries and make unity out of multiplicity" (*Three Guineas* 143). In this manner, the lesbian becomes the *spiritus mundi*, not only of Woolf's text but, ideally, of society and "the human spirit" itself. While her obdurate audience, each member obsessed to a greater or lesser extent with his or her own anxieties over the conflict to come, fails to recognize itself as the end of this panorama of national history—even when she quite literally holds up a mirror to it—she nonetheless persists. Even as she regards her failure, over her drink in the pageant's aftermath, she begins to plan her next play, a work, we may suppose, for a future beyond the end of the combat, an end Virginia Woolf herself would not see.

On January 21, 1931, Virginia Woolf addressed the London/National Society for Women's Service on the experiences of the woman writer. Her speech, which in a greatly shortened form became the essay "Professions for Women," includes a scenario in which the writer confronts her unruly imagination:

> The imagination has rushed away; it has taken to the depths; it has sunk—heaven knows where—into what dark pool of extraordinary experience. The reason has to cry "Stop!" The novelist has to pull on the line and haul the imagination to the surface. The imagination comes to the top in a state of fury.
>
> Good heavens she cries—how dare you interfere with me! . . . And I—that is the reason—have to reply, "My dear you were going altogether too far. Men would be shocked." Calm yourself, I say, as she sits panting . . . with rage and disappointment. We have only got to wait fifty years or so. In fifty years I shall be able to use all this very queer knowledge that you are ready to bring me. But not now. You see . . . I cannot make use of what you tell me—about women[']s bodies for instance—their passions—and so on, because the conventions are still very strong. If I were to overcome the conventions I should need the courage of a hero, and I am not a hero. . . .
>
> Very well says the imagination, dressing herself up again in her petticoats and skirts, we will wait. We will wait another fifty years. But it seems to me a pity.
>
> (xxxviii-xxxix)

Woolf would not live to see the day when the woman author could grant her imagination the freedom it demanded. Yet while her mathematical projection may not be completely accurate, for various authors have been able to record the urgings of their own imaginations sooner or later than others, the extent to which Woolf's scenario proved prophetic—particularly regarding the "very queer knowledge" that informs lesbian panic—becomes evident in the writings of postwar and postmodern British women writers.

CHAPTER TWO

"Are You a Lesbian, Mumbo?": Freudian Discourse, Shame, and Panic in Postwar Prefeminist Fictions

She thinks she is Providence, thought Sandy, she thinks she is the God of Calvin, she sees the beginning and the end. And Sandy thought, too, the woman is an unconscious Lesbian. And many theories from the books of psychology categorised Miss Brodie.

—Muriel Spark, *The Prime of Miss Jean Brodie*

Are you a Lesbian, Mumbo?

—Elizabeth Bowen, *The Little Girls*

Trout, are you a hermaphrodite?

—Elizabeth Bowen, *Eva Trout*

IN 1928, THE YEAR IN WHICH both Virginia Woolf's *Orlando* and Radclyffe Hall's *The Well of Loneliness* appeared, a year that Blanche Wiesen Cook pointedly calls "a banner year for lesbian publishing" (718), Woolf's younger colleague Elizabeth Bowen published her first novel, *The Hotel*. It is, like most first works, highly derivative, owing much to such earlier novelists of manners as Austen and Forster in its setting, tone, and sensibility.[1] Simultaneously, its plot might also be read as a revision of *The Voyage Out*, and while Bowen's novel lacks the intense hallucinogenic beauty and the striking representation of interiority that marks the earlier text, its narrative strategies provide its protagonist Sydney Warren and her older friend Mrs. Kerr with a possibility unavailable to Rachel Vinrace and Helen Ambrose: a means of negotiating lesbian panic without death or self-abnegation.

That this can be so must be attributed in part to the widespread questioning among the "Lost Generation" of traditional middle-class values in the wake of the carnage of the First World War and the ensuing economic crises in Great Britain. As historian Asa Briggs notes, a notable shift in British sexual mores accompanied the psychic and social upheaval, and, as a result, "many surviving Victorian certainties had gone" (264). Accordingly, the younger members of Bowen's cast of hotel guests idly wintering on the Riviera, loudly voice their disillusionment with the social expectations of marriage, family, career, and duty espoused by the older generation.[2] The most striking of these disaffected young people is the androgynously named Sydney, a taciturn, meditative, yet seemingly passionate young woman who, having suffered some form of nervous exhaustion in studying for college examinations, comes to the Riviera as the "poor relation" companion of her older invalid companion. Once there, she enters into an emotionally charged friendship with Mrs. Kerr, a widow whose modus vivendi seems, as her son suggests, a remnant of fin-de-siècle aestheticism. Whereas such an attachment would not have been readily or easily defined by Woolf's hotel guests little more than a decade before, the gossips among Bowen's characters are quick to ascribe morbid causes and consequences to such "very violent friendships" that "one didn't feel . . . were quite healthy" (53).

Despite these barbs, Sydney conspicuously continues her relationship with Mrs. Kerr until it is disrupted by a visit from the older woman's son, Ronald. While bereft by the ensuing exclusion from the mother-son bond, Sydney is simultaneously courted by James Milton, a middle-aged, socially awkward clergyman enchanted by her apparent inaccessibility and unlikeness to any of the other young women present. Not wishing to lose Sydney, Mrs. Kerr proposes a "maternal design" (115) of triangulation: a marriage between Ronald and Sydney. In this manner, she would be able to maintain her intimacy with Sydney on a permanent basis, under a more socially acceptable guise for all concerned. But Sydney, whose response to Ronald is basically one of jealous rivalry, intuits the underlying intent and is repelled by the suggestion that she "might have done something for him": "The attribution to herself of an irritable sex-consciousness vis-à-vis Ronald did not hurt, but sharply offended" (115, 118). Immediately thereafter, upon freeing herself from Mrs. Kerr's company, she seeks out Milton in order to accept the proposal of marriage she had earlier refused.

Even as she agrees to marry, Sydney admits that she does not love Milton, "but you know, I do want to" (124). Her agnosticism, moreover, would, in any rational situation, prove an obstacle to her ability to perform the duties of a clergyman's wife.[3] Therefore, her precipitate decision to capitulate to social conformity, to submit, like the other young women in the hotel, to the notion that "I must marry somebody. . . . I must have some children" (102), can be read as a form of lesbian panic, albeit lesbian panic arising from an ostensibly heterosexual source that she undoubtedly perceived to be otherwise. In contrast to Rachel Vinrace's fate in Woolf's novel, Sydney's acceptance of a proposal does not leave her with a bifurcated choice of marriage or death; rather, a close brush with death precipitates in

Sydney a form of heterosexual panic that frees her from the entrapment of an unwanted marriage. When a motoring party celebrating the engagement, comprised of the couple, Mrs. Kerr, and Sydney's cousin, barely misses a collision with a stranded lumber wagon and a drop off a steep cliff, Mrs. Kerr, to whom she reaches for physical consolation, displaces James Milton, at whom Sydney is unable to look, in the moment of danger. In the next moment, however, her gaze shifts to the male hysteria enacted by Milton, in whom "the crisis brought out . . . at the expense of his rationality all that was latently English" (159), as he berates and attempts to command the indigenous workmen—for whom he shows considerably less concern than he does for their horses. Just as Mrs. Kerr's design for a homoerotic family grouping had suddenly and forcefully impelled Sydney to accept the self-erasure of an ill-conceived marriage, so does this vision of stereotypically English masculinity disabuse her of its feasibility. This reversal of lesbian panic does not, however, constitute a return to the earlier erotic configurations. As both the novel and the tourist season draw to a close, Sydney returns to England and her studies, but not without a somewhat ambiguous valediction to Mrs. Kerr:

> What's most beautiful about you is your sensitiveness. If there's one thing one might hope to learn from you it would be to be sickened and turned cold by cruelty and unfairness. I hope that's what other people have learnt from you. I hope that's what someone where you're going next will be able to learn, too. . . . I am very grateful to you; you have done a great deal for me.
>
> (168)[4]

Mrs. Kerr, who seems unable to comprehend the meaning of this statement, grieves the loss of her companion in "desolation and loneliness" (169), while attempting to create yet another triangulation by encouraging a homoerotic bonding between Ronald and the bereaved Milton, with Sydney, presumably, as the "ghosted" third party.

While somewhat unlikely in its plotting and its mode of closure, *The Hotel* does mark a significant change in the function of lesbian panic as a disruptive mechanism in the context of the courtship plot. Indeed, heterosexual courtship here becomes the element of narratability that disrupts the homoerotic plot. There is never the suggestion that marriage to the socially and emotionally awkward Milton can offer a fulfilling or appropriate ending to this novel; rather, the crisis ultimately rests upon Sydney's ability to extricate herself from the very same self-defeating stratagem that had traditionally functioned as a means of the heroine's self-justification and exaltation. In this manner, Bowen's novel, with its marked skepticism regarding "Victorian certainties," refutes narrative ideologies that privilege only one mode of sexuality, one mode of being for all women characters, as well as ideologies that offer their female protagonists no options save those of marriage or death.

As if to underscore the need for wider narrative options for her female protagonist, Bowen brackets Sydney's plot with incidents involving Miss Fitzgerald and Miss Pym, two ardent and devoted spinsters who stand as fictional exemplars of what Lillian Faderman has termed "romantic friendship." At the outset of the novel, the two are presented in the wake of a sudden and vehement argument that sends them on their separate ways. Miss Pym takes up, momentarily, with Mrs. Kerr—who, upon discovering Sydney, has neither time nor attention for her erstwhile companion. The two "old pussies" (11), apparently reconciled, appear fleetingly and insignificantly at various junctures of the text, yet in the last pages, after the protagonists and most of the other guests have dispersed, Miss Fitzgerald and Miss Pym, who have at this point become Emily and Eleanor, sit and gaze at the hotel, contemplating "the day when we—so nearly lost each other" (175). The novel concludes with the image of the two women "hand in hand, reunited, in perfect security" (175). Thus, in *The Hotel*, love between women is accorded the position of privilege traditionally reserved in female-authored texts for the heterosexual wedding ceremony. While the desire that attains between Sydney and Mrs. Kerr, a desire that can never be completely or directly articulated, has no future without the manipulation of others, neither does heterosexuality in any of its manifestations within the text. Coupling in this novel, generally speaking, is motivated by a desire for the social aesthetic of correct form and for the success and approval that living up to expectations brings, and thus is rarely successful. Only the couple whose bonds have little connection to this symbolic order, therefore, are appropriately motivated and able to endure.

After beginning her novelistic career with this somewhat innovative narrative of female homoerotic desire, Bowen turned to fictions concerned primarily with what Jane Rule has seen as "decorous but clear . . . sexual relationships between men and women" (115). Rule's critique of Bowen's novels, for nearly two decades the only examination of the author and her works from a lesbian perspective, attempts to establish a mimetic relationship between Bowen's art and life. The "pattern" of Bowen's literary output, Rule posits, is similar to that with which "she seems to see in life, lesbian experience bracketing the heterosexual experience of marriage and children," adding that "it was not until late in her career, after the death of her husband, that Elizabeth Bowen returned to a concern for relationships between women" (115). Despite some biographical inaccuracy, Rule's paradigm has long defined the extent to which Bowen's novels might be considered "lesbian": the first and last (*The Little Girls* and *Eva Trout*) are, and those in between are not.[5] In a recent study informed by postmodern queer theory, however, Renée C. Hoogland has indicated that such distinctions are clearly oversimplifications; rather, in many of the intermediate novels Bowen creates subnarratives of "radically subversive desire" (301) that underscore or function as a counterpoint to the main heterosexual plot.

As Hoogland points out, the relationship between Lois and Marda in *The Last September* (1929) and that between Louie and Connie (as well as Louie's fixation on Stella, whom she encounters only once and accidentally) in *The Heat of the Day* (1949) are charged with homoerotic tension. Indeed, Louie's out-of-wedlock pregnancy, the result of promiscuous behavior arising from her anguished discovery of the admired Stella's own tarnished public reputation, might be read as a manifestation of lesbian panic. Similarly, Marda's superficial wounding by a Sinn Fein gunman while in the midst of her encounter with Lois surely echoes, albeit far more violently, the garden scene in *Mrs. Dalloway*, particularly as it is accompanied by Lois's reassertion that she "must marry" (125) her British soldier suitor and followed by Marda's "inconsequent" statement that she "hope[d] to have some children" and "should hate to be barren" (128). Even so, these homoerotic subplots and moments of lesbian panic are quite secondary in terms of their respective narratives overall; neither incident has any considerable influence on the novels' outcomes for their female protagonists. Indeed, the traditional closure of marriage is obviated for both heroines, not by the intrusion of other forms of desire but rather by the sudden and violent deaths of men to whom they attach themselves. This shift in focus in Bowen's works, however, cannot be adequately explained through the rather reductive means of the author's biographical facts. Rather, the development—or, as it were, the waxing, waning, and waxing again—of lesbian plots and subplots in Bowen's novels over the course of four decades is better evaluated in terms of the historical conditions prevailing during the various phases of her artistic production, conditions that inevitably affected the representation of female homoerotic desire not simply for Elizabeth Bowen but for women novelists in general.

The first and most obvious of these conditions involves the repercussions of the 1928 obscenity trial of *The Well of Loneliness*. While it would be an oversimplification to claim that lesbian themes in female-authored fiction simply disappeared or were only rendered in a highly surreptitious manner over the two decades between the suppression of Hall's novel and its 1949 reissue, the trial's verdict "restrain[ing] British publishers . . . from issuing lesbian propaganda" (Foster, 287) surely circumscribed the manner in which lesbians and lesbianism could be represented and narrated—and published—in the United Kingdom. In her groundbreaking survey of female homoerotic themes in literature, Jeannette H. Foster observes that the years immediately following the trial saw the publication of "a handful of more or less negative contributions, all by American women"[6]:

> Just how specifically the skirmish of censorship and its attendant publicity affected subsequent work is difficult to say. The few years saw in print nothing more outspoken than translations of Rachilde's *Monsieur Vénus* and Colette's *Claudine at School*. This can probably be attributed to caution on the part of both publishers and authors. That antagonistic voices, first largely women's and then men's swelled into a full chorus by 1933, might similarly seem a protracted echo of official disapproval.
>
> (288)

The ban on "lesbian propaganda" Foster cites did, of course, grant permission for a very different type of propaganda, the sensationalized representation of lesbian malignity. As Foster notes, such "negative contributions" appeared as a result of the "focusing of attention on the controversial subject . . . [and] an inevitably growing preoccupation with it" (288). Yet negative or sensationalistic representations of lesbianism are not, in and of themselves, necessarily analogous to the narrative strategies of lesbian panic, nor, as Foster suggests, do such representational extremes result in literature that calls for much in terms of critical inquiry. Rather, the narrative strategies of lesbian panic are based in great part on the assumption that lesbianism is both attractive and desirable—so much so that it is able to provide a tempting alternative to the compulsory heterosexuality that is deemed the appropriate, correct mode of ending—female homoeroticism is rarely a monstrous or pathological entity in texts informed by this strategy. Thus, if lesbian panic seems a less prevalent narrative strategy in British women's writing from the 1930s to the 1950s, it might well be that the lure of lesbianism inherent in that strategy could, ironically, be deemed "lesbian propaganda."

Another factor, often elided in overviews of literary history, is the growing conservatism in popular British literary tastes in the period between the two world wars, the same period in which modernism reached its peak. While female modernists might well be credited with a "body of work" that is, as Gillian Hanscombe and Virginia L. Smyers assert, a "magnificent testimony to the courage of women who refuse to be content with their assigned identities and functions" (248), forces other than modernism were simultaneously at work in British women's fiction as a whole. Indeed, as I have suggested in the previous chapter, Virginia Woolf's accomplishment in the writing of "women's bodies [and] their passions," while certainly influential for many subsequent female authors, was a personal triumph rather than one that necessarily spoke for her peers as well. Instead, as Alison Light argues in her examination of women and reading tastes in the inter-war years, for those not involved in the cultural and literary experimentations of modernism (that is, British women in the main), a new assertion of middle-class domestic values served to counteract the disillusionment arising in the aftermath of the First World War:

> [T]hose disturbances on the level of the emotional and ideological understandings of sexuality were more than just a local or minor kind of change. The strongly anti-heroic mood . . . characterising the aftermath of war made a lasting and deep impression right across cultural life and idioms at home. . . . [B]etween 1920 and 1940, a revolt against, embarrassment about, and distaste for the romantic languages of national pride produced a realignment of sexual identities which was part of a redefinition of Englishness. What had formerly been held as the virtues of the private sphere of middle-class life take on a new public and national significance. . . . [T]he 1920s and '30s saw a move away from . . . a dynamic and missionary view of the Victorian and Edwardian middle classes in "Great Britain" to an Englishness at once less imperial and more inward-looking, more domestic and more private—and, in terms of pre-war standards, more "feminine."
>
> (8)

Accordingly, the shift in focus in Bowen's work from the 1930s onward, from that of subversive desires in an antidomestic ethos (as in *The Hotel*) to that of subversive desires—lesbian and heterosexual alike—in the context of domesticity and its institutions, may be attributed, at least in part, to this particular aspect of the zeitgeist.

Nor did the Second World War, despite its "liberatory" effect of placing women in traditionally male industrial work and creating on the homefront an essentially homosocial environment, mark any significant resurgence in lesbian themes in literature. Foster points out that "the preoccupations of war—plus the paper shortage—crowded variant fiction almost completely from the market" (324). In the war's aftermath, female domesticity was once again resurgent—this time a socially enforced domesticity as men returning from war replaced and displaced women in the workplace. As a consequence, most popular and mainstream British women's fiction of the late 1940s and early 1950s focused on issues of marriage, home, and family, and, as Niamh Baker notes, either "censorship or self-censorship . . . led to an almost complete absence of lesbians" in these texts (78).[7] This emphasis on marriage and domesticity, however, did not necessarily function as an apotheosis of these institutions; instead, Baker observes, the women's novels characteristically "questioned the relationship between women and men, especially in the unequal partnership of marriage, reflecting doubts that many women held" (22).

To note this "almost complete absence of lesbians," however, is not to claim a *complete* absence. The three decades that separate *Mrs. Dalloway*, *To the Lighthouse*, and *The Hotel* from the novels discussed in this chapter saw the publication of an isolated number of narratives with lesbian themes. As early as 1933 Ivy Compton-Burnett created in the satirically comic *More Women Than Men* a microcosm, set in the context of a girls' school, in which homosexuality is the norm and heterosexuality an aberration. That she did so without incurring the opprobrium that had surrounded *The Well of Loneliness* only five years before might seem remarkable, until one considers that Compton-Burnett's novel is free of the "special pleading" for sympathy that contributes to the lugubriousness of Hall's book; indeed, considering that they quite literally get away with the murder of an inconvenient heterosexual character, one cannot deem Compton-Burnett's protagonists "nice" or particularly sympathetic. Moreover, while Compton-Burnett's novels acquired over time a certain cult appeal, they were hardly popular commercial successes.

Other novels, including Sylvia Townsend Warner's *Summer Will Show* (1936) and *The Corner That Held Them* (1949), Molly Keane's *Devoted Ladies* (1934), Mary Renault's *The Middle Mist* (1945, reissued as *Friendly Young Ladies*), and Dorothy Strachey's *Olivia* (1949), are notable exceptions to the novelistic "silence" surrounding lesbianism during this period—but they are exceptions all the same. Through historical displacement (her novels are set, respectively, in revolutionary France and medieval England),

Townsend Warner was able to create a context for love between women with relative freedom from twentieth-century constraints and phobias. Keane, like Compton-Burnett, employed the conventions of the comedy of manners, a mode that has long allowed gay male authors in particular to represent homosexuality through double-entendre and witty repartee.

Neither Compton-Burnett nor Townsend Warner nor Keane relied on the dynamics of lesbian panic to propel their narratives.[8] Conversely, elements of lesbian panic may be discerned in both Renault's novel and in Strachey's. In the former, the seemingly idyllic butch-femme relationship between Leo (Leonora) and Helen is disrupted by the intrusion of male presence in the person of Joe, who, curiously, "re-heterosexualizes" the butch Leo—who had turned to women after a traumatic experience with a man—in the course of one amorous night. Renault eventually dismissed the novel's unlikely plot and not necessarily happy ending, yet it is noteworthy as a rare example of lesbianism constructed, conceivably, as a result of *heterosexual* panic that, apparently, can be undone by the "right man."[9] Strachey's narrative of adolescent obsession might also be considered a somewhat sensational (but not particularly paradigmatic) example of lesbian panic within the conventions of the girls' school novel, a subgenre that will be more fully explored in the discussion of Brigid Brophy's *The King of a Rainy Country* in the next chapter.

These novels, along with a few works by male authors such as Lawrence Durrell and Anthony Powell, are nonetheless isolated examples of lesbian representation in the midst of the rigidly heterosexual literary milieu of mid-twentieth-century Britain. By the early 1960s, however, the discourse of Freudian psychoanalysis had achieved relatively widespread, even mainstream acceptance, conceivably as a result of greater educational opportunities for the masses in postwar Britain and America. Thus, in this period generally associated with sexual permissiveness, lesbianism gradually came to be seen not as an essential and monstrous state as the medical sexologists would define it but rather as an unfortunate condition stemming from a failure on the part of its female subject to negotiate properly the perilous but necessary shifts between love objects in the course of childhood and adolescence.[10] But while Freud's interpretations of female homosexuality is vastly more humane and humanistic than those proposed by most medical sexologists, his understanding of the condition is nonetheless a product of a culture informed by a compulsory, indeed hegemonic, heterosexuality. Accordingly, lesbianism, previously a signifier of chthonic anarchism with the potential of destroying civilization, is reduced to a mere sign of impotent failure.

When, in this period, lesbianism once again becomes a presence in female-authored fiction, particularly in the earlier novels of such authors as Iris Murdoch, Muriel Spark, and Doris Lessing, it is almost inevitably represented in terms of this by then commonplace perception and functions narratively as an ostensibly minor mode of being, clearly secondary to the central heterosexual plot.[11] Yet "ostensibly" is a key word here. A blatant and often errant pursuit of heterosexuality on their characters' parts propels the plots of texts such as Muriel Spark's *The Prime of Miss Jean Brodie* (1961) and Doris Lessing's *The Golden Notebook* (1962); yet the extent to which their frankly represented heterosexual encounters are the results of relatively apparent repressed female homoerotic desire have surely gone under-remarked, even by feminist critics.[12] Ironically, such critical lacunae, I would submit, are the result of a failure, if not a refusal, to incorporate other aspects of Freudian theory into the discursive mix, namely those articulated in "Some Neurotic Mechanisms in Jealousy, Paranoia and Homosexuality"—ideas that, even more ironically, Lessing quite openly probes in her novel.

Freud remarks that jealousy, in the context of romantic triangulation, is often "experienced bisexually. That is to say, a man will not only feel pain about the woman he loves and hatred of the man who is his rival, but also grief abut the man, whom he loves unconsciously, and hatred of the woman as his rival; and this latter set of feelings will add to the intensity of his jealousy" (*SE* 18:223). He goes on to explain that the repressed homosexual element of this jealousy leads in many cases to a projection of such feelings on the part of another or, in the worst case scenario, delusional sexual paranoia. But while Freud's use of the male subject position here might imply to some, albeit wrongly, that such jealousy and its effects are gender specific, a sexual reversal of this scenario is present at the narrative foundations of Spark's novel as well as Lessing's.[13]

As *The Prime of Miss Jean Brodie* nears its fateful denouement, Deirdre Lloyd, a woman whose husband functions as a token of both physical and metaphysical sexual exchange between the schoolteacher protagonist and the schoolgirl minions, remarks that "Miss Brodie sounds a bit queer, I must say" (152). While the speaker makes this assessment of a woman whom she has never actually met, in the Woolfian double-entendre brought to bear on "queer," she is nonetheless far from mistaken. A prototypical early twentieth-century "odd woman," Jean Brodie is a product of the post-First World War Britain populated by more women of marriageable age than men to marry them. Rather than accept the scorn and pity traditionally the lot of the spinster, she devotes herself, according to her own less than adequately informed lights, to a flamboyant if nonetheless ersatz Paterian pursuit of beauty and culture. As if to deflect any suspicion of her motivations in her interactions with her chosen group of students, her "crème de la crème" (15), she creates a image of herself as the tragic heroine of a disrupted heterosexual romance plot through her oft-repeated tale of Hugh Carruthers, her "felled fiancé" (21) who died in the service of king and country on Flanders Field. While the "Brodie set" eventually becomes aware of the mutability of this unverifiable and cliché-ridden tale, a mutability that corresponds directly to its teller's sexual intrigues of the moment, it nonetheless serves its initial purpose in exciting the erotic imaginations of its then preadolescent auditors. Thus, while the tellingly named Sandy Stranger and her classmate Jenny Gray invent their own fictions about liaisons between Miss Brodie and her lost lover, the mythic Hugh becomes an instrument by which to gain a fantasized carnal knowledge of their teacher—which, although unconsciously so, would seem to be precisely her intent.

This underlying intent is not lost on the highly perceptive Sandy, whom Miss Brodie predicts would one day "go too far" (35); nor is Freudian discourse. When, some years after this initial, metaphorical triangulation with Miss Brodie and her legendary lover, Sandy feels impelled to denounce her erstwhile mentor to the authorities of the Marcia Blaine School for Girls, she justifies her actions with a condemnatory assessment of Miss Brodie's dangerous, megalomaniacal sexuality: "She thinks she is Providence . . . she thinks she is the God of Calvin, she sees the beginning and the end. And Sandy thought, too, the woman is an unconscious Lesbian. And many theories from the books of psychology categorised Miss Brodie" (176). Like Deirdre Lloyd's estimation of the "queer" woman, Sandy's is hardly incorrect. In manipulating a sexual liaison between her former student Rose Stanley, a young woman she had predicted would be "famous for sex" (12), and her obsessed admirer Teddy Lloyd, the war-maimed, married art master whose sexual overtures she refuses, Miss Brodie forges a paradigmatic Freudian triangle. Through this complex arrangement, which she voyeuristically monitors through Sandy, she allows Teddy to consummate his fantasy with her through the mediation of Rose, while she achieves not only a surrogated adulterous *affaire d'amour* with Teddy through Rose but also a similarly surrogated homoerotic intrigue with Rose by means of Teddy.

Nor is Jean Brodie content to indulge merely in this Madame Merteuil-like sexual surrogation; she is also the unwitting instigator of a curious if generally unremarked marriage of gender (if not sexuality) dysphoria. Even as she renounces physical consummation with Teddy Lloyd (who, with his combat injury and his numerous progeny, is the sole embodiment of hyper-masculinity and unambiguous heterosexuality in the novel), Miss Brodie habituates the bed of the sentimental and basically feminized music master, Gordon Lowther. A Church of Scotland elder, Lowther seeks to "justify" their relationship and proposes marriage. When Miss Brodie refuses him, ostensibly out of her devotion to her young female charges, he marries the science instructor Miss Lockhart, presumably in spite. Although her appearances in the narrative are few and seemingly insignificant, Miss Lockhart functions both as a rival (for the affections of the girls as well as those of Gordon Lowther) and a foil to the protagonist. With her tweeds, her sports car, her golfing expertise, and her analytical mind, Miss Lockhart is, in her personal semiotics, the very type of the prefeminist academic lesbian. Accordingly, one might posit that by marrying her, the less-than-masculine Gordon Lowther substitutes for the "unconscious Lesbian" one who is relatively unproblematic if nonetheless latent.

The psychological dynamics at work behind these arrangements are not lost on their creator's most prescient student: "Sandy assumed that the reason why Miss Brodie had stopped sleeping with Gordon Lowther was that her sexual feelings were satisfied by proxy; and Rose was predestined to be the lover of Teddy Lloyd" (165). But while Sandy's assumption semantically posits Jean Brodie as the "God of Calvin" who predestines, Sandy usurps the position by giving her mentor the "nasty surprise" that the Calvinist God doles out in the end to "certain people [with] an erroneous sense of joy and salvation" (159) by reversing the preordained roles in the older woman's scenario: "in the event it was Sandy who slept with Teddy Lloyd and Rose who carried back the information" (161). Sandy, who would later become a contemplative nun and the author of a "strange book of psychology, 'The Transfiguration of the Commonplace'" (186), is able to discern the Freudian motivations in another woman. Jean Brodie, as Velma Bourgeois Richmond notes, "finds a romantic renunciation of love [i.e., heterosexuality] far more exciting than an actual experience" (19); moreover, neither her renunciation of a sexual relationship with Teddy Lloyd nor her enactment of one with Gordon Lowther are, as Bernard Harrison posits, "real," but rather "in the end they are both objects of her fantasy" (142). Accordingly, Miss Brodie, despite her self-presentation as a "sex-bestirred" individual (71), is not, strictly speaking, heterosexual in the actualization of her desires. Instead, she sublimates her latently homoerotic desires through her frequently announced "devotion" to the young women she wishes to recreate in her own image and likeness.[14]

Although Sandy is quite adept in fathoming the submerged homoeroticism of her teacher's designs, she herself falls into Freud's trap of jealous projection in her self-absolution, for her subsequent betrayal is based not so much on Jean Brodie's unquestionably problematic political sympathies or her obvious pedagogical irresponsibility as it is on Sandy's own long-festering lesbian panic. If we move beyond the Freudian paradigm of the pre-Oedipal phase and posit that lesbian girlhood is, in fact, qualitatively different from heterosexual girlhood, then it is possible to delineate in Sandy a mode of sexual curiosity that parallels yet diverges from that of her more commonplace peers and eventually brings her, in a social context that provides no expression of female homoerotic desire beyond the limited and infantilizing structures of girls' school homosociality, to her own extreme form of renunciation.[15] The earliest of her many pubescent fantasies, while she is still a junior school student, revolve around dubious visits to Miss Lockhart for the tactile pleasure of her removing (by means of her knowledge of chemistry) purposely acquired inkstains from sleeves, and around the visual aesthetics of the female body—primarily that of Jean Brodie: "Some days it seemed to Sandy that Miss Brodie's chest was flat, no bulges at all, but straight as her back. On other days her chest was breast-shaped and large, very noticeable, something for Sandy to sit and peer at" (18). Thus, through titillating contacts with the scientific (i.e., "masculine") Miss Lockhart and the dualistic ("masculine"/"feminine") Miss Brodie, Sandy intuitively absorbs that element of lesbian sensibility that Sue Ellen Case has identified as the "Butch-Femme aesthetic."

As Sandy's fantasies develop into narrative forms based upon canonical works such as *The Lady of Shalott*, *Kidnapped*, and that ur-text of heterosexual romance, *Jane Eyre*, her interactions with their characters are marked by sexual unknowing (she asks the Lady of Shalott "What can be the meaning of these words?" [33]) or a foreclosure of heterosexual consummation. This latter strategy is continued in the fantasy fictions she creates with her classmate Jenny about the loves of Miss Jean Brodie. While the more mundane Jenny would include a representation of sexual intercourse between Jean Brodie and Gordon Lowther, for example, Sandy disrupts all narrative expectations by inserting, despite Jenny's protests, "Miss Brodie yawns" at the moment surrender would occur, "in order to restore decency" (87). In effect, Sandy has, in Faith Pullin's words, a "general difficulty in seeing [Miss Brodie] as a sexual being" (89)—or, even more to the point, a reluctance to see her as a *heterosexual* being. This becomes even more apparent when a traumatic—if nonetheless exciting—episode in Jenny's life gives rise to a completely new fantasy narrative in Sandy's imaginary. After Jenny's encounter with an exhibitionist—an event of which Sandy would deny Miss Brodie the pleasure of knowledge—Sandy's curiosity focuses not so much on the man or the visual experience of male genitalia, but rather on the policewoman who questions and calms Jenny after the fact. Although Jenny can provide little information about and no name for this woman, and although she indicates that this official expresses herself with a less than refined accent, Sandy invents an idealized image of one "Sergeant Anne Grey" and posits herself as her "right-hand woman in the Force" in a campaign to "eliminate sex from Edinburgh and environs" (100, 101). At the heart of this fanciful effort, rendered in the language of crime reports, is an investigation "about the case of Brodie and . . . her liaison with Gordon Lowther, described as singing master, Marcia Blaine School for Girls" (101). Such fabulation, needless to say, entails a wish-fulfillment that would ultimately punish the otherwise beloved Jean Brodie for, if not prevent her from, her errant excursions into heterosexuality. Yet subsequently, as Sandy and her heroine rid society of the menace of heterosexual activity, their narrative closes in a cliché-ridden moment of homoerotic *jouissance*: "Sergeant Anne pressed Sandy's hand in gratitude; and they looked into each other's eyes, their mutual understanding too deep for words" (102).

In the older, more sophisticated Sandy, the dual impulses that inform this only partially whimsical fiction, those of punishing heterosexuality and coalescing with another woman, take on the more sinister characteristics of lesbian panic. Because she is prevented from any sort of union with Jean Brodie—indeed, precluded from even a surrogated union by the older woman's nomination of Rose as Teddy Lloyd's lover—she subverts and overrides her teacher's narrative with her own. Accordingly, she not only usurps the appointed place in Teddy Lloyd's bed and thus takes Rose's place in "becoming" Jean Brodie, she also, by manipulating and controlling the lives of others through self-created narrative, replicates—and thus in quite another sense "becomes"—Jean Brodie.[16] Having learned of the reversal of her own fiction, Miss Brodie is willing to capitulate, to substitute Sandy as the one "destined to be the great lover, although I would not have thought it" (181). But Sandy is herself at something of a loss to explain her affair with Teddy Lloyd. "He interests me" (180) is the best she can offer, but what in fact interests her, what she seeks to extract from him, is "the mind that invented Miss Brodie on canvas after canvas" (181), for each of his portraits, regardless of its sitter, is a portrait of the object of his obsession. In effect, Sandy's liaison with Teddy Lloyd is nothing more, and nothing less, than the merging of a shared obsession.

But as this union can never be more than the surrogation of inaccessible desires, it cannot and does not overcome the need to punish heterosexuality also present in Sandy's adolescent fantasies—and because her desire to bond sexually with Jean Brodie has led to her own excursion into heterosexuality, Sandy's need to punish becomes both destructive and self-destructive. Accordingly, her mode of betraying Miss Brodie to the authorities of the Marcia Blaine School, an event that follows immediately upon the revelation that the teacher knows of the liaison between Sandy and Teddy Lloyd, is curiously appropriate in its obfuscation of motivation. While Sandy admits to the headmistress that she is "not really interested in world affairs . . . only in putting a stop to Miss Brodie," she proposes that "you won't be able to pin her down on sex. Have you thought of politics?" (182). Given Miss Brodie's naive but nonetheless baneful fascist inclinations in the political climate of 1939, denouncing her on political grounds is surely more expedient than doing so by means of exposing sexual misconduct; and given Sandy's need to disguise her own motivations and actions, it would surely be inexpedient to expose those of her teacher.[17] It is not enough, however, for Sandy to punish the object of her own unattainable desires; she must also inflict self-punishment, for which the religion she takes from Teddy Lloyd while discarding the man himself offers particularly pertinent mode of enactment. Her conversion to Roman Catholicism and her subsequent life as a cloistered nun offers her not only a form of desexualized homosociality that replicates that of the girls' school—a structure generally unavailable to adult women in Protestant culture and society—but also a dogma that advocates self-abnegation and penitence.

While some critics have chosen to interpret *The Prime of Miss Jean Brodie* as primarily a religious conversion narrative, albeit a less than comforting one, Sandy's ultimate enclosure lacks the resolution expected of novelistic closure.[18] In effect, Sandy's betrayal of her mentor and model is nothing less than a successful attempt to render both of them non-narratable and thus impose a permanent ending on their ongoing and conflicting sexual self-fictions. The final representation of Sandy, now Sister Helena of the Transfiguration, "clutching the bars of the grille" in her cloister indicates that she has found neither peace her acquired religion and vocation would offer nor a metaphysical answer in "The Transfiguration of the Commonplace." Rather, as she admits that her greatest influence was not "literary or political or personal" but rather "a Miss Jean Brodie in her prime" (187), the homosociality of the convent becomes itself a surrogate for the Marcia Blaine School, a locus for the tortured preservation of the memory of Jean Brodie. For while the other members of "the Brodie Set" settle in the end for the mundane and conventional structures of institutional heterosexuality, Sandy, in her extreme and quixotic dedication and renunciation (to use two of her teacher's favorite words) ironically not only keeps the spirit of Miss Brodie alive but, in effect, "becomes" Miss Brodie in merely another form.

Much critical commentary has been devoted to Spark's complex structuring of time in this novel.[19] While the narrative present is, for all intents and purposes, the late 1950s, at which time the former schoolgirls are approaching middle age and Miss Brodie has been dead for over a decade, most of the action takes place either in the early part of the 1930s, when the girls are Miss Brodie's students in junior school, or in the latter part of the decade, when the political climate allows for the denunciation that ends the teacher's career. These two "historical" settings are juxtaposed with the events of the late 1950s, so that episodes function not only as flashbacks but also as what David Lodge has termed "flashforwards" (157). As a result of this disrupted chronology, a technique Spark previously employed in *The Girls of Slender Means*, future events are revealed to the reader in advance; only the motivations behind those eventualities remain to be seen. But, as Bernard Harrison rather subjectively argues, "the enigmatic and incomplete fragments of information which the novel drops casually . . . puzzle and irritate; [they] create in the reader a spirit of nervous dissatisfaction, of not knowing quite where he [*sic*] is going or what he [*sic*] is supposed to see when he [*sic*] gets there" (140). While no doubt irritating to some readers, the effect of this ever-shifting episodic narrative scheme is to defeat any clear-cut sense of bildung. The girls' development—which might well be expected in a novel set in the context of an educational institute—is nonlinear; indeed, they seem simultaneously both extraordinarily precocious and naive, and even the representation of the former schoolgirls as adults indicate that they perhaps know less as adults, perhaps as the result of willful obfuscation of past perceptions and motivations, than they did as children. Consequently, the dynamics of lesbian panic are "not quite known" to many readers or, for that matter, to the characters themselves; rather, they are obscured, in great part through the apparently revised concepts of Miss Brodie, her pedagogy, and the meaning thereof in the minds of her former students. Indeed, Sister Helena's own personal "transfiguration of the commonplace" would seem nothing less than an elaborate sublimation of the sexual nature of her betrayal of and relationship to Jean Brodie.

As a factor in a novel with a lesbian panic subtext, this broken chronology serves other purposes as well. While the narrative present is that of the beginning of an era of relative social and cultural permissiveness—indeed, perhaps the first in which sexual matters could be represented with relative frankness since the 1920s and the high modernism of which Woolf's novels were part—the settings of the greater portion of the novel are in those years following the obscenity trial of *The Well of Loneliness*, years in which, as I have discussed, lesbianism became so forbidden a topic that it all but disappeared from literature, save that of the least reputable sort. Accordingly, as the product of the dawn of a cultural period that at last saw the end to this mode of literary self-censorship, *The Prime of Miss Jean Brodie* is a fictionalized investigation of the convolutions of the sexual imagination in the context of widespread repression, convolutions that overdetermine all sexual impulses simply because all are forbidden. As a result, what might otherwise be relatively normal or commonplace adolescent fantasies become repressed perversions, giving way to pernicious plots and schemes, not only in Spark's novel but also in Beryl Bainbridge's later *Harriet Said*. And while such fantasies might be problematic in and of themselves, they are, as both *The Prime of Miss Jean Brodie* and *Harriet Said* demonstrate, even more potentially baneful when abated by the fantasies and desires of adults who have themselves never progressed beyond immature fabulation.

That Miss Brodie manipulates her charges with her own personal romance plot, a story that varies in its details according to her enacted metafiction of the moment, is a case in point. But here the romance plot, with which the strategies of lesbian panic are generally juxtaposed, is not only reduced to a matter of the past—much as it is through the use of flashbacks in *Mrs. Dalloway*—but is also exposed as the fiction it truly is. The romance plot is not a scenario Miss Brodie lives but rather a credential of sorts that allows her to appear worldly, courageous, long-suffering, self-sacrificial, and, indeed, "romantic" in every sense of the word—and, above all else, unquestionably heterosexual.

Alan Bold remarks that "one of Spark's most effective conceits is the notion that characters, in actuality as well as art, can only face facts through fiction" (13). While it is doubtful whether Jean Brodie ever recognizes either truth or facts on their own terms—she would appear incapable of gaining the self-knowledge that would qualify her as a true tragic heroine—fictions, whether youthful fantasy or various later transfigurations, allow Sandy to arrive at a condition of stasis, even if not necessarily the most optimal one. But that the fact of lesbianism and the panic it almost inevitably inspired, which had for three decades prior to the 1960s been rendered unrepresentable in literature, can be conveniently articulated by means of characters' metafictions is evident not only in *The Prime of Miss Jean Brodie* but also in a nearly contemporaneous text, Doris Lessing's *The Golden Notebook*.

Because of the extraordinary critical attention given to *The Golden Notebook* over the past three and a half decades, any new critical approach to the novel is almost inevitably predetermined and overdetermined. One is confronted not only by the overwhelming volume of structuralist and post-structuralist critiques of its elaborate, fragmented, multilayered metafictions but also by those critiques establishing its position in the feminist counter-canon as a foundational text in what has become a tradition of postwar female bildungsromans that explore "how sex fits into a modern woman's life" (Snitow, 158).[20] And because such critical explorations almost exclusively define female sexuality as heterosexuality, any attempt to discern a lesbian subtext in a novel that has elicited highly personal responses from the first generation of feminist critics can hardly avoid taking a stance of oppositionality.[21] I would nevertheless argue that the various narratives of protagonist Anna Wulf's sexual self-discovery, replete with numerous and relatively explicit representations of heterosexual acts and fantasies, is undergirded by the plot structures of lesbian panic. Moreover, Lessing's narrative fragmentation serves to obscure the incidents of lesbian panic whenever it arises; as the novel shifts in regular cyclic movements from one of its central "realist" text "Free Women" to the various "notebooks" that compartmentalize Anna's daily life and experience, her homoerotic anxieties fall into the structural fissures.

In many ways a typical feminist critique of *The Golden Notebook*, Ann Barr Snitow's overview deftly presents both the triumphs and shortcomings of Lessing's novel while defining its historical position in women's writing. Thus it is worth considering in some detail:

> That great study of social fragmentation *is above all the story of the many ways in which women are disappointed*.... Lessing ... made several observations about women's sexual situations ... that continue to be made in more recent women's novels: deeply arousing sex is scarce; sex that calls forth those deep feelings is the kind worth having; sexual arousal is an impulse that comes from the whole configuration of a person's experience. . . . The way in which *The Golden Notebook*

> develops these themes embodies the two major stylistic strains to be found in subsequent female writing about sex. On the one hand, Lessing is encyclopedic in her description of social texture; on the other, Lessing uses sex symbolically. In the realm of metaphor Anna's sexual experience is more positive than in its more literal embodiment. At this level, sex has the power to reassure and rejuvenate. Anna's final love affair is the occasion of a mental reorganization and *passes* as a happy ending.
>
> (159–60, emphases mine).

While the novel can certainly be seen as a breakthrough as it forthrightly discusses sex and sexuality with a frankness and exactitude not previously manifested in mainstream Anglophone women's writing, the sex represented is hardly ever satisfactory for Anna or other female characters. Circumscribing this dissatisfaction and disappointment are the self-limiting perceptions of fulfilling sex and the sources thereof, articulated through Anna's fictional alter ego Ella and encapsulated in Lessing's now notorious apotheosis of the "vaginal orgasm":

> When Ella first made love with Paul . . . what set the seal on the fact she loved him . . . was that she immediately experienced orgasm. Vaginal orgasm that is. And she could not have experienced it if she had not loved him. It is the orgasm that is created by the man's need for a woman, and his confidence in that need. . . . A vaginal orgasm is emotion and nothing else, felt as emotion and expressed in sensations that are indistinguishable from emotion. The vaginal orgasm is a dissolving in a vague, dark generalised sensation like being swirled in a warm whirlpool. There are several different sorts of clitoral orgasms, and they are more powerful (that is a male word) than the vaginal orgasm. There can be a thousand thrills, sensations, etc., but there is only one real female orgasm and that is when a man, from the whole of his need and desire takes a woman and wants all her response. Everything else is a substitute and a fake, and the most inexperienced woman feels this instinctively.
>
> (186)

While some critics have argued that Lessing, speaking here through the fictional persona of her own fictional persona, is being deliberately ironic, this notion of "real" sexual fulfillment nonetheless thoroughly informs Anna Wulf's sexual quest.[22] That the concept of the vaginal orgasm, while giving an anatomical locus for the sensation, is based on metaphysical rather than physiological processes for its production goes without saying. But despite its lack of clear physical causation, the vaginal orgasm, according to these lights, can only be activated by the combined presence of male "need and desire" and phallic penetration. Accordingly, a "real" female orgasm is essentially and exclusively the product of heterosex: the "more powerful" clitoral orgasms, which, not coincidentally, can also result from sexual interaction between two women or from autoeroticism, are dismissed as substitutes and fakes that a presumed Everywoman would "instinctively" recognize as such.

Yet, as Snitow notes, the ideal of "vaginal orgasm" is rarely realized by Anna or her alter ego, and disappointment almost inevitably ensues. Not surprisingly, Lessing's protagonist perceives a causal connection between disappointment and lesbianism; in the wake of being abandoned by her lover Michael, Anna records her emotional state as one that could lead to several apparently unhappy conclusions:

> A year, two years, five years of a certain kind of being can be rolled up and tucked away, or "named"—yes, during that time I was like that. Well now I am in the middle of such a period, and when it is over I shall glance back at it casually and say: Yes, that's what I was. I was a woman terribly vulnerable, critical, using femaleness as a sort of standard or yardstick to measure and discard men. . . . I was an Anna who invited defeat from men without even being conscious of it. . . . I was stuck fast in an emotion common to women of our time, that can turn them bitter, or Lesbian, or solitary.
>
> (410)

The ideas that inform this assessment, particularly that lesbianism is ultimately a manifestation of lack, is, as I have previously indicated, in accord with the Freudian-influenced perceptions of the period. Yet, as Adrienne Rich notes, this "quasi-feminist" definition of lesbianism *via negativa* "goes back to that notion which [Lessing] evidently has, that women become lesbians—bitter and full of hatred—not because there is a fulfillment in loving women, but because there is this terrible battle of the sexes going on and men just get to be too much to deal with" (Bulkin, 182). Thus Anna Wulf, if not Lessing herself, would outwardly posit that lesbianism has no reason for being in and of itself but rather exists as a mode of rejection of "real" (that is, heterosexual) sexuality. At the same time, however, Anna's "understanding" of lesbianism functions as a disavowal of her fear of being perceived as a lesbian, a fear that influences her self-destructive disruption of her relationship with her friend and erstwhile flatmate Molly, perhaps the only valuable and sustaining adult relationship in her life, and a fear with which she only belatedly and partially comes to terms.

The narrative patterns of lesbian panic may be discerned in *The Golden Notebook* when the novel is read not in the author's established sequence of interspersed and interrupting texts but rather as five individual if related texts—the "Free Women" story and the four notebooks that allow Anna to separate various aspects of her life and experience—augmented by the penultimate and eponymous "Golden Notebook." This last text may be seen as an idealized and surrealistic alternative ending to the final section of "Free Women," which, as Snitow suggests, merely "passes as a happy ending." Given its function as a framing narrative to the various notebooks, "Free Women," one might justifiably argue, is the central, privileged narrative within the whole, while the notebooks serve as Anna's self-generated glosses on the third-person biographical plot of which she is the protagonist.[23] While all the various texts are devoted in great part to the representation of Anna's numerous heterosexual encounters, "Free Women" (and, by extension, *The Golden Notebook*) in its circular structure begins and ends, significantly, with a moment of separation between two women.

As the novel commences, Anna and her friend Molly meet for the first time after a separation of some considerable time for which little immediate explanation is offered. The opening pages nevertheless reveal that the relationship between the two is based on a series of triangular exchanges. Claire Sprague aptly notes that Anna and Molly were "once so close as to be mistaken for sisters or lovers . . . both are over thirty-five, divorced, 'free' women currently living without men. . . . They have shared an apartment, the services of [the psychoanalyst] Mrs. Marks/Mother Sugar, and sometimes men. . . . Molly sends men . . . to Anna" (69). In what might be seen as a utopian gesture, one that corresponds with their romantic and relatively unreflective embrace of Communism, the women attempt to construct an exchange of men, an almost direct transference across sexual lines of Sedgwick's paradigm. Yet despite their economic independence, their capacity for pursuing nontraditional careers, and their ability to exist with relative impunity outside the structures of matrimony, both women are thoroughly male-identified, depending on men not only for the previously discussed sexual gratification of the vaginal orgasm but also for psychological approval and affirmation. Accordingly, their experiment in an exchange of men does not disrupt the patriarchal order; rather, both women are themselves ironically recirculated as objects of exchange while their relationship, one of the few positive or supportive connections in the novel, is rent asunder by the male disapprobation that underlies most lesbian panic.

Most of "Free Women 1" is devoted to a few hours on the day of the reunion of Anna and Molly. During this time, they discuss, with an air of regret and resignation, their various recent liaisons and are interrupted in their visit by the intrusion of Molly's ex-husband, Richard, a former Communist turned business tycoon. The women put up a spirited and united—if at times naive and illogical—defense against his misogynistic barbs, and the rapport between the two would seem to betoken a sense of solidarity and shared sisterhood. Only at the end of this first section of the novel is the cause for their past rupture attributed. At the end of their visit, Molly sadly surmises that "All this is simply because of Michael" (51), a suggestion that leads Anna to depart hastily in an air of agitation. In the course of her return home, past events are recalled through terse third-person narrative: "Michael had persuaded Anna, four years before, to move into her own flat. It was bad for her, he had said, to live in Molly's house, always under the wing of the big sister. When she had complained she could not afford it, he had told her to let a room. She had moved, imagining he would share this life with her; but he had left her shortly afterwards" (51).

Michael's rationale is, to say the least, irrational. Only through their domestic arrangement of shared household and child care are the two women able to maintain their status as "free women," an arrangement that allows Anna to devote an extraordinary amount of time to her paramour while remaining an apparently devoted mother. As he suggests that Anna could "let a room" as compensation for the economic hardship such a move would incur, his motive cannot be based on a desire for greater privacy, to have Anna to himself alone. Rather, it is Molly, specifically, who is "bad for her," despite her role in facilitating their liaison. Thus, by implication, Michael positions Molly as his rival for influence over Anna, if not for her affections and loyalty.

Even so, in the "Free Women" narratives, in which Anna functions as the third-person protagonist, Michael's judgment that living with Molly is "bad for her" is never explicated more fully. Nevertheless, in one of the "Yellow Notebook" sequences, those in which Anna explains her failed romantic and sexual relationships to herself through the medium of fiction, her protagonist, Ella, has an epiphany of sorts as she attempts to analyze for her friend Julia her reasons for moving out:

> There is now a moment of discomfort: Ella lets slide, out of cowardice, the chance of saying that Julia has behaved badly about her leaving; the chance of "getting it all out into the open." And in the silence of this discomfort, there is the thought . . . is it possible they thought us Lesbians?
>
> (387)

Yet Ella never articulates this thought aloud; rather, she answers her own question, her "bitter words" (387), with denial. Nonetheless, she soon thereafter "decides not to indulge in these conversations with Julia, thinking that two women, friends on a basis of criticism of men are Lesbian, psychologically if not physically" (389). Again, the perception that lesbianism is the result of embitterment toward men comes to the fore. But regardless of the inaccuracy of this perception, its force is sufficient, particularly when augmented by the projected disapproval of a male lover, to compel Anna/Ella to abandon her friend, her home, and the mutually supportive structures of her everyday existence. Accordingly, Anna's actions are nothing less than a very veiled form of lesbian panic. Ironically, the upheaval thus precipitated is all for naught; Michael leaves her soon after her move to the larger flat, which becomes an economic burden.

Anna's method of coping with both the material and psychological uncertainties that ensue is nothing if not suggestive. As if simultaneously to conceal, sublimate, and transfer her own feelings of lesbian panic, she rents a room in her flat to a male homosexual. This information is first related in a flat, matter-of-fact tone, as if it were of little significance, to Anna or anyone else: "Sometimes Anna thought that it could be said she was sharing a flat with a young man; but he was a homosexual, and there was no tension in the arrangement. They hardly saw one another" (52). Several implications may be discerned between the lines, implications that Anna would not be likely to examine directly. Because Ivor is male, she enjoys the scandalous frisson of the appearance that she lives with a man; yet because he is homosexual, he is, as Anna later articulates, not a "real man" (334). But, at the same time, because he is not female, like Molly, there can be no implication of lesbianism in their living arrangements, and, accordingly, there is "no tension."

While they are related in juxtaposition, as if to indicate their connectedness, the significance of Anna's departure from Molly's flat and her subsequent situation with Ivor (who, at this point, remains unnamed) is virtually obliterated as soon as the two events are presented. Coming at the end of "Free Women 1," these two incidents drop from the narrative consciousness as the various notebooks interrupt the "Free Women" plot. Only after more than half the novel has elapsed does the "homosexual" reappear; only then is he given a proper name. In the meantime, however, Anna's highly ambivalent feelings about male homosexuality are revealed through the "Black Notebook," in which she recalls the events of her earlier life in Africa, events that inspired her one published and highly successful novel. Three young RAF airmen, who "at Oxford . . . had been homosexuals" (70), enliven the meetings and outings of the small local Communist Party group. On one level, as members of this egalitarian group, they share a bond of comradeship with Anna and the others. Yet they are men who enjoy an ironically class-based and decidedly male power and privilege from which Anna is excluded. More subtly, Anna resents the sexual inaccessibility of these men. Accordingly, she can be open to the arrogant and often supercilious Paul, who, having basically dismissed his "homosexual phase" (70) as an undergraduate phenomenon, has a transitory sexual encounter with her shortly before his grotesque accidental death. At the same time her disgust is relatively unrelenting for the "truly homosexual" Jimmy (74), who is pathetically and unrequitedly in love with Paul and thus acts, albeit futilely, as her sexual rival.

This ambivalence is echoed in later developments in Anna's domestic situation. If there was indeed "no tension" between Anna and Ivor early in the novel, there surely and ironically is when he reenters the plot. In "Free Women 3," Ivor is first represented in a feminized role, acting as a caretaker for Anna's daughter, Janet, while Anna is preoccupied with Molly's distress in the wake of her son's attempted suicide, a gruesome event with which most of "Free Women 2" and "Free Women 3" is occupied. While Anna gives attention to Molly, the woman she previously shunned for fear of imputations of lesbianism, Ivor's "maternal" care is welcomed, if not to some extent exploited—until Ivor introduces onto the scene a lover, the unemployed, flamboyant, campy, and effeminate Ronnie. While tension did not exist between Anna and a desexualized, celibate, and dispersonal Ivor, once he is seen as part of a couple, Anna clearly feels a loss of control over her environment. This growing feeling of chaos, already exacerbated by the previously mentioned events in Molly's family, is deepened by Ronnie's demeanor. Positing himself vis-à-vis Anna as just another beleaguered female put upon by men, Ronnie seeks a common bond with her, even to sharing and discussing cosmetics. On a political level, Anna recognizes the oppression homosexual men share with women and racial outsiders and thus feels a social responsibility toward them: "Anna could not ask a couple of young men who were disturbing her peace of mind to leave, because they were homosexuals, and they, like a coloured student, would find it hard to get a room" (344) Still, she recoils in revulsion, seeing Ronnie's behavior as "mocking 'normal' love; and on a jeering, common, gutter level" (335). But Ronnie, who is completely dependent on men economically, psychologically, and sexually, is, in his outrageousness, little more than a camp parody of Anna's modes of dependence on men, an aspect of her that he, in his attempted "sisterhood" with her, no doubt recognizes. Accordingly, this perverse mirroring sends Anna into a state that is clearly one of panic.

Anna, in turn, projects much of her own anxiety over the two men onto concerns for her daughter's well-being, that Janet would be "corrupted" by contact with Ivor and Ronnie and that she "ought to have a real man . . . for Janet's sake, let alone mine" (334). Indeed, on some extraordinarily wry level, Ivor does influence Janet and introduce her to the homosocial life—through the medium of the girls' school novels with which he diverts her. Anna's panic is thereby intensified when, almost simultaneously with her eviction of the two men, Janet insists "out of the blue" on going to a boarding school, where she can be "ordinary and normal" (464). Anna's response of sadness and rejection is curiously apt, for in choosing for herself a homosocial adolescent environment, Janet effectively rebels against the outward nonconformity and random heterosexuality of her mother's "free" lifestyle. But Anna's reaction to Janet in her new schoolgirl persona is telling, inasmuch as her sorrow in losing intimacy with her female child is underscored by a fear of an apparently renunciatory mode of lesbianism:

> The young girl's quality, the petulant, indulged-child's charm, which she put on like a pretty dress about a year ago, vanished the moment she put the uniform on. . . . [She] was a nice, bright little girl in a hideous uniform, among a herd of such young girls, her young breasts hidden, all charm vanquished, her manner practical. And, seeing her, I mourned for a dark, lively, dark-eyed, slight young girl, alive with new sexuality, alert with the instinctive knowledge of her power. And at the same time I notice I had a truly cruel thought: my poor child, if you are going to grow up in a society full of Ivors and Ronnies, full of frightened men who measure out emotions like weighed groceries, then you'll do well to model yourself on Miss Street, the headmistress. (467)

In language that provocatively suggests her own homoerotic attraction to her daughter, she mourns what she sees as the loss of Janet's still-nascent sexuality—one that, for Anna, would be essentially heterosexual—without considering that Janet herself might view Anna's own sexuality with distaste. Rather, Anna returns to her previous concept of lesbianism, projecting that Janet's precocious rejection of heterosexuality is based on a bitterness toward men, whether sexually inaccessible and parodic homosexuals or unfeeling and exploitive heterosexuals.

It is noteworthy that neither Lessing nor her protagonist is unaware of the Freudian implications of the triangulation and jealousy the underscore many if not most of the relationships in the novel. As Anna is in the process of her mental breakdown, an episode that, suggestively, follows closely upon her eviction of Ivor and Ronnie and Janet's departure for girls' school, she ponders her seeming obsession with the other woman with whom Saul Green, her latest lover, is involved:

> I remember Mother Sugar and how she "taught" me about the obsessions of jealousy being part homosexuality. But the lesson at the time seemed rather academic, nothing to do with me, Anna. I wondered if I wanted to make love with that woman he was with now.
>
> Then there was a moment of knowledge . . . he was looking for this wise, kind, all-mother figure, who is also sexual playmate and sister; and because I had become part of him, this is what I was looking for too, both for myself, because I needed her, and because I wanted to become her. . . . I sat there in my dark room, looking at the hazed wet brilliance of the purple London night sky, longing with my whole being for that mythical woman, longing to be her, but for Saul's sake. (502)

Anna can come to this realization regarding a "mythic" woman, one whom she has never met, one whose described characteristics exist primarily, if not exclusively, in Anna's imaginary. All the while, the dynamics of her exchange of men with Molly, whom she knows far too well, are subjected to the mechanisms of denial.

If "Free Women," the story of Anna and Molly, is, as the novel suggests, the product of the affair between Saul and Anna, the end result of their artistic collaboration and their sexual liaison is, ironically, a reinscription of narrative structures of lesbian panic. Neither woman is able to maintain or endure her "freedom," nor are the friends ever able to mend the rift they have allowed men to create between them. Rather, Anna, disillusioned with the Communist Party and with her writing block unresolved, joins the more mainstream Labour Party and assumes a new vocation as a marriage counselor. That her new-found occupation is an unlikely one for a woman whose disappointments with men continue to loom large goes without saying; yet her willingness to take on the task of rescuing institutional heterosexuality in some sort of meaningful way would indicate that a belief in the courtship plot and the possibility of its traditional "happy" ending nonetheless persist, however incongruously, in her own subconscious. Molly's fate is even more traditional. Although Anna regards Molly's Jewishness with something approximating envy, the ties to her patriarchal culture and religion do, in the end, indeed bind. Exhausted by the strain of her blinded son's demands and his political ideologies, she finds relief from her "freedom" by marrying "the poor Jewish boy for the East End who got rich and salved his conscience by giving money . . . to progressive causes" (567). When Anna wryly observes that "Getting married to a man who has a house in Hampstead is going to make you very remote from the emotional rat-race," Molly quite forthrightly responds, "Yes, thank God" (568). Almost immediately after this exchange, "the two women kissed and separated" (568), bringing the novel to an end. If this conclusion does not necessarily indicate that traditional marriage is not only what women want but what they need, it certainly indicates that there exists little choice for women other than their eventual subsumption (or re-subsumption) into the patriarchal order. Accordingly, *The Golden Notebook* in the end presents yet one more repetition of the courtship plot after recording, throughout its long course, the failure of that very narrative convention.

When the lesbian subtext—typically configured as lesbian panic—reappears in mainstream British women's writing in the early 1960s, it is, as in these novels by Spark and Lessing, placed in juxtaposition to some remnant of the courtship plot. But if the courtship plot was already in decline in Woolf's middle novels and in Bowen's *The Hotel*, then it is certainly in shambles some three decades later. Both Spark and Lessing effectively reduce the courtship plot to a relic of the past that is clearly futile yet cannot easily be discarded. Accordingly, some purpose for it is inevitably found. For Spark's protagonist, the disrupted courtship plot functions as a means of creating a public image of dedication and heroism, while for Lessing's protagonist it would appear to be a familiar trope to which one can return for lack of a better plot. In either case, it serves the respective heroines as a mode of cynical metafiction. And as the courtship plot in either case serves to obscure the desires that its manipulators fear to articulate, it creates the conditions that have historically found their narrative shape as lesbian panic.

Conceivably, the recurrence of lesbian panic as a narrative subtext in the early 1960s is merely a newer and, in a sense, angrier exploration, after a long hiatus, of ground broken by modernist women writers. It is perhaps appropriate, then, that the task of moving lesbian panic from the position of subtext to that of central plot fell to one of the last surviving modernists. During the last years of her life and career, Elizabeth Bowen returned to the subject matter that informed her earliest novel, that of unarticulated or semi-articulated desire between women and the potentially dangerous behaviors that arise from the individual's inability to express or act upon those desires in any socially coherent fashion. That it was possible for her to address these issues once again was, no doubt, facilitated by the relatively "permissive" social attitudes of this decade that allowed for not only the relatively open representation of heterosexuality in *The Prime of Miss Jean Brodie* and *The Golden Notebook* but also the oblique or limited representation of lesbian desire in these texts. Indeed, it is conceivable that the youth culture that characterized much of the artistic output of the decade is reflected in the emphasis on adolescence and its aftermath in both *The Little Girls* (1963) and *Eva Trout, or Changing Scenes* (1968). Many of Bowen's critics have seen this radical shift in subject matter—accompanied by an equally radical shift in the author's style—as evidence of a loss of artistic power, a "bend back," according to Hermione Lee (190), that is variously attributed to her grief over the death of her husband and the loss of her ancestral home, to financial distress, to increasingly ill health, and even to a desire to be "trendy."[24] I would argue that these assessments, of dubious accuracy at best, fail to see—or avoid seeing—the revolutionary accomplishment of Bowen's last two works: the thorough displacement of the romance plot, the de-essentialization of heterosexuality as a social or narrative norm, and the establishment of lesbian panic as a narrative in and of itself, no longer a secondary mode of narratability vis-à-vis the main plot.

Early in *The Little Girls*, as the triad of protagonists are reunited after fifty years, one of them, Clare, gazes at a child's swing and ruminates: "Those were the days before love. These are the days after. Nothing has gone for nothing but the days between" (56). In this narrative quest for what might best be described neologistically as "recovered memory," the "days between," those that would have traditionally formed the romance plot and the quiescent state of matrimony thereafter, in fact "go for nothing." For the trio of aged school girls, as Edwin J. Kenney notes, "even heterosexual love no longer counts" (89). The tripartite structure of Bowen's novel, which effectively collapses chronology, moves from a seemingly incongruous problem in the historical present to its origins during the summer of 1914, then back to the unresolved issues of the past still influencing the present. It simply omits the period called "love" and thus renders it insignificant in comparison with the narrative of homoerotic attachment lost and, conceivably, regained. In doing so, Bowen, like Spark, challenges the Freudian notion that the development of female sexuality "proceeds from an emotionally pre-Oedipal female-centered natural world to the heterosexual male-dominated social world" (Abel, "Narrative Structure[s]," 164), albeit to quite different ends than those we have seen in *The Prime of Miss Jean Brodie*.

The novel begins, farcelike, with the exposition of a problem that seems inexplicable to all concerned, even to its originator. Dinah Delacroix (née Diana Piggott), a sixtyish widow of means, launches a highly eccentric project of collecting personal objects from her acquaintances and sealing them for posterity in a subterranean cave. The motivation for this strange activity ostensibly lies in a fear of war, that most frequent force of destabilization in Bowen's works. Here, however, this anxiety takes on configurations peculiar to the historic moment, as the gesture is one of defiance and preservation in the face of the Cold War threat of nuclear annihilation: "It's for someone or other to come upon in the *far future*, when practically nothing about any of us—you or me, for instance—would otherwise be known. . . . I'm looking forward to when *we* are a vanished race" (14, italics original). Yet this frenetic behavior, which serves to mask a very palpable macrocosmic panic, is merely a repetition of an earlier event enacted in the face of a war that ultimately decimated the child Diana's microcosm and left her with an unresolved and traumatic yearning. Only when this yearning is identified, relatively late in the novel, through the process of lesbian panic, can it find some form of resolution.

Before revealing the child Diana (nicknamed "Dicey") who internalizes this rupture, Bowen presents the woman she has become. A well-to-do if markedly frivolous matron possessed of a large country home, with a handsome and idealized retired military man functioning as her neighbor, admirer, and self-appointed protector, Dinah is the mother of affluent grown sons and the grandmother of two adoring young girls. Having acquired all the rewards of domesticity and having virtually none of its duties left to discharge, she would seem to have achieved the ideal if ultimate aftermath of the romance plot and to have little reason for discontent. Her oddly disturbing and apocalyptic project, then, is greatly at odds with the expectations of those around her, particularly those of the devoted

Major Frank Wilkins, who attempts to dissuade her from this and the antics that ensue.

In a Proustian moment, a glimpse of a swing—the same swing that inspires Clare's reflection—triggers Dinah's memory of a chest filled with symbolic items and buried by her and her classmates at the dawn of the First World War. The recollection becomes an obsession, and she becomes absorbed in her need to find the classmates she has not seen in fifty years. But because she has become, over a lifetime, a frivolously willful woman, she goes about this quest in a fairly absurd manner, by publishing advertisements such as the following:

> Sheikie and Mumbo, where are you? Your former confederate Dicey seeks you earnestly, in connection with the matter known so far only to us. Whole affair now looks like coming to light. Essential we meet before too late. You or anyone knowing the present whereabouts of Sheila née Barker and Clare née Burkin-Jones, who in 1914 were at St. Agatha's, Southstone, should at once write to Box—
>
> (27–28)

The tone of innuendo and urgency that informs this notice and others like it quite predictably cause alarm to the addressees, who are eventually revealed as having secrets of their own. As the two meet, for the first time since 1914, to discuss this strange turn of events, they are presented not as "Sheikie" and "Mumbo" but rather, like Dinah, as the women they have become. Sheila, now Mrs. Trevor Artworth bedecked in pink roses, is a male-identified, hyperfeminine, and slightly hysterical provincial middle-class lady who constantly refers to her estate agent husband's authority and fears anything that hints of unrespectability; consequently, she suspects "Dicey" of malicious intent. "Mumbo," however, remains Clare Burkin-Jones, large, overly chic in her tightly fitting suit and turban, and abruptly direct, with a tendency to bully others and an air of "sombre jollity" (32). Unlike Sheila, she is vaguely amused by Dinah's plot. She retains her original name, she explains, "for the best of reasons": "Mr. Wrong came along, all right. That was a mess. So when I wrote that off, I took back my name. ... Or rather, my father's" (32–33). Thus, tersely, she explains all the personal history she cares to reveal in the course of the novel, though in reclaiming the name of her father, an army major, she has apparently reclaimed his military bearing as well as part of her own mode of being.

The contrast between these women is of particular significance in the context of the novel, for while the text is ultimately a narrative of lesbian panic, the focus of the past and present contexts is not so much on sexuality—only Sheila's sexual history receives any specific scrutiny—but rather on gender. When the three are at last reunited, their perceptions of one another, juxtaposed with their recollections and expectations, are revealed as performances of the gendered roles that each, according to her own inclinations and circumstances, found to her advantage to play. The origins of these roles become apparent in the second part of the novel, a distant third-person narrative comprising the collective memories of the three over the course of the summer marked by the advent of the First World War. Students in a girls' school on the southern coast of England, each one, aged eleven, has already assumed her own gendered pose. Sheikie, the most superficial, is not only "Southstone's wonder, the child exhibition dancer" but also the spoiled and flirtatious daughter of her affluent "Dad-*dy*" (69, 107). As such, she has learned early to rely on her physical charm and to look to male authority for personal gain. Mumbo, by contrast, is a discontent, subversively rebellious child, given to intellectual pursuits. Repelled by the dutifully conventional domesticity and propriety of her mother, she models herself on her military officer father. This emulation includes an infatuation with Diana's mother, the widowed and romantically tragic Mrs. Piggott, who plays Debussy and reads novels in genteel poverty as the denizen of the romantically named Feveral Cottage, to which Major Burkin-Jones "would not be coming . . . for the first, second, or even third time . . . as each visit becomes one more" (84). Dicey, whose nickname indicates the less than upright domestic situation surrounding her, is the least exceptional or unconventional of the three. The child of a father who committed suicide before her birth, she evinces much of the romantic impracticality of her mother and, as if to emulate her mother, becomes emotionally attached, albeit in a confused, indirect way, to the Major's daughter. It is hardly accidental, then, that the man Dinah permits to be her admirer late in life—and who eventually posits himself as Clare's rival—holds the same military rank as did her mother's lover.

During a chance encounter with a suffragette, the spinster aunt of a classmate and a woman legendary among the girls for having been "chained to railings" (90) during demonstrations, Diana's own fantastic imagination is stirred by a discussion of local excavations of Roman artifacts. Impressed by the witchlike appearance of the aunt, who wears "a largish black straw hat which . . . had upon it what could only be magpie's wings" (88), Diana hatches a scheme with her friends to bury personally significant objects for future anthropological interest, a plan whose execution, with incantations in a "secret language" concocted by Clare, seems like nothing so much as a parody of the witches' scene in *Macbeth*.[25] But while this ritual serves as a prompt to the older Dinah's recovery of memory and subsequent actions decades later, it pales in significance to a later event, the memory of which is even more repressed for Dinah and, conceivably, the other participants.

As the summer draws to a close, the children and their parents are invited to a picnic outing on the beach to celebrate the birthday of Olive Pocock, a classmate from a well-connected family. After this occasion, the girls and their families will go their separate ways, presumably for the summer holiday but in fact, as matters transpire, permanently. This festive interlude, overshadowed by world events that are not completely within the children's reckoning, takes on sinister, mournful, and even chaotic overtones. Boys and girls, disregarding their parents' promptings to jollity, launch spontaneously and incongruously into a balefully grotesque rendition of Stephen Foster's "Old Folks at Home," while the organized games the parents plan disintegrate into hooliganish enactments of gender reversal. Dicey and Mumbo menace the already feminized and put-upon Trevor—who will, eventually, become the adult Sheila's husband—by trampling his eyeglasses underfoot, threatening him with matches, and forcing him into the dubious shelter of a sewer drainpipe. This carnivalesque behavior, in Clare at least, is a defiance of encroaching doom. She is aware, more than the other children, that the assassination of an Austrian archduke will have some inexplicable effect on their lives and that her father, invited to but absent from this outing, will be posted abroad the next day. Accordingly, she is distant and abrupt with Diana. Major Burkin-Jones finally appears, with the dual purpose of collecting his daughter and bidding Mrs. Piggott farewell. As the doomed lovers part—the Major soon to become one of the first British casualties at Mons, Mrs. Piggott to fall victim to the flu epidemic at the end of the war—Dicey watches with a growing realization of the arrangements of the adult world. Thus transfixed and confused, she misses the opportunity to say goodbye to Clare and runs desperately and wailing, too late, toward her friend as she slips out of sight. Clare's parting gesture, as she leaves the beach with her father, is cold and inadequate: "The rough child, up there against the unkind sky, on the rough grass, glanced at and over the sands once. She threw a hand up into a rough, general wave. Then she leaped down on the land side of the sea wall. She had disappeared" (133). With the parting of the Burkin-Joneses, the Piggotts, mother and daughter alike, lose the objects of their love. More than the burial of the chest, this rupture becomes the core of the adult Dinah's repressed memory, the psychic wound that goes unhealed.

The final part of the novel not only places lesbian panic, the response to this long unarticulated desire and loss, as denouement, but also gives the characters an opportunity for self-narrative, in which each justifies, as it were, herself—and, by extension, the gender role to which she has adapted—to the others. Having recuperated her lost friends, Dinah sets about the dubious recreating of old relationships, particularly with the ever-elusive Clare, now a successful entrepreneur and the proprietor of a chain of boutiques. Combining the "masculine" realm of business and self-sufficient individualism with the "feminine" realm of the ornamentality, triviality, and domesticity of the "Mopsie Pye" giftwares she markets, Clare deftly balances her own gender dysphoria for public consumption. Indeed, Clare effectively elides the private element of her life, existing in the text almost exclusively in her public persona. Unlike Dinah and Sheila, Clare is never represented at home. Instead, her various shops become her *loci vivendi*; thus, it is in one such shop that Dinah invades Clare's private sphere. Surprised by this intrusion, Clare is abrupt, even hostile, replicating her mood on the day of the beach picnic years before. Although the pretext of Dinah's visit is to engage Clare, as well as Sheila, in further playful adventures, their banter soon comes to reflect the sexual tension between them, particularly as Dinah provocatively laments Clare's lack of social reciprocation:

> "I wondered whether you'd telephone."
> "Well, I didn't."
> "No.—Last night, when I rang up, you sounded so cross."
> "You made me jump, suddenly coming through like that."
> "That's the worst of telephones. What were you doing?"
> "Well, I was in my flat."
> "Of course you were, else you couldn't have answered. What were you doing?"
> "Thinking about you," said Clare crossly.
> "And why not?—What's your flat like?"
> "Well, it's a flat."
> "Can't I come and see it?"
> "If you like. If I'm there."
> "Oh, you're so genial."
>
> (143)

The utter banality of this exchange masks not only Dinah's erotic aggression but also Clare's repressed inclinations. Through childlike plaintiveness, Dinah attempts to position herself as a significant presence in Clare's personal life while looking for specific details about exactly what that personal life entails. With the reticence characteristic of one who has spent a lifetime closeted, Clare divulges little in terms of specific information. This façade of indifference nonetheless has a fissure; Clare's statement that she was thinking of Dinah at the moment of her call reveals the reciprocal yearning she has almost completely concealed. Suggestively, Dinah follows up on her visit by writing Clare a note requesting a peculiar butter knife she has seen in the shop: "The more I think about it, the more I want it" (152). Alluding to the witches in *Macbeth*, Dinah describes the instrument's handle as "a pilot's thumb, wreck'd as homeward he did come" (180), and the phallic shape of this object of exchange between the two women does not fail to disturb both Frank and Dinah's houseboy Francis once it arrives by post.

This mounting erotic discomfort is relieved, momentarily, by yet another farcically comic episode. Three matronly women set out with picks and shovels to excavate their buried chest—which, as a result of postwar suburbanization, is situated in the garden of a private home. They recover the chest, only to discover it emptied of its contents—and to be accosted by the homeowner upon whose property they have trespassed. After manipulating their way out of their embarrassing situation, the three retire to Sheila's home—in the same street as her childhood home—for drinks and conversation. But what should be a lighthearted and sociable evening after this absurd escapade quickly turns dour. The purpose for reunion having been accomplished, they must confront what reasons exist, if any, for any continuing relationship. The congeniality among them is, at best, strained. Dinah, dismayed by the emptiness of the coffer, experiences the onset of an ontological crisis in which she is confronted by the emotional emptiness of her life and seeks a hasty departure. Sheila's jest that Dinah's home "won't run away" precipitates her exposition of her newly-emerging anxiety:

> That's what it *has* done, Sheikie. . . . Everything has. *Now* it has, you see. Nothing's real anymore. . . . Nothing's left, out of going on fifty years. . . . This has done it. . . . Can't you see what's happened? This us three. This going back, I mean. This began as a game, *began* as a game. Now—you see?—it's got me! . . . And now . . . the game's collapsed. We saw there was nothing *there*. So, where am I now? (163)

The nothingness of which Dinah complains is no less than the sum total of "going on fifty years" that she has repressed the homoerotic desires of her youth and has settled instead for an uneventful life of empty, if privileged, propriety that stands as the reward of the romance plot.

Despite Clare's admonition not to be "a fey bore"—to which she replies, "You're so military" (166)—Dinah sets out on a late-night long drive home, leaving Sheila and Clare to their own round of dissembling, which eventually settles into Sheila's personal narrative. While the future had seemed far more promising to Sheikie than to the other two in 1914, the fame of "Southstone's wonder, the child exhibition dancer" never reached beyond local parameters. At eighteen, she left for dance school in London, only to be informed at her audition that she had acquired through her provincial celebrity "certain ways," vulgar ways that left her with "too much to unlearn" (172). As a result, she turned to other "certain ways" of gender for which she had been rewarded early on, becoming the mistress of a surrogate for her father, an older, affluent man (for whose lingering death, she later reveals, she was indirectly responsible). Subsequently seeking social redemption, she married, at thirty-two, the previously put-upon Trevor, by then a widower with two children and a partner in her father's business. The girl who would go far, by performing the gender roles she adopted early on, ended up, ironically, in the street where she was born, living a life of cautiously protected respectability. After telling her tale, she expels her guest abruptly, having noticed that Trevor has returned home unexpectedly.

Despite the pronounced unease that permeates all their interactions, the three women continue their contact with one another, whether individually or collectively. Although distraught at the close of their expedition, Dinah nonetheless invites Clare for a visit soon thereafter for the ostensible purpose of Clare examining the wares of a local artisan for sale in her shops. With the business aspect of this excursion concluded, Dinah, on a highly contrived pretext, entices Clare into Major Wilkins's momentarily unoccupied cottage where, through inquiries about the marriage of Clare's parents, she attempts to evoke memories of the illicit if discreet liaison at Feveral Cottage. Clare, in a moment of candor, describes herself as "a muddle," as far as marriage is concerned. But ever the repressor, she gives no answer to Dinah's provocative suggestion that "the non-sins of our fathers—and mothers—have been visited upon us" (186) and eventually puts an end this interlude of oblique seduction by asserting, "this is not *like* Feveral Cottage!" (187). Yet before they reach Dinah's house, Dinah asks Clare to retire and come live with her, a request that is met with a sarcastic reference to Major Wilkins as a kept man. Still later that evening, when the two are alone together in the house, Dinah returns to the subject of "love," again indirectly and by positing the heterosexuality (although in term of "boredom") of her relationship with Frank Wilkins: "But then, boredom is part of love." The conversation I cite in my introduction then ensues, in which Dinah first accuses Clare of having "no affections," then directly asks, "Mumbo, are you a Lesbian?" Clare's answer, or nonanswer, is telling. She equates the question with Dinah's speculation about whether or not "Sheikie had killed anyone," with the answer to both being "not exactly" (197). Yet as Sheila did, in some sense, precipitate a man's death, this analogy would indicate that Clare, in some sense, is a lesbian—presumably one who, given her intense repression that manifests itself in abrupt anger, has never allowed herself to act upon her desires.

Still, as Dinah attempts to clarify, she would not castigate Clare for being a lesbian; she does not care what Clare is. This note of acceptance does not, however, find a receptive audience, and Clare further rebuffs her "bewildered" interlocutor, who nonetheless persists in attempting, even if awkwardly, to explain what she means: "I wanted you. I wanted you to be there—here, I mean. Whatever you think of yourself, you are very strong; and, also, I thought you would understand. Who else am I to talk to, without frightening them? Stay with me for a little, can't you?" (197). Perceiving Clare as a lesbian, Dinah mistakenly presumes she could, without "frightening" Clare, make her desires understood, if not through her earlier indirect approach then through relative forthrightness. To do so would be to break completely with the "safe" learned gender role of frivolous femininity she had performed over the fifty years she has come to see as nothingness. Clare, on the one hand, understands too well what is asked of her, the very act she has spent a lifetime avoiding. But at the same time, because a lifetime of repression has cost Clare whatever compassion she may have had for others, she does not understand Dinah's entreaty at all. Consequently, her response is a brutal projection of her own fear and a dismissal of Dinah based on a resentment of her past gender-based "games":

> Look, Dicey, what *are* you frightened of? . . . All your life, I should think, you have run for cover. "There's Mother!" "Here's my nice white gate!" Some of us have no cover, nothing to run to. Some of us more than *think* we feel. . . . Never once have you played fair, all along the line. Simply you play your particular kind of game better than you did; so, well by now, that you probably hardly know that you *are* playing it when you are.
>
> (197–98)

Yet Dinah, in earnest perhaps for the first time in her life, persists in her plea, only to remind Clare of Mrs. Piggott, her "enchantress" mother. Calling Dinah "Circe," she leaves, while Dinah responds with the inculcated graciousness and civility of accustomed gender role, that of a proper English lady: " 'Very well, said Dinah gently, turning away" (198).

While coming relatively late in the novel, this crucial encounter functions as the turning point for the entire plot, both past and present, and stands as a relatively rare representation of mutual lesbian panic. For the repressed lesbian Clare, Dinah's entreaties and inquiries act as an exposure of her long-secret sexuality, compounded, in this case, with the memory of parental secrets and dishonor. Accordingly, Clare responds to being "found out" through disavowal and abusiveness to cover her distress and flees Dinah's house in spite of the late hour and long drive from Somerset to London. Dinah's lesbian panic, though, is a far more complicated matter. Bowen creates a gap in the narrative, as if to replicate a series of new gaps in Dinah's memory, requiring the reader to reconstruct her subsequent actions through the perceptions of other characters. On the morning after Clare's departure, Dinah is discovered unconscious with evidence of a blow to the head, apparently self-inflicted. Her failed proposal *qua* seduction, based on the assumption that the "very strong" Clare was somehow at ease with her own sexuality, was configured through an attempt to romanticize and recapitulate the "non-sins" of her mother and Clare's father; but Dinah mistakes the "masculine" gender Clare performs as a sign of a secure lesbian sexuality. Thus, when her effort brings humiliation and an awkward disclosure of her own sexuality, Dinah seeks to emulate the sin or "non-sin" of her own father, that of suicide.

In *The Hotel* Bowen allowed for the reversal of lesbian panic by plotting a release from its immediate effects for her protagonist. In *The Little Girls*, however, the author takes this process further. The lesbian panic here, unlike that in any other previous novel in this study, is not only reversed but effects a closure of homosocial and homoerotic amelioration. Dinah emerges from her semicomatose state to discover Sheila in attendance as her nurse. For the male-centered and over-feminized Sheila, the act is a reversal of her abandonment of her paramour, the man she did not *exactly* kill, on his deathbed; only now the loyalty she could not extend to a man is realized through sympathy bestowed upon another woman. Sheila also functions as the tacit mediator through whom a reconciliation is effected between Dinah and Clare. Clare has returned to the scene, but she is barred from the house, not only by the clearly hostile male presence of Dinah's sons and Frank but also by Dinah's express wish. As Sheila enacts surrogate motherhood with Dinah's sons, a role she has long coveted, she allows Clare access to her patient. Contemplating the recumbent woman, Clare assesses her own emotional failure in her relationship with Dinah, past and present: "I did not comfort you. Never have I comforted you. Forgive me" (236). This basically metaphysical gesture of enlightenment and regret in a darkened room is intended as a valediction "for now and then," a making of amends for not taking leave, either on that day on the beach in 1914 or on that recent night. But Clare's enactment of closure, which immediately precedes the close of the novel, gives way to a new opening: Dinah wakes, and the text concludes with a brief dialogue:

> "Who's there?"
> "Mumbo."
> "Not Mumbo. Clare. Clare, where have you been?"
>
> (237)

By ending her narrative with this exchange, Bowen stops short of a state of quiescence. More *must* transpire between the characters after this interlude, but the plotting of further interaction—not to mention the judgment as to whether or not this is a "happy" or even satisfactory ending—is thrown back upon the reader. Therein, no doubt, lies much of the critical dismay with this text. In the only previous lesbian reading of *The Little Girls*, however, Jane Rule posits that the closure marks the beginning of a new, homoerotic rapport between Dinah and Clare: "That question ends the book with the suggestion that these two will now deal with the relationship the one has longed for, the other longed for but dreaded" (121). While idealistic, Rule's interpretation is nonetheless feasible; given the relative implausibility of a directly "lesbian" ending in a "mainstream" women's fiction at this historical juncture, it seems an apt explanation for the conclusion's abruptness. At the very least, the three lines the characters articulate, particularly Dinah's final utterance, indicate a desire for a reconfigured mode of affinity. By identifying herself as "Mumbo," Clare positions herself as the repentant child, abashed by her refusal to comfort her friend at the long-ago beach picnic, the act from which the original rupture ensued. Until she remedies the shame and injury connected with this incident, she remains "Mumbo," an angry child unable to function as an adult with another adult. But Dinah's repudiation of the childish nickname and her enunciation of the adult name indicate an acceptance of Clare's unspoken apology and a forgiveness of the offenses of the both the distant and recent past, just as the final question invites the presence of one long absent.

Although Sheila retires to another room immediately before the ultimate reunion of Clare and Dinah—in order, in a manner of speaking, to perform the role of mother to Dinah's *two* "enormous boys"—the conclusion of *The Little Girls*, as well as the use of crucial "moments of being" in its plotting, structurally recalls *Mrs. Dalloway*. Both move toward the reunion of three old friends, and the near-hysterical intrusion of Frank into Dinah's sickroom, as the male lover who resentfully senses he is less significant than the female lover to the loved one, is analogous with the actions of Peter Walsh. Yet while *Mrs. Dalloway* could offer its characters little more in terms of closure than the ability to acknowledge and mourn a past founded upon lesbian panic and its repercussions, *The Little Girls* indicates, however belatedly, the possibility of resolving such past disruptions and, by extension, the potential for a new narrative beyond lesbian panic.

If *The Little Girls* is, in effect, a narrative of gender roles acquired in and performed since preadolescence and the ongoing ramifications thereof, *Eva Trout*, Bowen's final novel, presents an exploration of the epistemological and ontological implications involved in a complete de-essentializing of gender and sexuality that calls into question the foundational reality of biological sex itself. That even the latter can be called into question, that it is not the proverbial "truth universally acknowledged" is evident in the question put to the eponymous heroine early in her personal history by one of her classmates at school: "Trout, are you a hermaphrodite?" To this impertinent inquiry, one that indicates that its subject is neither *essentially* male nor female, Eva can only respond, "I don't know." The enigmatic nonassertion of identity leads to an exchange that allusively configures the dislocation of those undefined by sex, gender, or sexuality in society:

> "Joan of Arc's supposed to have been [an hermaphrodite]."
> "Never established," one of the boys put in. "How could it be? *Elle fut carbonisée.*"
> "Then canonized," said one of the other girls.
> Eva pondered. "I'd like to be Joan of Arc."
>
> (51)

As the "giantess" protagonist cannot "know," much less articulate or identify her physical sex, it follows that she is equally indefinite regarding her gender and sexuality, if not more so. In this instance, the naive speculation of schoolchildren conflating the categories of sex and gender underscores the notion that even the underinformed and not completely initiated members of society perceive in some abstract manner that their classmate does not fit neatly on either side of the binaries of male/female and masculine/feminine in any traditional "normative" sense. Thus the narrative end for such an individual seems already predetermined, for Eva's possibilities already seem limited to quixotic displays of the bizarrely heroic; her desire to be Joan of Arc—that is, extraordinary and, ultimately, martyred—will be ironically fulfilled as the only conceivable outcome for the unwitting gender outlaw. As a character who functions as if she were completely oblivious to any "normative" concepts in terms of gender and sexuality, Eva Trout, described by an acquaintance as "ethically . . . a Typhoid Mary" (179), inspires many forms of panic in others; in her former teacher Iseult Smith, later the unhappily married Mrs. Arble, she evokes a particularly lethal manifestation of lesbian panic.

Bowen's text questions, in effect, whether any individual reared without a sense of the absolute binaries of male/female, masculine/feminine—much less any perception of heterosexuality as a norm—would instinctively or automatically recognize those social constructs as inherently "normal." As the novel begins, Eva, in the act of showing a putative castle, a "pile [that] resembled some Bavarian fantasy," makes a pronouncement to her newfound friends, the children of an Anglican vicar: "This is where we were to have spent the honeymoon" (11). Although this statement, which repeats itself ironically in the denouement, is later revealed as the result of Eva's "passion for the fictitious for its own sake" (242), it is nonetheless reflective of a not completely realized mimesis of the romance plot, one of the various metanarratives the character continually attempts to employ in her abortive quest to find a place within the symbolic order of society. But Eva, never having experienced the structures of the purportedly "normal" as an integral part of her environment, cannot, by the age of twenty-four (as she is at the beginning of the novel), create for herself any self-narrative that aspires to the condition of anything other than a parodic mimesis of normative.

Through a series of flashbacks early in the text, Bowen relates Eva's history. The only daughter of the masochistic but fabulously wealthy Willy Trout, she had been motherless since the age of two months, when her mother, a "skite with a paramour" whose "fantasies . . . were [her] undoing," "bolted" upon learning of her husband's homosexuality and was soon after killed in a airplane crash (40). Subsequently she was raised in genteel neglect by a male couple, her father and *his* paramour, Constantine Ormeau, who, by the beginning of the text, has become Eva's guardian. Her education, such as it was, was provided by a geographically isolated experimental school—on the site of the putative honeymoon castle—for "wealthy little delinquents who knew everything" (49). Rather than serving some altruistic educational purpose, the school was founded by Willy as a means of banishing Constantine's other lover, Kenneth, whom he appointed as headmaster—until the inevitable scandals took their toll. After the closure of the school, necessitated by, among other incidents, the attempted Ophelia-like suicide of Eva's first love object, a "fairylike little near albino who had for some reason been christened Elsinore" (52), she accompanied Willy and Constantine in their international travels, until, at the age of sixteen, she announced her desire to attend "an English boarding-school: one for girls" (57).

This exchange of the male homosocial world of Willy and Constantine for the female homosocial ethos of Lumleigh brought the protagonist under the tutelage of the "wonderful teacher" Miss Iseult Smith:

> She could have taught anything. Her dark suit might have been the habit of an Order. Erect against a window of tossing branches she stood moveless, but for the occasional gesture of hand to forehead—then, the bringing of the finger-tips to the brain seemed to complete an electric circuit. Throughout a lesson, her voice held a reined-in excitement—imparting knowledge, she conveyed its elatingness. The intellectual beauty of her sentences was informed by a glow; words she spoke sounded new-minted, unheard before. With her patient, sometimes ironic insistence upon fact, as fact, went what could be called her opposite capacity—that of releasing ideas, or speculation, into unbounded flight.
>
> Fearless of coming to an end, she allowed pauses, during which she thought, or picked up a book and turned over a page abstractedly, almost idly. Meantime, there was suspense in the glassed-in classroom; nobody stirred.
>
> (58)

With her nunlike "habit" and quasiphallic "erectness," Iseult Smith represents what is semiotically configured simultaneously as the female homoerotic and "masculine" intellectual principal within this homoerotic ethos. Through her dramatic, almost theatrical self-presentation, she imparts a quasi-erotic *jouissance* to her charges, particularly through the medium of language. It is hardly coincidental, then, that Iseult's first insight into the inarticulate Eva, is that language, particularly in written form, "panics" her "out of all proportion" (61).

The "new-minted, unheard before" words Iseult Smith articulates serve to waken latent desire in the unformed and unsocialized Eva, who soon becomes her devotee, possibly because the teacher, unlike anyone she had previously encountered, is willing to extend personal attention to her. This "pact" between teacher and student, while nurturing—indeed, humanizing—for Eva evokes another sort of panic for Iseult:

> Something disembodied Miss Smith. . . . [Her] *noli-me-tangere* was unneeded in any dealings with Eva—who *could* have touched her? In fact, at that time, that particular spring at Lumleigh, the young teacher was in a state of grace, of illumined innocence, that went with the realization of her powers. . . . No idea that they could be power, with all that boded, had so far tainted or flawed them for her. About Iseult Smith, up to the time she encountered Eva and, though discontinuously, for some time after, there was something of Nature before the Fall. There was not yet harm in Iseult Smith—what first implanted it? Of Eva she was to ponder, later: 'She did not know what I was doing; but did I?'
>
> (61)

For Iseult, the *jouissance* of her intellectual expositions, although apparently homoerotic for her students, is basically an autoerotic enterprise; her "disembodied" sexuality is turned inward in her presumed state of "innocence" so long as it is directed toward no one else, so long as no one else attempts to direct it. But "Iseult Smith had gone out of her way to establish confidence" in her pupil, "for her own reasons" (17), and, as a result, the ungendered and, for the most part, unsexualized Eva, in keeping with the biblical allusion of her name, becomes the temptress, albeit a thoroughly unlikely and unwitting one. The girl's relentless devotion, expressed through an intense desire for the acquisition of language, the agent of her own panic, culminates in a perversely absurd recitation of a fragment of metaphysical poetry, concluding with the ambiguously sacred and profane lines, "O let my Soule . . . suck in thy beames/And wake with thee for ever" (66). Iseult, in whom this display evokes the ineffable emergence of lesbian panic, feigns ignorance of the poetic double entendre, remarking instead on "how pure language can be" and claiming not to "understand" Eva—and, by extension, the poem. But Iseult's attempt to withdraw herself from the girl whom she has provoked, even manipulated, with language, which has by this time become subliminally analogous with sexual desire for both of them, elicits Eva's distress and an abjectly desperate demand that the teacher care for her: "*You*, not understand me?—that cannot be possible. All that I know of me I have learned from you. What can you imagine that I would hide from you, *could* hide? What can you imagine?" (66).

As in Woolf's novels, and in Bowen's previous texts, lesbian panic is constructed around a given critical moment; in *Eva Trout*, moreover, as in *Mrs. Dalloway*, the ur-narrative of lesbian panic is rendered in a series of fragmented flashbacks that comprise only a small portion of the text, yet it serves as the basis for the eventual denouement and most of what occurs in between. This particular exposition, related as an extension of Iseult's troubled memory, is such a pivotal moment, that moment of "the Fall," the moment that implanted "harm in Iseult Smith." As the novel moves into the narrative present, other fragmentary revelations bring Eva's history up-to-date: after Eva left Lumleigh, she maintained her devotion to and, intermittently, contact with her teacher, even when "Iseult Smith's abandonment of a star career for an obscure marriage puzzled those for whom it was hearsay only—but the reason leaped to the eye: the marriage was founded on a cerebral young woman's first physical passion" (18). As Hoogland notes, "in the patriarchy the masculine mind and the feminine body are mutually exclusive" (238); accordingly, Iseult, a translator of "ultra-new French novel[s]" (18) and "a D. H. Lawrence reader and . . . a townswoman" (22), succumbs, under the internal pressure of lesbian panic, to traditional notions of femininity by annihilating the "masculine" intellectual aspect of her character through her marriage to Eric Arble, a relatively uneducated, failed fruit-farmer turned mechanic.[26]

Whether or not the language-impaired Eva is equally affected by this relationship is shrouded in ambiguity. Indeed, whether or not a word for the definition of erotic desire between women exists in her own personal epistemology is questionable. Late in the text Eva confides in Constantine's latest love, the Anglican priest Father Tony Clavering-Haight, that Iseult "abandoned me. She betrayed me." Yet when, in response to this dramatic statement, he asks if they had "a sapphic relationship," Eva's first reply is "What?," as if to indicate ignorance of the term itself, then a tremendous non sequitur: "No. She was always in a hurry" (184). Ironically, in a novel in which time itself is skewed through gaps and nonchronological sequences, Eva apparently associates time with lesbianism, the lack of the former being an obstacle to the latter. In the portion of the novel that details Eva's rather surrealistic adventures in America, she re-encounters her lost love, Elsinore, who has, since the rupture of their acquaintance, become an almost stereotypical psychotic upper-class American matron. At the end of their reunion, the women embrace and Elsinore sobs, "*Take me with you, Trout! . . . You never left me, you never left me before!*" (142). But Eva decides, after some reflection, that Elsinore "came back too late . . . came at the wrong time" (143).

As the novel begins *in medias res*, the twenty-four-year-old Eva is residing with the childless Arbles while awaiting the inheritance that will come to her on her twenty-fifth birthday, the legacy of the recently deceased Willy, who, it is implied, committed suicide in response to Constantine's ongoing manipulations. Because of the Arbles's continued economic distress, Eva's status as paying guest seems financially beneficial; yet the strains already present in this "obscure marriage" of unequals are exacerbated by the addition of a third party—which, not surprisingly, leads to the typical configuration of erotic triangulation. With time and money, Eva's odd mannerisms have become far more outlandish. The awkwardness of her unsocialization has given way to lavish displays of wealthy self-indulgence, including a penchant for expensive if tasteless attire and constant outings in her Jaguar, which, like its various successors, becomes a quasiphallic fetish for its owner. Iseult's immediate response to this prolonged exposure to this strange young woman in her own home is a withdrawal into a state of neurasthenia and apparent (hetero)sexual frigidity. Eric, in turn, reacts to Iseult's debility by making Eva an object of his sexual interest. On a subliminal level, Iseult's psychosomatic condition can be read as a subconscious manipulation of Eric in an attempt to engineer an "exchange in men"—or, more precisely a man—between herself and Eva, a means of achieving indirectly the lesbian relationship socially and ethically forbidden between teacher and pupil. But Eva, for whom neither masculine and feminine gender roles nor heterosexuality has historically had any normative force, does not respond "normally" (that is, submissively) to Eric's yet-unarticulated interest; rather, she revolts against the growing sexual morbidity of the household by running away—and buying for herself a simulacrum of home and normalcy, a lavish if decaying seaside resort house, romantically named "Cathay."

This extravagant gesture is the first of Eva's various attempts to acquire—or, more precisely, to purchase—the vestiges of social normalcy, in this case a home. Indeed, Eva, who has led a desultory life with her father and Constantine, cannot rightly be said ever to have had a home as such. Her only models of the concept of home—like her only models of the concept of heterosexuality—are the Arbles and the family of the Reverend Dancey, homes and marriages that are, respectively, unhealthy and eccentric. Eva's home, which she quite deliberately establishes without marriage, is thus modeled after little more than fantasy and, as a result, only achieves a bad mimesis of normalcy. That this is so is readily evinced by her choice of home furnishings, which might best be described as early postmodern:

> Outstanding examples of everything auro-visual on the market this year, 1959, were ranged round the surprised walls: large-screen television set, sonorous-looking radio, radio-gramophone in a teak coffin, other gramophone with attendant stereo cabinets, sixteen-millimetre projector with screen ready, a recording instrument of B.B.C. proportions, not to be written off as a tape recorder. Other importations: a superb typewriter shared a metal-legged table with a cash register worthy to be its mate; and an intercom, whose purposes seemed uncertain, had been installed.
>
> (118)

This collection of expensive and impractical objects, like her earlier attachment to her Jaguar, outrageously demonstrates the extent of Eva's fetishism, a trait that Freud defines as a male response to the discovery of the mother's lack of a phallus.[27] Indeed, a Freudian interpretation of her household decor—which is not even remotely related to any "feminine" notion of domesticity—would deem it as inherently "masculine," an exhibition of "penis envy" in which her wealth permits her to indulge. Hence, in the eyes of the other characters, Eva is a dangerously defeminized woman who must be brought back under the control of a masculine social order. And although this woman's home is, both literally and figuratively, her castle, she faces various attempted invasions from the forces of this order.

While the overly solicitous and uxorious estate agent Mr. Denge, who is little more in Eva's eyes than an intruder, represents the regulating norm of heterosexuality peculiar to middle-class domesticity and pride in property, he is rendered feckless and effectually castrated by the young heiress's unsociable rage and insistence on her own rights of domain. Likewise, the homosexual Constantine, who, as Hoogland suggests, does not so much subvert heterosexuality as function "as an exception to confirm the rule" (266), would have her submit to the law of the fathers; he discovers, however, that in the process of coming into her majority, Eva has become a law unto herself. Thus the most problematic of these invaders is Eric, who comes with the Lawrencian intention of returning her to his home by means of physical seduction. But, weary from his long drive, Eric falls asleep, and, aside from an absurd display of "masculine" aggression in which he grabs Eva and shakes her, nothing transpires physically between the two—and Constantine's discovery of the sleeping Eric not only places the would-be seducer in the position of class-transgressor but also renders him subject to blackmail.

It would seem, then, that Eva is impervious to the threats of the male hierarchy, a type of the "monstrous" lesbian historically represented as a danger to the social order.[28] Her ultimate vulnerability, however, is set in motion by the fourth—and only female—visitor, Iseult. Encouraged by Constantine's insinuations, Iseult chooses to believe that the triangulation she has both dreaded and subconsciously desired has been consummated, thus giving her a quasihomosexual tie to Eva. But while Eva indulges in fiction for its own sake, the literarily astute Iseult prefers fiction to reality and, as she continually demonstrates, interprets the events around her in terms of the masterplots of canonical literature. It is with some ironic justice, then, that Iseult, in a supposedly reconciliatory gesture, arranges to meet Eva in what was once the home of Charles Dickens, the author of orderly closures in which virtue triumphs—and that Eva, the ostensible author of Iseult's chaos, finds nothing disrespectful in settling herself in the chair in which Dickens once wrote. Whether intentionally or not—for Eva's true intentions are generally only ambiguously articulated—Eva does nothing to dissuade Iseult from the fiction she has internalized, even while Iseult, following Dickens, asks if they can't "start again," as if they could simply begin a new narrative that would obviate the earlier lesbian panic. Consequently Iseult accepts Eva's sudden and final pronouncement, "In December I shall be having a little child" (121), as proof that she had been impregnated by Eric's visit in March.

Iseult's interpretation of this information, although inaccurate, serves her purposes. As a reconciliation with Eva—which would complete the triangulated homoerotic arrangement—proves an apparent impossibility, she uses Eric's presumed infidelity as a pretext to terminate her relationship with him as well. Yet Eva's December child is certainly a virgin "birth" and another exercise on Eva's part in parody mimesis of normalcy, in this case of motherhood. As she admits much later, she has her child by what, at the time, "seemed the best means," means that obviated going to "all that trouble" of heterosexuality that would conflict with her "disagreeable impressions of love" (222). Rather, she becomes a mother asexually—by purchasing her child Jeremy from an American blackmarketeer. And, as he is, in a sense, acquired through her patrimony, she becomes, in effect, both his mother and his father. As a literal object of exchange, Jeremy becomes one more fetishized possession; as a male child, moreover, he facilitates Eva's new status as the phallic mother.[29] That he proves to be a bad bargain when his condition as a deaf mute becomes apparent is perversely appropriate for this relationship. Eva, for whom language remains an ongoing obstacle, is content to live with the nonverbal child for eight years in a wordless state that closely resembles the Kristevan semiotic, during which time their main activity is roaming around the United States and watching movies. In effect, America becomes for Eva a space outside the law of the fatherland, and its cultural heritage of the cinema provides a realm of the imaginary in which the two can live in fiction for its own sake while retaining the outward appearance of "normal" mother and child. As a result, the two become virtually non-narratable for the duration of this period—Bowen relates the events of this American sojourn only tangentially through flashbacks. But unlike Eva's other objects Jeremy cannot remain in a condition of stasis, as he grows in age and size, Eva strikes upon the uncharacteristic notion that her son must, as a Trout, take his place in the symbolic order and, to this end, returns to England with him. The influence of the cinema from the American years nonetheless entails deadly consequences and facilitates Iseult's final, indirect act of lesbian panic.

As Eva attempts to reconnect with her former acquaintances in England, Iseult is curiously absent. Her flight from Eric—and the idea of his supposed liaison with Eva—is not so much an attempt to rid herself of lesbian panic as it is a means to indulge in it. Removing herself to France where she resumes her occupation as a literary translator, she positions herself as a yet-embodied manifestation of Terry Castle's concept of the "ghosted lesbian" in a situation of mutual ghosting. Through a rather overdetermined and quasisecretive relationship by correspondence with Constantine—to whom she nonetheless refuses to reveal her whereabouts—she remains connected not only to Eva through the younger woman's quasi-stepfather but also to homosexuality through its most visible representative in the text. Indeed, in the convoluted prose and overwrought judgments of taste that characterize her letters to Constantine, she seems determined to outdo her exquisite counterpart in the stereotypically homosexual male behavior that might best be described as "queenieness." Thus she allows herself a connection, albeit a distrusting and at times antagonistic one, with the one "legitimate" (that is, male, patriarchal, powerful, and affluent) mode of homosexuality in the novel. Yet all the while her motivation is informed by the memory of the "illegitimate" (that is, female and eccentric) homosexual desire evoked by Eva.

While, as Hoogland observes, "the figure of her lost love object continues to haunt the heroine's narrative itinerary" (263), the "lost love object" is equally haunted. Throughout Eva's long self-imposed exile in the semiotic world of America, an absence that renders Eva the ghosted lesbian in Iseult's perceptions, Iseult maintains an almost obsessive interest in the "reputed foetus" thought to be the result of the consummation of her feared and desired triangulation. That Iseult exhibits no such interest in the very real children Eric has subsequently fathered by the Norwegian woman who has become his common-law wife is not surprising, given the dynamics of lesbian panic; this nameless woman is connected to Eric alone and not to any preexisting homoerotic attraction on Iseult's part. Consequently, Iseult surreptitiously attempts to infiltrate Eva's artificially constructed mother-son relationship, initially through the suggestively disembodied and thus "ghosted" subject position of a mysterious voice on the telephone, in order to replace Eva with Jeremy as the object of her poisonous pedagogy, thereby creating yet another triangulation across sexual boundaries.

Although some critics have faulted Iseult's transitory abduction of Jeremy and its drastic consequences as overly contrived—a rather ironic criticism in the context of a novel that is, to a great extent, about epistemological and ontological contrivance—its symbolic valences are apt.[30] Iseult's "pedagogical" legacy to Jeremy, through which she effectively corrupts his Edenic innocence as she did Eva's, is one of fetishism involving that most phallic object, the loaded gun. While a toy gun in Jeremy's hands fills Eva with anxiety, Iseult exploits the child's interest in the mere simulacrum of this deeply inscribed symbol of male sexuality by planting the thing itself for his eventual enjoyment. More significantly, the gun she bequeaths the boy is one that had formerly belonged to his supposed father Eric. Thus, through this transfer, Iseult symbolically composes an Oedipal scenario for the bright if inarticulate child, one through which she effectively emasculates her former husband, the facilitator of her unwanted but nonetheless compulsory heterosexuality, and bestows maleness on Eva's basically feminized child. In doing so, Iseult on one level attempts to appropriate a maternal role, the role she did not—indeed, could not—achieve with Eric, and thereby displace Eva from her pseudoheterosexual familial position with the child. On another, ostensibly semiconscious level, however, Iseult sets in motion a new twist on the Oedipus myth; in a narrative thoroughly permeated with gender confusion, Jeremy uses this sign of masculinity not to sleep with but rather to kill his mother—who is also, in some de facto sense, his father.

Doubly ironic are the circumstances surrounding this fatal and seemingly foreordained denouement. As if to parallel Iseult's precipitate, incongruous, and obviously insincere reconciliation with Eric (and thus with heterosexuality), Eva concludes that she can only "normalize" Jeremy's situation and provide him with access to the symbolic order through her own assimilation into institutional heterosexuality—although she is initially quite content to achieve her purposes through a parodic mimesis of the actual form by means of a staged enactment of a wedding breakfast and honeymoon departure with Henry Dancey. Once the precocious child-confidant who facilitated Eva's schemes (and thus, in some sense, Jeremy's predecessor) and now a Cambridge undergraduate, the sardonically frank Henry is the only character able to analyze Eva's situation forthrightly. And while he is at first willing to abet Eva in her latest fiction, he understands the ultimate futility of her various simulacra. Consequently, with the self-abnegation that is generally characteristic of a romantic heroine, he volunteers himself for the actual role of husband in the improbable if not impossible hope of granting Eva the "normalcy" that has ever alluded her.

The structures of fantasy and unreality that have so informed Eva's life, and, by extension, Jeremy's, will not permit closure or enclosure in any form of social normalcy, much less the most visible of its forms, that of institutional heterosexuality. As if a figure in one of the American films that has formed his personal ontology, the gun-toting Jeremy saunters unrestrained through the railroad station toward the couple, while the crowd, its members no doubt influenced by the same films, "st[an]d back respectfully, according space and free play to the child star and not obstructing . . . the rigged-up cameras which . . . they took to be present and in action . . . for, how should there *not* be cameras?" (265). Eva's life ends with a puzzling question, a circumstance that echoes her initiation into Iseult's chain of lesbian panic. Asking Constantine to define the meaning of the "favourable concatenation of circumstances" he wishes on the couple, Eva falls victim as the final link in her unlikely narrative chain is forged. At the same time, as she stands as an ostensibly passive bystander at this spectacle, Iseult witnesses the conclusion to her own metafictive concatenation by which she destroys the object of her lesbian panic through the agency of one of its purported by-products.

As a bizarre congeries of gender and sexuality confusion, fetishism, consumerism, and contemporary culture rendered through non-linear plotting, metafiction, and a parodic deconstruction of traditional metanarratives, *Eva Trout* is perhaps the ur-text of postmodern lesbian panic upon which such works as Beryl Bainbridge's *Harriet Said*, Emma Tennant's *The Bad Sister*, and Fay Weldon's *The Heart of the Country* subsequently expand.[31]

But just as the critical reception of the novel has evinced an unwillingness to accept the brave new narrative world of Bowen's final literary statement, so have certain writers and readers preferred the "closeted" atmosphere that informed earlier narratives of lesbian panic. As a result, the legacies of Henry James and Virginia Woolf and their stratagems of silence and repression have yet to be entirely consigned to the realms of literary history. That such is the case can be deduced from the recent popular and critical success of the novels of Anita Brookner.

In slightly more than a decade, Brookner has produced more than a dozen novels that render in fine detail the mundane and uneventful existences of lonely women of acute sensibility. While most of Brookner's fictions focus on passionate but celibate spinsters who futilely cling to the ideals of the romance plot, *A Friend from England*, according to its author, is concerned with "female friendship," which Brookner deems "an undervalued and underfictionalised topic" (Kenyon, 23). This description, however, is not without a certain disingenuousness, as the relationship between two women represented in the text is hardly one of mutual support, companionship, or affection. Rather, it is the conjunction of a grudging and judgmental obsession on the part of one participant with the passive indifference of the other.[32] In this manner, the willful and highly sophisticated suppressions of the knowledge of sexuality inform the plot of Brookner's suggestively enigmatic reworking of "The Beast in the Jungle." More reticent than her modernist literary predecessors, Brookner eschews any use of any term denoting homosexuality in her text, thus harkening back to the nineteenth-century uses of non-denotation previously discussed. Yet the evident if unnamed male homosexuality that Rachel alternately ignores or abhors as it suits her purposes points to the repressed lesbianism latent in her own purposes, and the Jamesian elision of self-knowledge that underscores the text serves to illustrate the impossibility of enacting a nineteenth-century plot in a twentieth-century epistemology.

A Friend from England chronicles the rather uneventful history of the attachment between Rachel Kennedy, an unmarried, financially independent woman in her mid-thirties, and the Livingstones, an unimaginative and conventionally bourgeois nouveau riche family who look to Rachel to oversee their unsocialized, sheltered, and seemingly dull daughter, Heather. Despite a profound lack of common interests or even more than rudimentary conversation between the two women, Rachel willingly agrees to this pointless and thankless task, in part because she regards the

Livingstones as a fixed point in her otherwise unfixed universe. In contrast to the Livingstones' predictable and comfortable life, Rachel's own life outside the bookstore she runs—with a discreetly if nonetheless apparently closeted gay male business partner—is shrouded in mystery and only obliquely represented through elisions in the narrative and in purposefully vague references to her "adventures." But here the conditions of unreliable narration—and Rachel is a prototypically unreliable narrator—demand close scrutiny.

With the exception of *The Golden Notebook*, the previously discussed twentieth-century texts all rely on third-person narration and thus represent the dynamics of lesbian panic from a purely external, safely distanced perspective. Unlike Lessing's novel, which posits itself as the highly conscious self-analysis of an artist temporarily unable to create and in which lesbian panic is merely one of many subplots, *A Friend from England* functions as the extended dramatic monologue of an isolated and alienated individual. Utterly detached from the most basic human relationships, Brookner's narrator functions in an emotional vacuum. Given this almost complete interiority, it follows that Rachel's primary audience in this narrative self-justification of a series of apparently irrational behavior is Rachel herself. Consequently, the minor and seemingly inconsequential details of her self-narrative attempt to conceal her motives and fears while nonetheless revealing them. Rachel creates an aura of heterosexual romance, albeit one of disappointment and secrets around herself. She relates, for example, numerous trivial incidents, such as meeting a man on an airplane with whom she exchanges addresses and makes plans to meet for dinner. Yet these incidents are never more than tangential to her obsession with Heather, and Rachel's narration never directly represents any form of active participation in heterosexuality on her own part. Indeed, the only men with whom she has any sustained interaction are either elderly and paternal, or presumably homosexual.

Her association with Heather seems no more than a somewhat burdensome social kindness until Heather rather precipitately marries Michael Sanderson, a convivial if vapid young man who immediately incurs Rachel's inexplicable animosity. Her insistence that he is "unfit" for marriage is not clarified until Rachel accidentally encounters Michael, wearing gaudy makeup, in a "peculiar wine bar" (113) habituated by gay men, where she was to meet her business partner. Her response to this milieu is one of suggestive disavowal rendered in painfully trivial detail: "I took a seat at the bar and ordered some fruit juice, then, thinking I looked too obvious, or rather, thinking I looked obvious when I had no plans for being obvious, I moved towards a table near the door. The place had filled up while I had had my back to it" (113–14). Rachel goes to great pains to deny her knowledge of the ethos of the place, yet, if her narrative purpose is to explain herself to herself, it becomes a futile exercise in self-deception.[33] Others are not necessarily so fooled; Michael, upon seeing her there, winks at her as if she is complicit in the secret they are keeping from Heather and her family, just as he has earlier encouraged a greater intimacy between Rachel and his wife. Rachel, however, turns once more to disavowal, asserting that "I had never come across this little idiosyncrasy before," and claims as her first concern protecting the Livingstones—at least Mrs. Livingstone—from "the burden of this secret" (115).

Consequently, Rachel drops out of sight for an indefinite period of time, leaving a large gap in her personal narrative, as if the discovery of a sexual secret—one too fearful or repulsive to name directly—drives her more deeply into her psychological closet. At some later point, upon hearing of Mrs. Livingstone's unspecifically diagnosed but seemingly serious illness, she renews her contact with the family—only to discover that Heather has, as suddenly as she married, announced her intent to divorce Michael (without giving any specific reason) and marry Marco, a man she had recently met in Italy.

A double reversal of the Sedgwickian triangle forms the basis of Heather's relationship with Marco. Unknown to Rachel, Heather had embarked on a close friendship with Chiara, Marco's sister, whom she visited in Italy while still married to Michael. Thus Heather had formed with Chiara the female-female bond Michael had wished her to have with Rachel, and, once Michael is dropped from this triangulation, Marco takes his place. Rachel's immediate response to Heather's plans is to form deep if indefinite suspicions about "this Chiara" (150). Typically, Rachel makes an attempt at quadrangulation, just as she has already done by superimposing herself on the tripartite structure of the Livingstone family and by fabulating Colonel Sanderson's erotic interest toward her on the occasion of his son's marriage to Heather. She insists that Rachel must not marry and go to Italy; but because she cannot articulate her own desires, she positions the ailing Mrs. Livingstone as a fourth party. When this rhetoric fails, she uncharacteristically offers a bit of self-narrative. In the only instance in the novel in which Rachel reveals herself directly to any other character, she presents herself as a woman with a "past":

> Listen, Heather, I wanted to get married once. Of course I did. But he was married, and nobody made it easy for me. Yes, I thought like you once. I wanted the same things. But since then . . . Well, he taught me a lot. He taught me to take care of myself, to give nothing away I couldn't spare. He taught me to see to it that I was the one in control. That's a grim lesson to have to learn. But I learnt it. And I'm still here. And I'm not likely to end up supporting someone else's widowed mother in the back streets of Venice, miles from home.
>
> (157, ellipses original)

The function of this interpolated narrative is, at best dubious. The scenario Rachel presents is hardly analogous to Heather's situation, and Rachel's inability to form a marriage in the past is no reason for Heather to eschew marriage at the present moment. Although ostensibly related to convince Heather that she is the more worldly and knowing of the two, Rachel's story of a past adulterous affair (to which she never otherwise refers) is, essentially, her presentation of her heterosexual credentials at the very moment she attempts to dissuade a woman from leaving her for both a man and another woman. But the logic at work is typically false. Rachel's "confession" does not "normalize" this most unusual interlude, any more than the image of Marco's dependent mother as a bugbear proves effective while she evokes filial piety and the needs of the emotionally dependent Mrs. Livingstone as a reason for staying. Nonplused, Heather excuses herself: "I'd give you a lift, but you're going in the opposite direction" (157).

Heather is expectedly unmoved by Rachel's self-abjecting demonstration, yet even after Heather has departed for Italy, Rachel remains obsessed by the thought of retaining her in her "rightful" and infantilized place in the family triangle. Although she resolves to break her connection with the Livingstones, the sentimental tears of Mrs. Livingstone over her "lost" daughter provide Rachel with a much desired if decidedly incoherent pretext for running off to Venice with the curiously aggressive intent of "arresting" Heather. While her ostensible intent is to return the delinquent daughter to her grieving parents, Rachel's fantastic self-projection and inappropriately overblown passion betray the erotic desires she would otherwise deny:

> I saw myself sweeping [Marco] aside, taking her by the wrist, throwing her on to the plane . . . I nurtured my anger as if it were a sacred flame, a talisman that would protect me throughout this journey into

> the unknown. . . . with it I felt cold, hard, a bully, a brute. With it I could commit murder and while my victim, in all innocence, sat at a table in some dingy apartment, waiting for her prospective mother-in-law to serve her with a plate of soup, I armed myself with courage, sought out my finest clothes, smoothed the leather of conqueror's boots against the calves of my legs, slammed the door on my flat . . . and walked out into the street . . . my face haughty with disapproval. (186–87)

Despite her uncharacteristically and theatrically "butch" pose, Rachel arrives in Venice without any premeditated or systematic plan and is shaken by a reply from Heather agreeing to meet her.

Their confrontation and its aftermath provide an exemplum of a purely interiorized and self-destructive mode of lesbian panic. Heather appears with Marco, whom Rachel envisions as Heather's androgynous—and conceivably homosexual—lookalike: "I remembered with a jolt how closely she had resembled Michael at her wedding, and I . . . wonder[ed] whether this twin-like capacity of hers might not play her false in exactly the same way as it had before" (196). Rachel's arrogant self-assurance is further eroded by Heather's nonchalance as she indicates that she has already surmised the reason for Rachel's visit: "I'm afraid you've had a wasted journey" (197). Moreover, Heather explains that she has learned to arrange her private life—away from her parents—according to the example Rachel imparted at their last previous meeting, which, from Heather's perspective, is that of "Deceit. Control. Arrangements. Mismanagement" (198). Heather apologizes for her lack of hospitality but explains that Marco "wasn't too keen on my meeting you," adding, "He knows about you and why you came here" (202). Heather walks away, but Rachel, stung by the fear that her secret life and motivations are common knowledge, rushes blindly and hysterically through the darkened streets of Venice, futilely searching for the woman now permanently lost to her: "I had failed, but that was not what counted. What counted was that I was guilty of an error. It was not Heather who was endangered, but myself. I felt shame, penury, and the shock of truth. Something terrible had happened. I did not see how I could ever face those who knew me" (203). Consequently, Rachel acquires the not quite tragic sense of insignificant outsiderhood experienced by one who has kept her secret sexual life in the closet only to discover that others have known of and have manipulated that closetedness in order to make their own lives seem more significant, real, enriched, and honest: "No one would know the inner workings of my life, nor would anyone inquire, thinking me to be a creature without mystery. . . . I would become 'poor Rachel.' Perhaps I already was" (201).

It would be difficult to deem either Brookner's novel or her aesthetic sensibilities postmodern.[34] Indeed, much of Brookner's current popularity would seem based on her stalwart retention and preservation of older, more traditional literary forms as a bulwark against the chaos of the present. But if the "first lesson of Postmodernism," is, as Patricia Waugh suggests, that "it is impossible to step out of that which one contests . . . one is always implicated in the values one chooses to challenge" (33), few texts illustrate the point as well as *A Friend from England.* The determined inexplicitness of Rachel Kennedy's narration and her fear that being regarded as "a creature without mystery" is the ultimate sign of abjection that merely underscores the impossibility of living according to a nineteenth-century moral and social code long after the narrative ideologies inspired by that code have been superannuated.

CHAPTER THREE

"The Proper Names for Things": The Lesbian in Postmodern Women's Fiction

If it sounds wrong it's because of the way it's written, not what it means. All the best parts in the book were written years ago when we didn't know the proper names for things. We are limited now by knowing how to express ourselves. It sounds worse perhaps, but we can't go back.

—Beryl Bainbridge, *Harriet Said*

IF VIRGINIA WOOLF'S PROGNOSTICATION about women authors' ability to employ their "very queer knowledge" freely were to prove prophetic, then the 1980s would mark a turning point in literary representations of female sexuality; such a development would potentially, by extension, allow writers to move beyond the limited and limiting strategies of lesbian panic as a source of narratable conflict and disruption. That certain British women writers of the 1980s, particularly Beryl Bainbridge, Emma Tennant, Fay Weldon, and Jeanette Winterson have, to some extent, succeeded in doing so would lend credence to Woolf's assessment; yet to affirm her statement as a universal truth falls far short of accuracy. As I have indicated in this study, even within the parameters of a literary subgrouping or sub-subgrouping (in this case the female-authored twentieth-century British novel), there is no uniform, chronological "progress." Individual authors do not necessarily develop their narrative strategies synchronically; variables of economics, social class, political or religious ideologies, sexuality, and just plain idiosyncracy all determine the extent to which a given author responds to the issues that inform the *Zeitgeist*. Consequently, even the basic literary movements into which this study is divided overlap chronologically: Virginia Woolf, as a representative modernist, wrote from 1909 until her death in 1941; the study of authors informed by postwar sensibilities extends over nearly sixty years, from Elizabeth Bowen's *The Hotel* in 1928 to Anita Brookner's 1987 novel *A Friend from England*; the examination of lesbian panic and postmodern British women writers begins, in this chapter, with Brigid Brophy's *The King of a Rainy Country* in 1956.

To define certain works as "postmodern" and other, contemporary works otherwise is, of course, a matter of conjecture; even the application of the label "postmodern" is rendered problematic by the wide variety of definitions given the term in current critical discourse—perhaps the inevitable result of any attempt to delineate cultural phenomena without the luxury of historical hindsight.[1] Compounding this apparent instability of signification is the notion, held by many feminist and postmodern critics alike, that feminism and postmodernism are mutually exclusive terms. The last of these concerns still persists to some extent; it has been addressed, quite effectively, by Molly Hite and in two separate studies by Patricia Waugh.[2] Following Waugh's example in *Feminine Fictions*, I am distinguishing the writers whose works are addressed in this chapter from those in the previous one, in great part according to their use of experimental (i.e., postmodern) technique or their adherence to more traditional modes of women's narrative.[3] Because the trends in women's fiction under scrutiny in this chapter reach their high point in the early 1980s, I am using the term "postmodern" according to the "description of a range of aesthetic practices" that, according to Waugh, predominated at that time; namely, "playful irony, parody, parataxis, self-consciousness, [and] fragmentation," rather than "pervasive cynicism" the designation has since come to signify (*Practising Postmodernism*, 5). It is hardly coincidental, then, that the texts under consideration in this chapter all share, to greater or lesser degree, the trait noted by Carol McGuirk as characteristic of much postmodern British women's writings, a "strong . . . element of parodic allusion [to canonical 'classics'] in plot, characterization, and style" (947).

But if Waugh and Hite have reconciled feminism and postmodernism, they have done so with virtually no attention to or consideration of the role lesbianism plays in either. Hal Foster suggests that postmodernism mourns the loss of the "phallocentric order of subjectivity . . . leading to narcissistic laments about the end of art, of culture, of the west. But for others, precisely for Others, this is no great loss at all" (78). Responding to Foster, Waugh posits that this non-loss is precisely what would render postmodernism appealing and useful to members of marginalized groups:

> Those excluded from or marginalized by the dominant culture—for reasons of class, gender, race, belief, appearance, or whatever—those

> Others referred to in Foster's essay, may *never* have experienced a sense of full subjectivity in the first place. They may never have identified with that stable presence mediated through the naturalizing conventions of fictional tradition. Such Others may, indeed, *already* have sensed the extent to which subjectivity is constructed through the institutional dispositions of relations of power, as well as those of fictional conventions. (*Feminine Fictions*, 2)

This assessment not only suggests congruity with Rachel Blau DuPlessis's assertion that "heterosexuality is not a natural law . . . but a cultural and narrative ideology" (xi), it could also be seen as a tacit argument that postmodernism is an almost obvious mode of discourse for the doubly-"Othered" lesbian, a concept that lesbian critics have only recently begun to explore.[4] In Waugh's text, however, lesbianism falls into the gap of "or whatever" and remains unexamined, even in her analyses of the novels I consider here. Hite, similarly, limits her discussion of lesbianism to two sentences about the "triply marginalized" Shug and Celie in Alice Walker's *The Color Purple* (118). Thus, in response to this lacuna, I am adding to the criteria dividing the "traditional" from the "postmodern" the element of lesbian sensibility. By this I do not mean the author's own sexuality; rather, that the author actively—and, optimally, explicitly—engages the dynamics and consequences of such marginalized desires, as opposed to the retreat into fear that inheres in more traditional narrative forms.

Given that the resurgence of traditional writing during the period discussed in the previous chapters occurred, for the most part, in response to renewed societal pressures requiring marriage and heterosexual conformity, the work of postmodern women writers in moving beyond the narrative pitfalls of lesbian panic resumes, almost of necessity, the efforts of Virginia Woolf at an earlier stage than that at which Woolf herself left off. In her 1956 novel *The King of a Rainy Country*, Brigid Brophy, for example, employs the narrative strategies of epiphanic and repeated "moments" and the backgrounding of a lesbian past against an ostensibly heterosexual present pioneered in *Mrs. Dalloway*. If the stratagems by which the characters in Brophy's novel operate seem as fraught by silence and unspeakability as those in Woolf's earlier novels, it is a reflection of the mores of the first post-World War II decade. A pervasive if grossly exaggerated fear of the imminent extinction of the "British race," stemming from declining birthrates in the 1930s and reinforced by the considerable number of British war casualties, resulted in a renewed social enforcement of compulsory heterosexuality in the wake of the armistice.[5] But while lesbianism (indeed, homosexuality in general) exists as an unnamed presence, a signified without a signifier, in Woolf's fictions—and while it tends to function as a pernicious free-floating signifier with a generally disembodied or absent referent in the works of an intervening generation of British women authors—Brophy is able to unite signifier and signified as a sign, to name the desire directly, even if the name is the then-pejorative "queer." At the same time, Brophy, unlike the modernist Woolf, does not seek to create a new mode of narrative to circumvent the expected heterosexual closure inherent in traditional linear narrative; rather, she assembles a pastiche of familiar novelistic genres, exhausting and discarding each as it proves incompatible with the narration of homoerotic desire and replacing it with another.

The tripartite structure of *The King of a Rainy Country*, while recalling that of the superannuated Victorian "triple-decker," in fact delineates the shifts from one "master narrative" to another. These transitions, moreover, are not only carefully manipulated on Brophy's part but are also self-consciously metafictive on the part of her literarily aware protagonists who, given a lack of conventional, established fictions by which to plot their own desires, hopelessly attempt to "normalize" themselves through conformity to available narratives.[6] Thus Brophy's novel begins as an off-beat courtship plot *à la vie de Bohème* in the present tense, backgrounded (in a manner reminiscent of *Mrs. Dalloway*) with a homoerotic girls' school narrative. Once the protagonists push the conflicts of those modes to their logical points of climax without achieving the prerequisites for any resolution to ensue, they embark on a new plot, a picaresque travel *qua* quest narrative, simultaneously recalling Henry Fielding's *Joseph Andrews*, Mark Twain's *The Innocents Abroad*, and Frances Trollope's *Domestic Manners of the Americans*. When this strategy also fails in achieving the socially and narratively prescribed outcome of heterosexual consummation, the main characters, now expanded in number from two to four, attempt to enact their desires and, as a result, come to varying levels of self-knowledge through the adoption of a plot from opera, in this case Wolfgang Amadeus Mozart's *Le Nozze di Figaro*. Through this most self-consciously artificial mode of fictional representation—certainly the only "respectable" mode of providing for a purposely cross-gendered representation of erotic desire—the characters are able to "perform" their irreconcilable forms of otherness and achieve various degrees of closure that, perhaps inevitably, fall short of resolution.[7]

Until its denouement, *The King of a Rainy Country* chronicles the unsuccessful courtship of Susan and Neale, a young couple who are ostensibly "in love" (13) and, without any formal declaration of intention, assume that they will eventually marry. Although both are the products of a relatively privileged educational background, they assume a "Bohemian" lifestyle of voluntary poverty, Neale working as a dishwasher and Susan as the secretary to Mr. Finkelheim, a pornographer functioning under the guise of a rare book dealer, a Gentile pawning himself off in the business world as Jewish. Finkelheim's disreputable game of appearances versus reality serves not only as a reflection of the couple's own naive game of "passing" but also as a conduit for the subtle expression of the troubling reality behind their veneer of acceptable, indeed avant-garde, heterosexuality. While Susan and Neale do, in fact, share a bed, they are never in it simultaneously. Their shared fiction that they are prevented from consummating their presumed betrothal by the exigencies of work schedules (Susan works during the day, Neale late nights and early mornings) could, potentially, provide the foundation for a comedy of manners and a series of jokes revolving around the familiar bed trick. Yet in this context (in which the couple contrive, despite the demands of their employment, to spend a significant amount of time together), it provides not the basis of endless jokes but rather a shield to deflect suspicion. When Susan balks at the idea of having any of her old school friends "snooping round our flat," Neale inquires whether she is "afraid they'll think we go to bed together," when, in fact, she fears that "they'll guess we don't" (64). For Susan, the raised eyebrows that might result from this simulacrum of an unsanctioned and therefore daring heterosexuality are preferable to a revelation of the celibate condition that in fact attains.

The trappings of Finkelheim's shop, where Neale regularly visits in the proprietor's absence, provide the means by which the inexplicable obstacle to consummation becomes clarified. Susan, while disinterested in the volumes of male nudes in stock, discovers in her perusal of a striptease picturebook the likeness of her schoolmate Cynthia Bewley, the obsessive object of the girls' school narrative constantly present in Susan's memory. Homosocial school fictions, though given relatively little attention as a novelistic mode, have their own particular conventions and narrative expectations.[8] Usually concerned with the bildung of one particular and often troubled girl, they feature the highly emotive attachments and conflicts of the adolescent female psyche in an atmosphere of ubiquitous sexual awakening. The relationships among students, or, in the most extreme scenarios, between a student and a highly attractive and unmarried woman teacher, easily lend themselves to a form of lesbian panic peculiar to this genre. Separated from the world of men and boys, the students conduct themselves in a type of lesbian utopia, minimally aware of but generally oblivious to social disapprobation of same-sex love until discovery or intervention, usually by an authority figure, exposes the "inappropriateness" of the affection. This disruption of an Edenic situation, which generally precipitates the separation of lovers, ends, at worst, in tragic consequences, particularly the suicide of one of the parties. At very least, as in Susan's memories of Cynthia, the result is one of unresolved and ongoing hurt and shame.

As the events of Susan's day-to-day life with Neale plod on, the narrative of the past surfaces, in nonsequential and fragmentary fashion. As she is in Neale's presence when she discovers Cynthia's picture, some explanation of her visceral response is required. Thus it is revealed that, a few years before, the adolescent Susan became enamored of the slightly older Cynthia, and, over the course of a fall term, the two entered into a close romantic friendship that culminated, on the last night before the winter break, during a performance of *As You Like It*, in a passionate kiss.[9] While the cross-dressed Rosalind makes her speech to her "pretty little coz," Cynthia, sent with Susan into the storage space beneath the stage to retrieve, suggestively, "Hymen's crown," finds a faded silk rose among the old props and, placing the flower in Susan's lapel, suddenly kisses her friend:

> I stood in Cynthia's arms, with my arms round her, trying to see her face. . . . I had known that people kissed, but I had never involved the fact with myself. I found I had no idea how I had come into Cynthia's arms, how that space had been leapt which had always seemed sacrosanct. I had been not only without anticipation but without desire; and now all the desire I had in the world had been fulfilled beyond its own horizons.
>
> I found that the desire had formed to kiss again. I cast my mind back to find out how it had been done and copy it; but I could not discover any means behind the act. As my memory played on the immediately past moment, it became irrevocable.
>
> I was left with a new moment, and with desire. Plotting clumsily, I bent my head towards Cynthia, my lips bitterly closed together.
>
> We heard the door open and Miss Falconbridge say: "Haven't you found it yet?"

> As we convulsed apart I felt a kind of guilt I had never experienced before. We filed out . . . and I was dissimulating in an entirely new way.
> (89–90)

In a moment recalling the scene in the garden in *Mrs. Dalloway*, Susan is propelled into sexual awakening, her attachment transformed from childish affection to adult desire. Yet the moment is lost almost as soon as it occurs, as she is unable, in her confusion, to repeat the spontaneous, accidental kiss as a deliberate act. The voice of authority, here in the person of the sympathetic Miss Falconbridge the spinster schoolmistress, intrudes upon the pair, and immediately Susan experiences guilt and shame in relation to the act—feelings that she had never before connected with her love for Cynthia—and intuits that somehow such behavior must lead to a game of appearances versus reality. But before Susan thoroughly understands the extent of this "dissimulation," she must endure the separation of the winter break, anticipating the results of this awakening. As we discover from another fragment of her recollections, what later transpired was an inexplicable alienation on Cynthia's part, a refusal to communicate—a manifestation, it would seem, of subtle lesbian panic on the part of the older, more worldly girl in response to Susan's awakened desires. Subsequently Cynthia, who publicly rejects and humiliates Susan, enters into a superficial attachment of dispassionate sex play with Susan's erstwhile friend Gill, and Susan is left alone, without solace or an explanation of a series of events that, because of their unspeakablity, must go unquestioned.

Neale, who, under usual circumstances, might be expected to become jealous or suspicious of a past female love who continues to hold so strong an attraction for his presumed intended, not only encourages Susan's apparent obsession but joins in it himself, encouraging Susan to find the "lost" girl and urging her to call all the Bewleys in the London telephone directory, to contact other former schoolmates for information, and to visit the art school where Cynthia was last known to model. Indeed, in this slippage-filled text, the absent Cynthia becomes one more example not only of the "ghosted lesbian" but also of the erotic connection between Neale and Susan that stands in lieu of a heterosexual relationship, another excuse for delaying what would otherwise seem inevitable in this relationship.[10] For Neale, whose interest in sex and marriage seems primarily a matter of discourse, is as undefined in his orientation as Susan. This is readily apparent early in the novel when Susan returns home to discover François, a mysterious French houseguest with whom, at Neale's invitation, she is to share a room for the night. Affronted by this unwanted bedfellow, Susan balks; but François, in the course of an episode rendered almost entirely in French (contributing even further to the narrative slippage that permeates the novel) informs her she need not fear for her virtue: "Pas impuissant, non. Pas impuissant—comment dit-on en anglais? C'est un des mots que je connais—*quair*" (35).[11] But while Neale's "quair" friend soon vanishes from the text, this interlude, along with his interest in Finkelheim's male nudes and his distaste for the shop's "marriage manuals" indicates the extent of Neale's own dissimulation and suggests that what brings Susan and Neale together is nothing more or less than a shared latent homosexuality.

Susan and Neale could, conceivably, continue their game of deceptive appearances and shared obsessive fantasies of Cynthia interminably; but such a scenario would soon become static and, accordingly, non-narratable, the avoidance of conflict ultimately allowing no hope of resolution. Accordingly, two events put an end to the stagnant courtship plot. A police raid of Finkelheim's shop leaves Susan bereft of employer and employment. Almost simultaneously, a letter from Gill (in response to Susan's letter at Neale's instigation) brings a newspaper clipping announcing that the aspiring actress "Cynthia Beaulieu" will be attending a film festival in Venice; it also brings word of Gill's own disastrous attempt at heterosexuality and the warning "Don't ever write to me again" (96). Given these motivations, the pair falsify their qualifications, obtain employment as tour guides conducting American tourists from Nice to Venice, and, accordingly, exchange their exhausted narrative for a new one, that of the quest; but what is found in this journey is merely a variety of means by which heterosexuality can be postponed.

The exigencies of travel almost inevitably give rise in the picaresque to numerous and various occasions for illicit sexual encounters. If the restraints of British middle-class mores were all that had prevented carnal knowledge between Neale and Susan, surely the context of another country would allow for a release from these inhibitions. But, as we have seen, this is only ostensibly the case; ironically, exposure to the boorishly libidinous Americans only reinforces the pair's stereotypically English reticence, an attitude that seems to grow in proportion to the Americans' expectations. Sexual union becomes, for Susan and Neale, a highly articulated (and thus artificial) fantasy that can only occur at an optimal moment. The very real possibility of rape—which, in the minds of the young American men of the traveling party, is merely a matter of fulfilling social expectation—serves the purpose of minimizing the likelihood of this "moment" for

Susan; yet Neale persists in seeking, presumably for no other purpose than to provoke rejection and thus perpetually postpone the seeming inevitability of heterosexual consummation.

Once they have arrived in Venice and are relieved of their charges, however, there seems little excuse left for deferral. Outside the hotel lobby, as Neale badgers her with a series of tired poetic clichés, Susan reluctantly assents to the "moment," distracted all the while by the scene around her: "Out of the corner of my eye, I saw a cotton dress move in the hotel foyer. I turned. So did Neale. . . . Inside the hotel, Cynthia was facing us, but not looking out: we were the direction, not the object of her gaze" (198). Although Neale whispers "Let her go," in the moment that Cynthia turns her back toward them, both burst through the door in pursuit of her. In this rendering of the interrupted moment, Brophy's unsubtle use of the deus ex machina (or, in this case, *dea*) underscores the sheer contrivance—on the characters' part—almost invariably involved in such episodes. Here and in other novels, moments of epiphany, while seemingly accidental, are generally convergences of desires and plots (usually sexual in nature) set in motion long before; yet because they usually occur in inopportune places and times, the interruption of the sublime by the mundane is bound to occur. Thus the characters involved can only realize enough of their desires to articulate but not actualize them. Accordingly, they can explain their unfulfilled existences through a sequence of events ostensibly beyond their control, when it is unlikely that the characters were ever completely willing to take the responsibility for all that the completion of the moment would entail. In "finding" Cynthia, Susan and Neale in a sense fulfill their quest but then must face what they hoped to achieve in doing so. Conventional literary wisdom dictates that the end of the quest narrative must result in some sort of self-knowledge to the seeker. Would the "resolution" of an earlier interrupted moment and the lesbian panic that arose from it clear the path for heterosexuality in the present? Would it offer an explanation of Neale's problematic sexuality as well? Or was the fantasy in itself more pleasurable than its fulfillment, as Neale later suggests? As the end of the travel results, in any case, in merely one more reason to defer the closure of heterosexual union, yet another generic plot fails the characters, and a new one begins.

Part 3 commences with the entrance of Cynthia for her reunion with Susan. Neither seems willing or able to face this meeting alone; just as Susan is accompanied by Neale, so Cynthia, too, brings a friend, the fading operatic soprano, Helena Buchan. As Cynthia proves herself the stereotypical starlet, a form virtually devoid of content, Helena comes to the fore. Once known for her portrayals of the tragic Tosca and the betrayed Donna Elvira in *Don Giovanni*, Helena, who deems herself "not feminine enough" (252), has over time settled into the role of the Countess Almaviva in Mozart's *The Marriage of Figaro*, a woman, like Helena, for whom romantic love and marriage has proved a disappointment. Accordingly, the other three assume various "operatic" demeanors as the plot shifts into a miscast version of Mozart's opera, a *Marriage of Figaro* without a Figaro to manipulate the excesses and foolishness of the rest of the characters. The result is a romantic rectangle in which all the parties are sexually ambivalent and thus unsure of their own desires.

With her childish dreams of fame and glory, Cynthia has become little more than ancillary to the grand diva; as such, she functions as the page Cherubino to Helena's Countess Almaviva. Neale, for his part, becomes churlishly aggressive as the sole male in this ensemble. He would assert his "right" to dominance over the women, even suggesting that Helena run away with him, just as Count Almaviva in the opera would reassert the traditional droit du seigneur; but thoroughly lacking affluence and power—and really desiring an erotically tinged mother-son relationship—Neale, too, becomes Cherubino.[12] In her critical study of Mozart's operas, Brophy makes a point of explaining "Who is Cherubino, What is He?" (*Mozart*, 103), but she omits one salient point about this character: while Cherubino is literally a sexually overwrought adolescent male and figuratively, according to Brophy, a variation on Cupid (Eros), "he" is performed, both in Mozart's opera and, historically, in Beaumarchais's original play, by a woman. Thus, while the staged "reality" of the opera presents a boy attempting to romance a woman, the overriding appearance of what transpires on stage is a simulacrum of lesbianism.[13]

But with a Countess, no Figaro (or Count), and two Cherubinos, Susan's part in this "opera" remains unclear. The adulation around the ever-present Helena not only prevents Susan from gaining any explanation from or resolution with Cynthia—who seems to have acquired a highly selective amnesia about the past—it also results in an alienation of Neale's affections. Only after Helena kindly but resolutely declines Neale's proposition can Susan assume her designated role, that of her operatic namesake Susanna, the Countess's confidante. Intuiting Susan's resentment, Helena invites her, alone, on a day trip to Padua, for the ostensible purpose of having a publicity photograph taken. In the course of their travels they discuss the intimate details of their lives. Helena tells of her failed marriage, in which she "wasn't really the girl," "wasn't the type," and simply "gave a performance" (245); and, dropping all inhibition, Susan explains "about Neale. And Cynthia" (246). Just *what* she explains, however, is a matter of critical interpretation; Brophy provides only an orthographic "white space" in lieu of direct discourse.

In the wake of this confession, Brophy departs from the Mozartean plot to restage the foundational narrative. As Helena waits for the photographer, she and Susan rummage through the studio props and find a wreath of silk roses; Helena takes one and places it in Susan's lapel, thus replacing Cynthia's rose, which Susan had preserved and Neale had since appropriated as his own. In this case, however, the photographer does not intervene, nor is there panic; rather, the two women acknowledge their mutual "sympathy" (254). Subsequently, they stay the night at a local inn, and Helena pays a curious visit to Susan's room. Terry Castle calls the episode "a tender lesbian scene between diva and female fan" (219); indeed, the encounter is suggestive, taking place as Susan lies naked in bed and Helena speaks of her own recent nakedness, proscribed by her need to traverse the corridor. Yet while no sexual act is directly represented, the symbolic resonances serve their purpose: the women exchange acknowledgements of their otherwise covert sexuality. In achieving this self-knowledge, Susan effectively puts closure on all her previously abortive plots.

Upon her return to Venice, Susan discovers that Neale and Cynthia have mutually succumbed to a peculiar form of heterosexual/lesbian panic. Cynthia, having failed her much-sought screen test, and Neale, stung by Helena's rejection and seeming "conspiracy" with Susan, turn to each other. At Cynthia's demand, Neale beds her, immediately becomes engaged to her, and makes plans to go into business and assume an appropriately middle-class existence—with Cynthia as housewife—upon their return to England, thus accomplishing in a moment what could never occur with Susan. But if this *Marriage of Figaro* lacks a Figaro, it will not lack for a wedding, the conventional ending to a comedy. Neale explains to Susan that he is not really in love with Cynthia, but "at the back of my mind I have the faintest feeling—as if I had, once, been in love with her" (261–62). Unable or unwilling to take the risks that a still-illegal male homosexual existence entails, he opts for a simulation of lesbianism instead, appropriating Susan's past so as to become her and thus write a "happy ending" to her earlier narrative. Yet, because it lacks the self-knowledge inherent in Susan's revision of the "moment," Neale's conclusion can offer little in the way of resolution or closure.

Back in England to begin a new plot, Susan places the rose from Helena in a drawer for safekeeping. Her friend Tanya, who helps her set up new housekeeping arrangements, remarks that she has "brought back" Cynthia's old rose. She replies, "No. It's a replacement" (270). In the end, Helena—quite literally—replaces Cynthia as the lesbian ghost. Susan, having earlier declined an invitation to join Helena in her travels, finds in the older woman a resolution rather than a continuing narrative; indeed, as Helena, unknown to Susan, is terminally ill, little in terms of continuance would be possible. Susan returns home to chart a new course for herself, only to discover that Helena has died en route to Vienna and that a parcel from the diva awaits her: Helena's own wedding dress, a fulfillment of her promise of a gift "you may have a use for . . . [o]r you may not. It doesn't matter if not" (255). Countess Almaviva does, after all, oversee the preparations for Susanna's wedding to Figaro. A conventional interpretation might assert that this gesture symbolizes a mother-daughter bond between the two women, a passing-on from generation to generation.[14] But this overlooks that the dress is the symbol of Helena's own failed marriage plot—and that the figure of Figaro is conspicuously absent. Rather, the dress is a symbol of shared knowledge and a union, metaphysical if not physical, between Helena and Susan; it is a memento mori, a reminder to keep alive the "moment" in Padua that has obviated the earlier painful one, a reminder of the "temporary shelter" (271) that the marriage plot, if embarked upon falsely, provides.

As *The King of a Rainy Country* recapitulates in its preliminary concerns many of the plot factors of *Mrs. Dalloway*, a move necessitated by the resurgence of repressive mores, it is perhaps necessary to consider what Brophy's relatively obscure novel accomplishes that was not already done by Woolf three decades earlier. On a purely narrative level, both novels create an interplay of lesbian panic in the past and an untenable existence—the performance of a false plot—in the present. Yet Woolf's protagonist, gaining insight into her situation at the age of fifty-three, can do little more to change her continuing narrative than to acknowledge the significance of what transpired in the past. Brophy's protagonist, conversely, arrives at this self-knowledge at the age of twenty and thus has the potential to create a new and different narrative for herself, one, by implication, not based on master narratives of the past. Thus, while Brophy gives no clue as to what will ultimately become of Susan, the relative optimism of the ending—that, having avoided the trap of the wedlock plot, Susan *can* do as she will—indicates a progression of sorts since Woolf's time.

Aesthetically, however, the difference between Woolf's novel and Brophy's is that which Patricia Waugh sees between modernism and postmodernism. Seeing the latter as a further development of—rather than a definitive break from—the former, Waugh describes postmodernism as "a recognition and account of the way in which the 'grand narratives' of Western history have broken down" (*Practising Postmodernism*, 5). Unlike Woolf, Brophy does not attempt to realign narrative sequence or create a new technique in order to express what earlier forms could not contain; rather, as I have shown, Brophy employs a variety of old narrative forms to demonstrate their emptiness, purposelessness, and, in the case of lesbian desire, their perniciousness. Thus she subverts them, exhausts them, and ultimately discards them; consequently, however, even Susan's future falls into the slippage of the white spaces, for there is no preexisting narrative, particularly in the 1950s, for what we would presume she will do next.

Brophy's subsequent texts, fictional and otherwise, suggest the future for one such as Susan. With the advent of the more "permissive" 1960s, Brophy produced a series of comedies of manners in which lesbianism is simply a given in the social milieu, in which lesbians quite openly speak of and enact their desires with impunity, and in which lesbian panic is a minor and distasteful activity indulged in only by narrow and unsympathetic characters, such as Nancy, the protagonist's wife in *Flesh*. Just as significantly, throughout the 1960s and 1970s, Brophy, in the role of polemicist, persistently affronted the Leavisites and other members of the British literary establishment through her essays not only on the function of the novel and narrow-mindedness of canonicity but also in support of bisexuality and pacifism and in opposition to the "immorality" of marriage, monogamy, censorship, and religious bigotry.[15] While her controversial views and her confrontational tactics have contributed, no doubt, to her own exclusion from academic discourse and critical attention, Brophy unquestionably paved the way for subsequent women novelists—perhaps male novelists as well—to represent lesbianism explicitly and without panic.

That Brophy had at her disposal a public forum from which to make her unorthodox pronouncements is an indication of the sweeping social changes affecting Britain in the middle of the 1960s. The decade from 1958 to 1968 produced, as Jeffrey Weeks records, a "complex body of legislation . . .

including reforms of the laws governing gambling, suicide, obscenity and censorship, Sunday entertainment, the abolition of capital punishment for murder, as well as liberalisation of various statutes governing sexual behavior" (249). Thus, British law moved from a model of enforcement of traditional Christian moral tenets toward one of relative toleration of private acts enacted with mutual consent. A key factor in this shift was, of course, the 1957 Wolfenden Report, which recommended extensive changes in British legal codes concerning male homosexuality and resulted, a full decade later, in the decriminalization of sexual acts between consenting adult males, by means of the Sexual Offences Act of 1967. Conversely, female homosexuality, as I have already mentioned in earlier chapters, had not been illegal under British law; yet changes in legislation increasingly brought homosexuality in general to public attention, thus increasing cultural interest in other alternative forms of sexuality. Changes in public attitude can also be attributed, in part, to the relative prosperity of the late 1950s and early 1960s; during a rare postwar period of economic stability, middle-class standards of saving and spending translated into sexual metaphors, resulting in an increased sexualization of the marketplace, particularly among the young and sexually restless, an ever-expanding group of consumers with considerable disposable income. While the so-called sexual revolution of the 1960s may well have been a result of increased capitalist consumerism as much as any movement of social reform, enlightenment, or altruism, its ethos of ostensible sexual freedom allowed for the production of numerous experimental fictions, many of which dealt quite explicitly with alternative forms of sexual behavior.[16] Prominent among these is *The Microcosm*, Maureen Duffy's account of lesbian bar life in 1960s London.

Through the deployment of multiple and diverse lesbian voices, including not only the patrons of The House of Shades bar but also a paraphrase of the narrative of eighteenth-century cross-dressing actress Charlotte Charke, Duffy fragments and decenters narrative. The result externally resembles such modernist polyphonic texts as Virginia Woolf's *The Waves*, James Joyce's *Finnegans Wake*, and T. S. Eliot's *The Waste Land*. In its purpose and theme, however, the novel bears little in common with these works; rather than a quest for a subsumption of the individual into a societal, spiritual, or cultural whole, *The Microcosm* is ultimately an exhortation to the formation of minority subjectivity, its experimental form resulting as much from its origins as a documentary case study as from literary experimentation.[17]

By turns, each of Duffy's various lesbian narrators—the closeted gym teacher Miss Stephens ("Steve"), the enterprising teenaged runaway Cathy, the "femme" factory worker Sadie, the retired vaudeville star Feathers, the military officer turned capitalist entrepreneur Kay ("Stag"), and the seductress Judy, among others—articulates either in first or third person her personal bildungsroman. In this manner, the novel stands as a mosaic-like compilation of stories for which no "master narratives" exist. All the speakers, most of whom are denizens of The House of Shades, are interrelated to one another by their connection to Matt, the bar-room philosopher who functions as a first-among-equals in this loosely knit, ghettoized community. Although the possessor of a degree in anthropology, Matt has accepted the minoritizing dictate that nothing fails like success and thus works as a service station attendant by day and frequents the bar by night, applying her considerable erudition and linguistic skills to the creation of elaborate metaphors by which she can understand her environment and her sexuality. Thus the spectral voice of Charlotte Charke, whose personal and professional successes in life were few, serves the frustrated anthropologist as an atavistic presence, reassuring her that she is not a creature *sui generis*. Matt has, moreover, so internalized the dictates of medical sexology on "inversion" that, as a "butch" lesbian, she is self-signified in a third-person narrative arising from her own consciousness by masculine pronouns.[18]

Given the profound psychic and social marginalization of the characters in *The Microcosm*, it is almost inconceivable that lesbian panic would not be a presence in their collective narratives. Duffy's handling of this specific problem is not only virtually without precedent in women's writings, it is metaphorically apt: she treats lesbian panic as a disease, isolating it from the greater lesbian community and placing its narration in the setting of a hospital. In a lengthy section (99–133), Marie, an unhappy housewife confined to a mental institution in the aftermath of a suicide attempt, struggles to recreate the sequence of events that led to her current state. Through the use of fragmented sentences marked by the absence of any punctuation save periods, Duffy represents orthographically the mental state of a woman seemingly bereft of any coherence and any possibility other than endings. Her first intelligibly articulated recollection is that of a summer vacation in Italy years before with another woman, one who protected her from the amorous importunities of young men. But this episode ends with rupture and sexual denial: "and we lost touch. never touched. what do i mean. i didnt understand" (100). In subsequent recollections of this Italian interlude, she echoes the frustration of Lily Briscoe in *To the Lighthouse*: "lost gone away no never nothing ever happened" (129). As her narrative unfolds, Marie reveals through the reconstruction of past conversations the pressures put upon her to take a secretarial job, to marry, and to bear a child. As marital heterosexuality proves repulsive to her, the voice of her husband, Guy, joins that of her mother in an undying onslaught of barbs and criticisms, and her marriage disintegrates into a façade maintained for propriety's sake. Yet Marie is able to establish a period of relative tranquillity in her life by prevailing upon Guy to take her and their daughter to a seaside resort for vacation, a trip that inevitably invites comparison with her earlier idyll in Italy. While at the seaside, Marie experiences a break-through of sorts, partially alleviating her confusion and constant inability to understand her situation. She is attracted by a young man she sees daily at the beach, looking, presumably, for female companionship. When she sees him instead in the company of a similar young man, she is, in what has become her permanent state of self-defensive unknowing, unable to understand:

> and first there was a sharp pang like an icicle inserted deftly into the soft flesh of the belly and passing straight through the intestines leaving a flush of cold oozing through the net hole while you thought i could have been his friend we could have said so much now theyll hunt together to give each other confidence youll see when the next pair of girls pass youre an old married woman who cares about you.
>
> (117)

Yet when the boys wrestle each other, Guy clarifies the situation for her beyond a doubt:

> those two boys. what about them what are they doing holding hands. i dont understand. hell marie for god's sake dont you know anything theyre a coupla queers. you mean theyre strange in some way. i said queer honey not strange you know pansies homos do i have to spell it men who go with men.
>
> (118)

Marie's response, surprisingly, is not shock; rather, she feels "almost relieved freed in some way" and immune from Guy's vituperation: "he cant touch me now he cant touch me anymore" (118, 120). The boys become a personal icon for her, appearing in dreams and "smil[ing] at me approvingly" (121), providing her with an inchoate knowledge that allows her to maintain a tolerable stasis in her day-to-day life for a number of years. It is only when the life of her daughter Linda, with whom she has maintained a sort of surrogated homosocial relationship, intersects with that of one of the novel's other lesbian protagonists that Marie is forced into a recognition of what she has constantly refused, in her own words, to "know" or "understand." Attempting to please her games mistress Miss Stephens, Linda stays late at school and, in order to compensate for her lack of athletic prowess, aspires to become an umpire. Her jealousy stung by this appropriation of her child's affection and attention, Marie shakes off her habitual indifference and attends an evening parent-teacher conference in order to protest. What Marie finds in facing Miss Stephens is a not a monstrous child-snatcher but a recollection of the Italian holiday and the lover—indeed, the self—she refused to realize long before:

> turn away stumbling sinking into the chair offered you the words the words beat in your head like surf the white light-washed walls spin as you drown green water closes over you. mustnt not here what would they all think mustnt and anyway it not the same quite different dark and she was what does it mean steady now breathe deeply there she is her back to you again just as Linda described her a little younger than you and with short crinkly hair then why memory drowning i dont i dont

While Miss Stephens matter-of-factly discusses Linda's school progress, Marie's recognition of what she "didnt understand" comes to the crisis point in the now-familiar language of panic:

> but the words are flooding over your head and youre not listening for their meaning only to the waves of sound breaking on a distant beach setting an echo booming in the empty caverns of your head you have left so long unexplored unvisited and the sting of salt in old wounds sets your flesh on edge the hair rising on the scalp pricking of sweat in the palms a million silver fish sport in your veins leaping and twisting and the trapped dolphin of the heart thuds its blunt snout against the bleached rib-cage.
>
> murmur something in understanding the words you would have used are dried and rattle like stranded popweed above the high water mark nothing you can do or say now except a polite thankyou and turn away . . . into the night. i cant go home i cant go home yet but why not why cant i and why cant i understand i must get away and think.
>
> (127)

After wandering in the streets, she returns home late to Guy's querulous consternation; unable to sleep, she begins to acknowledge her loss:

> i could have gone on to a training college too only and once i went abroad went south to the sun and all day we lay on the hot sand or splashed in the and she said sit over there marie while i but i dont understand was it the building i mean being at school again that made me think of her and where was she now teaching perhaps in a school like that
>
> (128–29)

In order to discover some means of self-explanation, or at least to regain a state resembling equilibrium, she embarks on a secret train journey the next morning to the beach resort, the locus, to her mind, of the source of secret knowledge. But while the vision of the boys could bring her a semblance of inner strength in the past, in the wake of this all-too-direct confrontation with embodied lesbianism, she finds no solace at the seaside:

> and then nothing came though i struggled on beginning to feel cold and hungry and tired there was nothing that was my answer nothing for me somewhere id lost my chance when i hadnt even known what it was and now i was just an insignificant figure pretending to battle with forces that didnt care or know i existed at some vital point i hadnt understood hadnt known and it had gone away from me and would never come back . . . . there was no answer i turned away back along the beach the magic beach which had failed to free me this time. it wasnt the beach it was you who should have freed yourself the answer is always the same we have to do these things for ourselves.
>
> (129–30)

Returning home, Marie attempts to do for herself by ingesting the contents of a bottle of sleeping tablets.

But while lesbian panic pushes Marie to the brink of suicide—an echo of the event Matt laments at the outset of the novel—it is the sight of the lesbian body that facilitates her return to consciousness, sanity, autonomy, and, literally, syntax. Throughout her hospital monologue, Marie periodically interrupts her narrative with an enigmatic observation to the effect that "over the wall there is a i dont know i dont understand" (114). When she regains a state of coherence, she explains to the nurse that she has reoriented herself by looking out the window: "There's nothing there except the wall and that isn't very high and a garden on the other side with someone digging" (132). That someone, the nurse explains, is Miss Birk, the ambulance driver who also tends the garden; who is eventually revealed as "Bill," the "butch" partner of Matt's friend Feathers, an elderly entertainer. Thus, while her panic results from and in isolation from the lesbian community, her recovery begins through this metaphysical communion with a kindred spirit. Indeed, Duffy suggests that for Marie, unlike most enactors of lesbian panic, recovery is a real possibility. Having established that Miss Birk is not a chimera and that she will be able to see her from the window again, Marie postulates that her life is only now beginning and that she will not be returning home "til I've thought it all out, till I've understood completely and know what to do" (133).

As Marie resolves to accept responsibility and self-knowledge, the narrative perspective shifts again to Matt, who is telling her current lover Rae about her first love, a schoolmate with whom she once traveled to Italy. This relationship was the catalyst in Matt's recognition of "why I should feel like this" (133), her first step in developing a lesbian subjectivity, the process that stands as the central narrative of this radically decentered text. But Matt does not know what has become of Marie, nor, in the scope of the novel, will she ever learn. Accordingly, Duffy has situated lesbian panic as an isolated narrative unto itself, one that ultimately has no bearing on the final outcome of the main plot. Rather, Marie's lesbian panic is merely one more of the unfortunate incidents inherent in the conditions of marginality. Like the suicide of "Carl" that Matt recalls as the novel begins—an act for which no motive is made explicit—or the wrist-slashing incident in the bar restroom early in the text, it not only serves as a reminder of the misery endured as a result of societal prejudices but also—and, for Duffy, more importantly—stands as a warning of effects of internalization of victimhood and the failure to take responsibility for oneself.

This movement from victimhood to subjectivity delineates Matt's bildung in the novel. While the microcosm of The House of Shades provides its denizens with a sense of community and shared values, the false security it imparts ultimately distorts its members' views of themselves and the larger world. Although Matt can readily accept her own sexuality, she internalizes, as part of this acceptance, the status of social outcast. As such, she makes no attempt to be anything but an outcast, working at menial jobs that will provide the minimal support needed to maintain her modest domestic situation with Rae and her nightlife at the bar. Consequently, she assumes moral superiority over successful lesbians like "Stag" who, in her estimate, have "sold out" to the larger heterosexual world, just as she assumes intellectual superiority over most of the other bar patrons and an attitude of negligence toward Rae.

A chance encounter with one of her former professors—whose car she fuels at the service station—forces Matt to question her comfortable and over-intellectualized marginalized status. Urging her not to waste her education or ability, Professor Finlay, who is well aware of Matt's lesbianism, offers her a position in an archaeological expedition in Italy, an undertaking that would not upset her domestic situation as it would also accommodate Rae, a freelance artist. With no compelling reason to refuse this opportunity, Matt is faced with the contemplation of whether her ready acceptance of the role of outcast is not, in fact, as much the result of her unwillingness to accept the challenges of being an outsider in the context of the rigors and responsibilities of professional life rather than the result of the relentless pressures of monolithic social prejudice. In accepting the position, Matt takes responsibility for herself, not merely as a lesbian but as a human being. She understands, consequently, the lure of the pseudo-utopia of the lesbian ghetto; but she also realizes that there can be no social progress, no end to prejudice and marginalization, if the marginalized elect their own segregation:

> I conceived this idea of the rockpool, of the gay world as a universe in little where you could find crustaceans and fish, dozens of different forms of plant and animal life in as many colours, a microcosm if you like. And you can sit beside the pool day after day studying them until you become an expert in your own little field. Then I found I wasn't studying them from a distance . . . but swimming about down there among them, subject to all the same laws and problems and I accepted this for a long time . . .
>
> For a time this was right and necessary because I still had enough consciousness of what I was doing for it to be valid but gradually I began to lose that consciousness and become a tiny organism in the life of the rockpool, gasping for an existence like all the rest, adding to the problems instead of helping to solve them and just as frightened of the open sea as everyone else. We're terrified of what's out there, of the competition, of being laughed at, of having to stand up and hold our own and so we make this little world for ourselves where we can be safe and comfort each other with what a dreadful life it is and how handicapped we are until being queer becomes a

> full-time occupation and there's none left over for anything else. But it's a fallacy. There's no such thing as a microcosm. You're walking along the shore and you come across the rockpool. You think it contains all you want, all the varieties of human experience and just as you're becoming thoroughly absorbed in it a great wave washes over it and you realise it's not complete in itself, it's only part of the whole and all the little fishes who've been swimming frantically round and round, and the crabs who've been hiding under the stones half buried in the sand with only a pair of frightened eyes peering out, have to make a run for it out into the open sea because that's the only place they'll ever grow up, and the only ones who are left in the pool are those who're too slow-moving, too firmly attached to their rocks and their way of life to get out. We're part of society, part of the world whether we or society like it or not, and we have to learn to live in the world and the world has to live with us and make use of us, not as scapegoats, part of its collective unconscious it'd rather not come to terms with but as who we are, pieces of humanity that go to make up the whole human picture.
>
> (286–87)

Having affirmed that "there are dozens of ways of being queer and you have to find what your kind is and then make something of it" (273), Matt takes control over her own destiny and eschews the ironic conformity that often adheres to groups the larger society deems nonconformist. Being a lesbian need not be defined by bar life, fear, self-pity, victimization, failure, or any of the other elements that motivate panic.

As she provides Matt with a new plot to enact, one relatively free from the encumbrances of traditional master narratives, it would seem to follow logically that Duffy has created a new master narrative to accommodate the lesbian in literature without resort to the presumed inevitability of panic. This, however, does not prove to be the case; for, as has often occurred with texts by writers from racial minority groups, the message the novel imparts was soon at odds with the expectations, desires, and ideologies of the group it was intended to promote and facilitate. Prior to writing *The Microcosm*, Duffy had achieved cult-figure status with the lesbian reading audience for her autobiographical bildungsroman, *That's How It Was*. An exploration of the processes by which one "becomes" a lesbian—in keeping with Duffy's belief in the social construction of sexuality—*That's How It Was* provides a rare insight into the dynamics of class and education in the formation of lesbian subjectivity. Only by acquiring education can Paddy, the adolescent protagonist, escape the rigidly and brutally compulsory heterosexuality that informs almost every aspect of working-class existence. While *The Microcosm* is considerably less accessible to what Virginia Woolf termed the "common reader" than its stylistically straightforward antecedent, it was initially hailed by Barbara Grier, one of the relatively few openly lesbian reviewers at the time, as "the definitive lesbian novel" and "the first novel to treat Lesbianism objectively" (9).[19] But *The Microcosm* appeared as a crucial historical shift in sexual politics was about to occur, the ramifications of which drastically changed the production and receptions of lesbian writing.

As the previous chapter indicates, during the two decades following the end of the Second World War, lesbianism was rarely a central theme in mainstream literature. Simultaneously, however, a veritable industry arose in mass-market cheap paperbacks, commonly known as "pulps," featuring sensationalistic and explicit representations of lesbian sex, ostensibly for a male audience but often written and read by lesbians.[20] Ersatz variations on the basic themes of Radclyffe Hall's *The Well of Loneliness* and Djuna Barnes's *Nightwood*, most followed a simplistic linear narrative structure of seduction, followed by "deviant" sex and sociopathological behavior, culminating in punishment. Despite the obvious sordidness of these violent texts, their plots, given such relatively undemanding narrative expectations, had no need for anything so complex as lesbian panic. With the rise of lesbian feminism in America and Europe in the early 1970s, however, a vastly different form of lesbian popular writing appeared. A combination of the traditional bildungsroman and the mass-marketed romance fiction, these texts, too, offered a predictable plot line in which two women meet, fall in love, reject the patriarchy, and elope to the utopian green world of Lesbian Nation.[21] Ironically, lesbian panic plays little part in these works, primarily because the inevitably unpleasant aspects of this process would perforce be at odds with the new prohibition against negative representations of women.

Duffy, who had never subscribed to the former paradigm, was hardly inclined to follow the latter; rather, she continued her exploration of sexuality differences—differences not limited to lesbianism—through a variety of experimental techniques, primarily the decentered cross-section-of-society model she developed in *The Microcosm*. In novels such as *Wounds*, *Capital*, *Londoners: An Elegy*, and *Change* she employs a panoramic point of view in presenting a wide cast of diverse characters, whose lives often only tangentially intersect. In doing so, she inculcates lesbians and gay men into the larger scheme of society, not, as Woolf did in her later novels, to subsume the individual into a larger community but rather to present the individual character as a unique combination of strengths and weaknesses who must take responsibility for his or her own mode of being and make his or her own way in the context of the mores of society at large. As such, her lesbian and gay characters are neither doomed miscreants nor the equally predictable and ideologized noble martyrs nor the sole focus of narrative attention. In *Wounds*, for example, the elderly lesbian Kingy appears sporadically, both as an individual attuned to and at peace with nature in an urban setting in a number of garden scenes, and as an at times unruly alcoholic who makes herself a convenient target for homophobic pub-goers. In a more ideologized or idealized mode, Kingy would, as a matter of course, become a representative figure who embodies both virtues inscribed as peculiarly lesbian and the universalized suffering of the marginalized. Instead, Duffy simply renders her as one more of the many individuals whose personalities each comprise a variety of positive, negative, and, for the most part, neutral traits for which she or he is held accountable.

Arguably, what Duffy attempts to accomplish through such representation is what Catharine R. Stimpson has termed writing "zero degree deviancy," a concept derived from Roland Barthes. In an early work, Barthes ponders the possibility of writing in a mode "freed from all bondage to a pre-ordained state of language" and "the existence of a third term . . . a neutral term or zero element . . . between the subjunctive and imperative moods (76)." Barthes speculates that such an "amodal" form of writing would "[take] its place in the midst of all those ejaculations and judgments, without becoming involved in any of them" (77). Stimpson does not suggest that this neutral language *as such* is pertinent, useful, or even possible in lesbian writing—indeed, Barthes realizes that such a use of language would ultimately result in a "state of a pure equation, which is no more tangible than an algebra when it confronts the innermost part of man" (78)—but instead contemplates the desirability and viability of a "zero degree" representation of "deviancy" that would avoid the pitfalls of the two demotic modes of lesbian narrative I have just described, modes based on the respective demonization and glorification of lesbianism. Conceivably, the realization of "zero degree deviancy" would not only provide a perspective on lesbianism free from the distortions of polar extremes but obviate the narrative strategy of lesbian panic.

But such attempts at neutral representation, as Stimpson recognizes, ran afoul of the paradigms of early lesbian feminist consciousness, which demanded uncritically positive images of women in general and lesbians in particular. Offering as an example the fate of American lesbian novelist Bertha Harris and her groundbreaking 1972 text *Lover*—a work whose critical reception and publication history parallels, in many ways, those of Duffy's novels—Stimpson acknowledges the irony of this "baffled response":

> Some people in the feminist and lesbian press have criticized Harris and others for [their literary] adventures. Harris has been called inaccessible, as if modernism were itself an indecipherable code. She is, therefore, supposedly ideologically unsound, stopping that illusory creature, the average lesbian, for using literature to articulate her experience and urge rebellion against its nastier aspects.
>
> (109)[22]

The response to Duffy's novels subsequent to *The Microcosm* could be similarly described. Within a few years of her acclaim as the author of "the definitive lesbian novel," Duffy had incurred the almost universal opprobrium of key figures in the then-nascent field of lesbian writing. With the publication of *Wounds* in 1969, Grier, who had previously hailed Duffy, found fault with the "wholly unnecessary" sympathetic treatment of a heterosexual couple and deemed the author "an experimenter in fiction . . . determinedly so" who "has been playing games with style and language" since the early *That's How It Was* (174, ellipsis original)—a statement that, in effect, reversed Grier's earlier assessment of *The Microcosm*. Subsequently Jane Rule, in the first major critical treatment of lesbian fiction as a distinct entity, delineated the extent of Duffy's ideological "heresy":

> Maureen Duffy's turning to psychology and sociology for perceptions about her world, to the history of literature and drama for forms and styles to imitate, is not, of course, odd behavior for a serious writer, but, since she is a lesbian, the solutions she finds in those traditions seem to threaten more than illuminate her experience. A number of younger women writers today, lesbian or not, have begun to refuse to offer up their emotions to Freud or their voices to tradition. The danger for them may be a thinness in such an entirely personal solution. The weight of education which has imposed such a burden on Maureen Duffy's experience and style need not finally obliterate the original authenticity of her vision and voice. . . . If some of Maureen Duffy's translations are melodramas of learned guilt, she has and will again translate truly.
>
> (182)

The privileging of "experience," "emotions," "authenticity" over literary tradition and "the weight of education" illuminate the greatest obstacle facing the lesbian novelist—and to some extent, women novelists in general—at the time. While Harris eventually retreated from the fray and remained silent as a novelist and critic for over a decade, Maureen Duffy, like Lily Briscoe, adhered to her vision, publishing more than a dozen eccentric but nonetheless "mainstream" novels over three decades.[23] In her 1983 "autobiographical" novel, *Londoners*, in which she returns to the issues that informed *The Microcosm*, Duffy, through the persona of a gay male author, offers her own apologia for what one critic deems her "conservative choices" and "implicit rejection of slipstream ideologies, however progressive they may be" (Brimstone 42):

> I decided life outside, and inside with my work, was too absorbing and exciting, and that I really couldn't take constant emotional and domestic upheaval. Too distracting. You get nothing else done. As it is one has to spend far too much time being a token "gay" when one ought to be writing.
>
> (121)[24]

The ideological stigma attached to Duffy early on nonetheless still attains; this most prolific and highly innovative lesbian novelist, who dared push lesbian narrative and representation beyond simple formulae, still receives scant attention from lesbian critics, and even in those rare instances is subject to critical caveats and apologies regarding her lack of conformity to ideological paradigms that are now, for the most part, superannuated.[25]

If lesbian authors were ideologically constrained, by the early 1970s, from explorations of the "nastier aspects" of lesbian life, of which lesbian panic is undoubtedly one, then it remained for heterosexual women writers—who, by this time, had grown increasingly aware of lesbian possibilities—to do so. In the hands of Beryl Bainbridge and Emma Tennant, the anatomization of postmodern female sexuality and sexual dread took the form of an inverted, parodic, or otherwise reconfigured retroping of the traditional Gothic mode. Historically a means by which homosexual men and heterosexual women authors (and, by extension, their respective audiences) could explore, express, indulge in, and subsequently, through the requisite closure in which social order is restored, reconceal their forbidden desires, the Gothic would seem an apt narrative structure through which to represent the dynamics of lesbian panic. But while the lesbian villainess, usually represented either literally or metaphorically as a vampire, has figured in the works of such minor male-authored Gothic works as Sheridan LeFanu's *Carmilla* and any number of "pulp" fictions, the concept of lesbianism as illicit sexual threat has played a very minor role in the development of the perennially popular and peculiarly female form that Cynthia Griffin Wolff has termed the "Radcliffean Gothic" (213).[26] This lacuna may be ascribed to the extreme polarization of sex and gender roles that attain in the Gothic tradition: all significant power, whether good or evil, is firmly invested in patriarchal structures, while the generally passive female protagonists, despite their usual identification as "heroines," are notably lacking in subjectivity and agency (Wolff 211–14). If the Gothic, then, were to represent the emergence of repressed and illicit female homoerotic desire, its long-established conventions would, of necessity, be subverted.

Beryl Bainbridge's fictions are informed by what one critic has termed "the gothic of everyday life," when, in an ultrarealistic contemporary setting "all the emotions go underground, when what has seemed like a logical if perhaps violent plot turns to outright nightmare, driven by forces that no one will name" (M. Wood 969). In *The Bottle Factory Outing* (1974), perhaps her best-known work, Bainbridge initially deflates the terror of Gothic convention by rendering, through a narrative tone of macabre humor, the misadventures of an ill-sorted pair of female factory workers in the mundane setting of contemporary industrial Britain—only to reinscribe that terror when the quotidian, the ordinary, and the supposedly safe become the sources of sexual threat and bodily harm. While the Gothic is traditionally set in "a never-never land, existing beyond the reach of spatial or temporal constraints" (Wolff 211), an "historical" Italy or France that never was, Bainbridge transplants the Italian villains (and, to the mind of her overimaginative protagonist, Freda, romantic heroes) through time and place, positioning them as the émigré proprietors of the wine-bottling works at which the two young women are employed. Although Freda's perceptions are certainly influenced by the ideals of romantic fiction, she is in her person everything that the Radcliffean Gothic heroine is not—vulgar, untalented, immodest, and, above all, unabashedly hypersexual. Brenda, her roommate and co-worker, is as cautious and chronically terror-stricken as any of Radcliffe's female characters; yet rather than express her fears through displays of exquisite sensibility, Brenda responds to danger with unspecific and insipid complaint, if not outright physical and emotional inertia. Brenda, moreover, finds the threat of physical danger omnipresent, even from sources where there is, in fact, none to be had—including Freda.

To protect herself from her roommate, with whom, through financial exigency, she shares a bed, Brenda, who has run away from a presumably brutish husband, takes extraordinary precautions:

> Brenda had fashioned a bolster to put down the middle of the bed and a row of books to ensure that they lay less intimately at night. Freda complained that the books were uncomfortable—but then she had never been married. At night when they prepared for bed Freda removed all her clothes and lay like a great fretful baby, majestically dimpled and curved. Brenda wore her pyjamas and her underwear and a tweed coat—that was the difference between them. Brenda said it was on account of nearly being frozen to death in Ramsbottom, but it wasn't really that.
>
> (308)

Thus a wryly incongruous form of lesbian panic undergirds the relationship between the two women. It goes no further, however, than these curious sleeping arrangements, and, in what Olga Kenyon has called the novel's "ironic contradictoriness of events" (*Women Novelists Today* 107), it completely pales in comparison with the very real heterosexual dangers that Freda heedlessly invites—and that Brenda fretfully neglects to call by name. As a consequence of their equally unrealistic perceptions of male sexuality, Freda ends up a murder victim—the fate of less-than-virtuous women in more traditional Gothic fare—while Brenda becomes an unwitting accomplice to the disposal of all tangible evidence—including the remains of Freda.

But if lesbian panic is merely a minor by-product of the larger heterosexual panic informing *The Bottle Factory Outing*, it is the central—if unnamed—dynamic of Bainbridge's earlier novel of schoolgirl love and duplicity, *Harriet Said* (1972). The history of this "elegant and troubling book" (M. Wood 968), perhaps the first to be marketed as a narrative of lesbian panic, is, moreover, as curious as any of its author's fictions. First written in 1958, and loosely based on a widely publicized case of matricide—supplemented with Bainbridge's own recollections of an adolescent friendship with "a clever art student who introduced [her] to such writers as Virginia Woolf," *Harriet Said* was rejected by a potential publisher who found the text "too indecent and unpleasant even for these lax days" (Millard 40, 41). The publisher further expressed the fear "that even now, a respectable printer would not print it" and registered amazement and horror over "what repulsive little creatures you have made the two central characters" (M. Wood 968). Consequently, Bainbridge withdrew the novel for a period of fourteen years, during which she published two highly experimental fictions of life in the "swinging sixties," *A Weekend with Claud* (1967) and *Another Part of the Wood* (1968). In 1972 *Harriet Said* was published in Britain by Gerald Duckworth (the publishing firm established by Virginia Woolf's much reviled stepbrother) to much critical acclaim. Its subsequent American first edition, published by George Braziller, was marketed with passages from the original rejection letter and the following excerpt of a review by Julian Symons from the London *Sunday Times*:

> Harriet Said is a sharp, chilling short novel about a suppressed Lesbian relationship leading to violence. Its origin lies in a famous case of the early fifties, in which two New Zealand girls "enacted how the saints would make love in bed," as one of them put it, and also made plans for what the same girl jokingly called "moidering mother," plans which they later carried out.[27]

The first sentence of Symons's critique has since been used to publicize *Harriet Said* on the flyleaves of all Bainbridge's subsequent novels under the Duckworth imprint. Thus has the novel that was once "too indecent" for publication been marketed with lesbian panic as a preeminent selling point—and not without a hint, however inappropriate or inaccurate, that promises the sensationalistic lesbian violence peculiar to much pulp fiction of the decade.

To summarize *Harriet Said* as "a sharp, chilling short novel about a suppressed Lesbian relationship leading to violence," is not inaccurate in and of itself. Nor, for that matter, is Michael Wood's encapsulated description of the novel as being about "two girls [who] ruin any comfortable ideas we may have about sheltered youth, as they taunt an old man and finally kill his wife" (968). Yet even taken together, these assessments hardly begin to explain the bizarre and complex psychological dynamics of Bainbridge's narrative. Her two young protagonists are far from innocent; indeed, the unnamed narrator expresses the wish that her younger sister, from whom she must distance herself "for her own sake, because of Harriet and me," will, unlike her and her friend, "grow up normally and be like everyone else" (16).[28] They are not, however, without some measure of primitive righteousness in their punishment of Peter Biggs, a closeted homosexual who sublimates his socially forbidden desires into the tolerated activity of heterosexual pederasty, and his wife, a physically grotesque and sexually demanding woman with the intellect of a pruriently minded child. Simultaneously, their treatment of the older couple allegorizes their struggle with their respective parents, adults who condone the irresponsibility and uncritically accept the testimony of other irresponsible adults (such as Mr. and Mrs. Biggs) rather than articulate, much less explain, inconvenient and embarrassing matters of sexuality to their daughters. Thus the girls become each other's source of sexual information and imagination, "living at second hand" (39), while the bond between them is the only one either values.

Set in a suburb of Liverpool in the early post-World War II period, the novel retains vestiges of Gothic trappings through a series of clandestine encounters in the woods, a centuries-old church with Norman tombs, the adjacent graveyard, and, ultimately, the Biggses' house, haunted, so to speak, by a history of sexual subterfuge. In keeping with the conventions of the Radcliffean Gothic, the events that transpire in these *loci* are, despite their unlikeliness, completely devoid of supernatural or preternatural interference and utterly human in their origin and motivations. Their unlikeliness, along with their humanness, moreover, are the very factors that make these occurrences completely inexplicable in terms of polite social discourse, thus adding still another layer of unspeakability to the multiplicity of lies and silences by which the figures of adult authority maintain their control over the protagonists. Thus, as the novel investigates the social milieu in which adolescent girls imbibe willful ignorance and manipulation of their own sexuality, as well as that of others, the stage is set for lesbian panic.

In their autodidactic quest for sexual knowledge, Harriet, who is slightly older and far more aggressive than the narrator, takes the lead. But while she boldly maintains that they "know the proper names for things" (123), the two girls' vocabulary and knowledge are limited by their sources—local gossip, the observations of older girls at school, voyeurism, and the novels of D. H. Lawrence.[29] Their parents, conversely, function as ineffectual models of a social decorum that attempts to deny the very existence of sexual matters, even as, through their extreme attempts to cope with their daughters' increasingly uncontrollable curiosity and behavior, they give these same issues undue emphasis and importance. When the narrator proves "a disgrace owing to the dirty stories found written in my notebook," her parents, apparently incapable of exerting any discipline or parental authority themselves, send her off to an expensive boarding school to remedy her being "out of control and going wrong and in need of supervision" (10). Yet the narrator intuits that the reason for this exile is not so much the "dirty jokes"—which, ironically, she learns at boarding school to commit to memory rather than to writing—but rather "that really they were scared of Harriet and me being so intimate. . . . Nothing else" (10). And while both girls' fathers are well aware of "incidents in the past never properly explained" (75) involving Peter Biggs, Harriet's father alternately fumes hysterically at the idea of his daughter's apparent attachment to the older man and fears the loss of Biggs as a valuable golfing companion, while the narrator's father is limited to mumbling to his daughter, with little provocation and no explanation, that Biggs is a "blighter" and "nothing but a damned scoundrel" (11).

Further contributing to this atmosphere of ignorance and shame is Mrs. Biggs, who, in order to conceal the debased conditions of her own marriage, becomes a self-appointed neighborhood censor, spy, and gossip and thereby teaches the girls the dubious lesson that their own nascent and undefined sexuality is something about which they should be both covert and ashamed. By constantly spying on the girls' activities and reporting them—with the worst possible interpretation—to their respective parents, Mrs. Biggs not only emulates the behavior of a jealous and self-seeking child but exacerbates and encourages the unsupervised experimentation that eventually—and ironically—results in her destruction.

Circular in structure, the novel begins with the parting of the girls in the aftermath of the yet-unspecified climactic event of their relationship. While what exactly has transpired is unclear, the event has clearly been one that has established a permanent and indelible bond between the two, a consummation, though not necessarily of the usual sexual sort. The emotional atmosphere surrounding the girls is simultaneously charged with trauma and the need for dissimulation and with the narrator's sense of physical and psychic intimacy with Harriet:

> I could feel her breath on my face, and over her shoulder I could see the street lamps shining and the little houses all sleeping. She brought her hand up and I though she was going to hit me but she only touched my cheek with her fingers. She said, "Don't cry now." . . . We stood for a moment looking at each other and I wondered if she might kiss me. She never had, not in all the years I had loved her.
>
> (7)

As the girls run away from each other with premeditated screaming, the narrative turns back in time to chronicle the events of the preceding summer vacation, during which the narrator and Harriet are reunited after the enforced separation of boarding school. While apart, the narrator has "heard new dirty jokes" (11) and Harriet has gone to Wales, where she has experienced a somewhat fanciful romantic adventure with a boy she met. Left to their own devices and plagued by boredom and a lack of suitable outlets for their curiosity and energy, the two resume their former occupation of writing elaborate quasifictions in their mutual "diary" and settle on an unlikely object for their fantasies, the feckless, aged, and ironically named Peter Biggs. Out of a need for anonymity in their writings, in the event of parental discovery, they dub him "Peter the Great"; but because "the name Peter was daft . . . we called him the Tsar" (10).

The precocious Harriet has, by this point, dominated her friend for a number of years; accordingly, she prompts the narrator to join her in more daring expressions of their adolescent awakening of sexual desire. The girls are, nonetheless, relatively naive in the ways of the world and thus unable to foresee the consequences of manipulating Mr. Biggs's own closeted and elaborately confused sexuality, which manifests itself in unexplained twilight wanderings around secluded ponds and seaside dunes, all-night assignations at home with the unctuous Douglas Hind when Mrs. Biggs is away, and an undue interest in and identification with pubescent females. The near-obsessive attention they devote to his every activity—as demonstrated by a grotesquely graphic episode of voyeurism during which they observe Mrs. Biggs forcing her sexual attentions on her passive and seemingly unwilling husband—provokes in turn the infantilized Mr. Biggs's own undue sexual interest in the narrator. The spectacle of the Biggs's copulation, an unseemly introduction to the "mysteries" of adult heterosexuality, combines with Harriet's ambiguous narrative of her adventures in Wales and her imperative that the narrator discover "love" during their summer interlude agitate the younger girl's already repressed and manipulated feelings for Harriet. While the narrator herself shows only minimal interest in heterosexuality, she feels compelled to fulfill Harriet's fantastic designs for her. Accordingly, she encourages Biggs's self-pitying attentions, all the while feeling that the reality of her encounters with this pathetic man fall far short of the fantasies that unite her with her friend. And when her motivation to proceed in the manipulation and "punishment" of Peter Biggs falters, she contemplates her hopeless love of Harriet as her first consideration: "I wished I could erase my love for Harriet as easily as my footprints. I spoke seriously to myself . . . resolving to be more adult in my emotions" (81). Although she deludes herself into believing herself "in love" with Biggs for Harriet's sake, when Biggs opines that Harriet has "an evil mind," she muses, "I could not love him after all if he hated Harriet. If I loved him when he thought Harriet evil, then I could not love her. . . . And if Harriet was in truth evil, then I was, and so was the Tsar" (86).

As a result of this forced and misbegotten desire, the thirteen-year-old narrator finds herself sexually violated in a mechanical encounter with Biggs on the beach, which she describes as "raptureless, a visit to the doctor, nothing more, and a distant uneasy discomfort of mind and body as if both had been caught in a door which had shut too quickly" (135). Yet Harriet's response to this news is not the triumphant gloating the narrator expects; rather, Harriet becomes violently upset, for she had intended her friend to experience not the physical actuality of sex but rather the vague metaphysical notion of "love." But because they do not, in fact, "know the proper names for things," one term is easily mistaken or substituted for another in the slippage-laden language of sexual experience, just as the narrator's virgin sacrifice to Mr. Biggs is in effect a surrogated act of love for Harriet. Confronted by the horrible reality of their misconceived fantasy, both girls become hysterical; when surprised by the sudden appearance of their erstwhile tormentor Mrs. Biggs, they panic. Harriet urges the narrator to "Hit her . . . hit her" (149), and, seizing a convenient walking stick, the narrator strikes a fatal blow. In the aftermath of this "accident," for which Harriet, with a perverted yet appropriate sense of justice, arranges to place blame on the dead woman's husband, the narrator's feelings for Harriet, so recently and sorely tested, are renewed: "I did love Harriet then. She was so wise, so good, so sweetly clever" (151). The indissoluble secret they now share in a society that treats sexuality itself as a dirty secret leads to an intimacy between the two girls that resembles sexual passion. The novel concludes as it began, with Harriet calmly and gently comforting her traumatized friend, who, in this moment, still seeks a kiss from Harriet, the reward of physical gratification in return for her misguided acts of devotion.

Unlike Ann Radcliffe and other early female Gothicists, Bainbridge offers no moral didacticism nor, for that matter, any ideal solutions to the problems confronting young girls and their desires. She nonetheless pointedly illustrates from the disempowered perspective of the female adolescent many of the factors leading to lesbian panic made manifest through uncontrolled violent behavior. In doing so, she creates an ironic version of Gothic justice and restoration of order in her denouement. Mr. Biggs is barely a shabby replica of a Gothic villain, much less a romantic hero; but in the metafiction of the girls' lives that finds its expression in their diary, he fulfills the role all the same, just as he eventually does in actuality through his act of statutory rape. Mrs. Biggs, lurking in shadows and using the authority conferred upon her by adulthood to thwart—and thus pervert—female friendship, is, in turn, an appropriate Gothic consort in the context of the adolescent imagination. Thus it is as a consequence of her own mean-spirited infliction of moral disapprobation—a means of deflecting social stigma from her marriage—that she is punished, as is her equally guilty husband. Consequently, in a social setting that encourages ignorance and fear of sexuality, and in which no one is capable of taking control of or even humanizing their sexual impulses, the narrator and her friend quite literally get away with murder. There may be little virtue on anyone's part to be rewarded by this outcome in this bleak narrative landscape. But in a situation in which no form of sexuality is permitted to be "normal" and adults both impose and blame their failures and irresponsibilities on children, it is difficult to suppose—or insist—that the conclusion of this novel be other than it is.

Bainbridge's rendering of the Gothic, in what Anatole Broyard terms her characteristic "thrift shop in English literature" perspective on "Things Out of Joint" (Johnson 30), is that of a well-worn, nearly exhausted trope that nonetheless retains a bizarrely anachronistic force in a milieu of absolute sexual repression. Through the seedy, mundane quality of the postmodern Gothic landscape, Bainbridge effectively drains the mode of what had formerly been one of its most salient features, that of decadent and aristocratic glamour.[30] Indeed, because it renders the forces of terror familiar through their domesticity and banality, this deflation of typical Gothic grandeur increases both the possibility and the relative level of insecurity, fear, and paranoia by draining the commonplace of the comforts assumed to reside therein. Conversely, while Emma Tennant retains much of this everyday horror, she looks, in her reappropriation of the nineteenth-century Gothic as a means of representing the sexual angst of late twentieth-century women, to the ur-texts of what Sedgwick calls the "paranoid Gothic" (*Epistemology* 188), as if to illustrate that no matter how much has changed over a century's time, for women far too much remains the same.

A self-styled literary recycler, Tennant has made a career of rewriting the master narratives of the male-authored canon from a postmodern, gynocentric perspective. "The point of writing for a woman," Tennant suggests, "is to take, magpie-like, anything they please from anywhere, and produce a subversive text out of the scraps" (Kenyon, *Women Writers Talk*, 176). Her knack for what Marleen S. Barr terms "feminist fabulation," the exposition, subversion, and rewriting of "patriarchal myth" (xii), makes her one of the foremost practitioners of parody and pastiche among contemporary women writers.[31] Thus a close reading of her texts reveals *The Queen of Stones* (1982) to be William Golding's *Lord of the Flies* from an adolescent female point of view; *Black Marina* (1985) as a post-colonial staging of Shakespeare's *Pericles* against the backdrop of the United States invasion of Grenada; *Faustine* (1991) as female version of Marlowe's *Dr. Faustus* set in the youth culture of the 1960s; *The Adventures of Robina, by Herself* (1987), which represents Tennant's own experiences as a 1950s debutante at the royal court, as a variation on a theme of *Moll Flanders*; and *Sisters and Strangers* (1990) as a feminist slant on the Book of Genesis and a congeries of other texts. In this manner, she questions the personal and practical ends of the ideological values the Great Tradition promotes and exposes both the dangers of adopting such plots as personal metanarratives and the advantages of subverting them.

In *Two Women of London: The Strange Case of Ms. Jekyll and Mrs. Hyde* (1989), perhaps her best-known novel among American readers and critics, Tennant obliquely addresses the dynamics of lesbian panic through a retroping of Robert Louis Stevenson's Victorian thriller, which Elaine Showalter describes as "a fable of fin-de-siècle homosexual panic, the discovery and resistance of the homosexual self" (107).[32] By rendering all the principal characters female and setting the action against the backdrop of a neighborhood terrorized by a rapist at large, Tennant explores, as she had previously in *The Bad Sister* (1978) and *Woman Beware Woman* (1983), the problems of women, already marginalized in a male-dominated society, who compound their own oppression through the abuse and denigration of each other. In creating this narrative, Tennant presents a scenario that might be said to set up the expectation of lesbian panic yet obviates all such possibilities through the elimination of key characters before such panic can be actualized. For this reason, a brief overview (rather than an in-depth reading) is in order here.

The phenomenon of multiple personality disorder, exacerbated by the abuse of supposedly psychotherapeutic drugs, forms the relationship, so to speak, between Eliza Jekyll, the manager of a trendy art gallery, and the welfare mother Mrs. Hyde, her next-door neighbor in Nightingale Crescent, a once-seedy area of London now in the last throes of "gentrification." Tennant's plot is a somewhat muddled one; given the overly ambitious nature of what she attempts, perhaps it cannot be otherwise. Accordingly, the reader is provided with the dramatis personae at the outset: the Austrian emigre Robina Sandel, who runs a trendy boarding house for women; Robina's friend Mara Kaletsky, a thirtyish film maker with a propensity for illegal drug use; Mara's erstwhile "school-chum" Jean Hastie, a Scottish solicitor, who has retired from her profession at a relatively young age to devote herself, somewhat incongruously, to family and the study of the Gnostic Gospels; Eliza Jekyll, the proprietor of a trendy art gallery and an acquaintance of Jean Hastie in college; Mrs. Hyde, a welfare mother with whom Eliza Jekyll has formed a dubious relationship; and Dr Frances Crane, another of Robina's friends, who, it is eventually revealed, has treated the mysterious Mrs. Hyde for depression. Although these women are all apparently linked by friendship or professional ties, their relationships with one another are all, in actuality, quite tenuous. Moreover, with the exception of Jean Hastie and several incidental lesbian characters, all are relatively ambiguous or undefined in terms of their sexuality.

As in Stevenson's original, the primary witness to the strange transformations of Ms. Jekyll/Mrs. Hyde is a solicitor with, in Showalter's words, "almost a dread of the fanciful, a fear of the realm of the anarchic imagination" (110). Jean Hastie, who is simultaneously positioned as an outsider through her marked "Scottishness" in this decidedly English setting and as a privileged insider by virtue of her social status, functions through the medium of her journal as first-person narrator for much of the text. Despite her very patristic and unquestionably heterosexual choice to exchange her career for domesticity, Jean considers herself a feminist, and she arrives in London to conduct research for a book on the origins of belief in free will and original sin that, she hopes, will reconcile feminism and traditional Christianity. Yet for Jean, whose own low-keyed transformation is in its way more significant than the spectacular metamorphosis of her friend Eliza Jekyll, a theoretical acceptance of feminism does not circumvent the revulsion and disdain she exhibits toward female "outsiders," including foreigners, welfare mothers, and, with some particular edge, lesbians. During her stay in the homosocial atmosphere of Robina Sandel's Nightingale Crescent bed and breakfast, her ever-increasing discomfort with her fellow guests, mostly affluent and unmarried professional women, becomes evident. Compounding her anxieties is her suspicion, based on little more than the environment, that Eliza, who has called upon her legal expertise to turn over the ownership of her flat to her impoverished neighbor, is being blackmailed as a result of a sexual liaison with the woman whom Jean considers little more than a beast. Thus Jean Hastie becomes drawn into an obsessional cycle of fixation upon the derelict Mrs. Hyde, whom she doggedly follows through some of the meaner streets of London and whose every move she documents in her diary. In effect, she enters into a triangulated relationship of attraction and repulsion with, according to her perceptions, two women who should have nothing to do with one another—but who are actually one and the same.

Only through a complicated turn of events does Jean avoid the looming trap of lesbian panic. The gruesome murder of a male neighbor at the hands of Mrs. Hyde, the disappearance of Eliza Jekyll, and the nervous breakdown and subsequent death of Dr Crane not only remove any immediate lesbian "threat," they also allow Jean to recuperate her traditional maternal role. Unlike the original Dr. Jekyll, Eliza, as an almost stereotypical female cultural entrepreneur reliant on the benevolence of wealthy male patrons of the arts, has no estate to leave her solicitor; rather, Jean is left with the care of Mrs. Hyde's (in fact, Eliza's) abandoned children. Yet despite this "escape" from the self-knowledge with which lesbian panic would, if realized, present her, Jean is nonetheless transformed. In the course of her painstaking observations, Jean witnesses brutal events and discovers the less-than-ideal conditions in which even "respectable" wives and mothers like Eliza Jekyll (whose bifurcated personae are result of drug use) may all too easily find themselves. These revelations force Jean to reconsider her beliefs about "the innate sense of moral responsibility in each individual." Acknowledging that she is "no longer certain on this—all important—point" and that a case like that of Eliza Jekyll must inevitably cause "a considerable rift in both Christian and atheistic feminist thinking" (120), she must eschew her convenient philosophies of good and evil, salvation and damnation, and accept the ambiguities that inform the lives of less privileged women if she is to understand the meaning of feminism at all.

But if the interlocutor Jean Hastie is saved from lesbian panic through the chaos of chance and accident and, conceivably, the disconsolations of philosophy, Emma Tennant effectively impedes any potential exploration of the theme of lesbian panic in what would seem its absolute embodiment: the doppelgänger relationship of Ms. Jekyll and Mrs. Hyde. In *Epistemology of the Closet*, Sedgwick observes that in Stevenson's novel, as in Oscar Wilde's *The Picture of Dorian Gray*, "drug addiction is both a camouflage and an expression for the dynamics of same-sex desire and its prohibition: both books begin by looking like stories of erotic tensions between men, and end up as cautionary tales of solitary substance abusers" (172). Tennant, likewise, shifts the narrative focus from Jean Hastie's semiarticulated homosocial discomfort and fascination—the "lesbian" relationship between Eliza and her unfortunate "neighbor" is, after all, only a product of her imagination—and ends with a polemic against the widespread use of prescription tranquilizers as an all-purpose panacea for women's discontents. But while Stevenson's novel, set in an all-male ethos in which not even a female name is spoken, represents the metaphorical splitting of a man at morals odds with himself in his pursuit of an illicit secret life, Mrs. Hyde is the unwanted by-product of institutional heterosexuality and the welfare state. In an oddly postmodern (if somewhat medically implausible) denouement, Jean discovers that her once-vital friend, having been abandoned with three children by a charming but errant husband, found herself on the dole and, consequently, transformed into the tired, aging, repulsive drudge, Mrs. Hyde. In her struggle to regain the youthful beauty and heterosexual appeal of Eliza Jekyll, qualities necessary for her to succeed in the male-dominated art world, she became addicted to medically prescribed antidepressants and, subsequently, illegal hallucinogens supplied by her male rock-star landlord. Thus Mrs. Hyde is not the subversive homoerotic creation of a sexually repressed female imaginary but, rather, is a result of male heterosexual domination and interference—an angry, repressed, and murderous alter ego who returns whenever Eliza Jekyll undergoes drug withdrawal. In this manner, what had been an allegory for social and sexual duplicity in the original (and thus open to a range of encodings) becomes ultimately a somewhat strained metaphor of multiple personality disorder emblematizing women's socioeconomic woes that effectively bars further interpretation in Tennant's revision.

But if *Two Women of London* is, in the end, not altogether satisfactory, it is not on account of any unwillingness or inability on Tennant's part to address the theme of lesbian panic. In an earlier novel, *The Bad Sister* (1978), Tennant, in keeping with her practice of textual revisioning, explores with surrealistic intensity the conditions of incestuous female homoerotic fear and violence through a systematic gender reversal of James Hogg's *The Private Memoirs and Confessions of a Justified Sinner*. Sedgwick describes Hogg's text as an exemplar of the "paranoid Gothic," a form that indicates, much as Freud would later postulate in the case of Dr. Schreber, "that paranoia is the psychosis that makes graphic the mechanisms of homophobia" (*Between Men* 91). By replacing all the male figures caught up in these mechanisms in Hogg's original with female ones and resetting the action in the presumably more self-conscious ethos of the 1970s women's movement, Tennant would seem to provide a lesbian analogue of Sedgwick's paradigm of homosexual panic. Instead, *The Bad Sister* demonstrates, albeit unwittingly, the extent to which Sedgwick's model of psychological and physical violence stemming from homosocial/homoerotic interactions between men, as I have indicated in the introduction to this book, is not applicable to the narration of repressed and forbidden female homoerotic desire in women's writing.

Tennant's novel maps, through a multiperspective narrative, the history of Jane Wild, the illegitimate daughter of a Scottish peer, from her childhood through her psychological disintegration in early adulthood, a process that culminates in the murder of her father and the legitimate half-sister who gradually becomes, in Jane's first-person account, her doppelgänger. Structurally, *The Bad Sister* carefully follows the contrivance of its antecedent, with a fictive—and ostensibly rational—editor's preface and afterword surrounding the central text, the increasingly hallucinatory and demented "Journal of Jane Wild." Yet the sex-reversal of the basic configuration of Hogg's novel, the struggle between the suggestively named Robert Wringhim and George Colwan, brothers with different fathers, to that between Jane Wild and Ishbel Dalzell, sisters with different mothers, in itself skews any systematic, one-on-one narrative transferal. While paternity may be rendered a matter of ambiguity, maternity rarely is. The elder Robert Wringhim, a "flaming predestinarian divine" (2) and the putative father of Hogg's protagonist, becomes, through his position of religious authority, a member of the Colwan household, forming, in effect, a ménage à trois. But as Tennant's sibling rivalry is based on separate maternity, Jane and Ishbel, while raised in geographical proximity to one another (as unacknowledged impoverished bastard and privileged daughter respectively), are members of different households. Indeed, the contrast between the conditions of these two childhood homes, like that between the treatment Michael Dalzell accords his legitimate and illegitimate families, is vital not only as justification for Jane's unrelenting anger but also as a basis for Tennant's feminist subtext. Yet neither Louise Dalzell, the laird's demure and repressed wife, nor the surnameless and woebegone Mary, his cast-off mistress, is in any position, psychologically or otherwise, to assume the function of the conventionally Gothic demonic divine that the elder Wringhim paradoxically performs as a factor of his illicit fatherhood. Thus, Tennant expands the original parental triangle with the creation of a new character, one much in keeping with the novel's 1970s setting. The presumably lesbian Meg, a megalomaniacal separatist feminist commune leader *qua* witch, effectively assumes the role of Jane's manipulative female father when the abandoned Mary, through conditions never defined in the text, becomes her follower.

The rupture that Tennant's sex-reversal forces in the original structure of the homosexual panic narrative, is not merely a matter of an addition to the dramatis personae, although Meg's cross-gendered role and her ostensible (as opposed to covert) sexuality certainly realigns the central narrative and representational dynamics of *The Bad Sister* in a manner far different from that of Hogg's novel. Rather, the respective structures of social and economic power informing character motivation in *The Confessions of A Justified Sinner* and *The Bad Sister* are at such polar extremes, by virtue of this sex-exchange, that virtually no narrative correspondence between the two is viable. As Sedgwick observes, the conflict at the heart of Hogg's narrative arises from young Wringhim's desire for incorporation into the male homosocial structure of the patriarchy, for proximity with men of power, while failing to recognize "that the ultimate function of women is to be conduits of homosocial desire between men" (*Between Men* 99). This exchange in women, which Sedgwick sees as the basis not only of male social, economic, and cultural domination but also of homophobia, has served the purpose of sublimating male homoerotic impulses while keeping women in an inferior, subjugated position.

Yet women, as a result of their traditional disempowerment, lack any analogous system of exchange in men beyond the relatively simple configurations of triangulation (or quadrangulation) we have seen in previous texts. Thus Hogg's principal characters—including, in a fundamental sense, both the elder and younger Robert Wringhims—all enjoy, by virtue of their biological sex, a place in what Julia Kristeva deems the symbolic order. Indeed, it is through the younger Wringhim's inability or unwillingness to observe the basic "rules" of the symbolic order that he "submit[s] to feminization" and thus becomes the homophobic initiator of homosexual panic. In the case of Tennant's female protagonists, however, the marginalization historically inherent in the condition of women is pushed to the extreme in their positions as denizens of a female homosocial world metaphysically controlled by the practice of witchcraft, an almost absolute and paradigmatic example of the Kristevan semiotic.[33]

Consequently, Tennant's narrative, unlike Hogg's, is not based on the protagonist's frustrated desire to enter into a same-sex realm from which she is excluded, nor does Tennant create an alternative system of exchange of men in which her characters can participate. Rather, Jane apparently excludes herself from the female homosocial world by entering into a less than fulfilling and seemingly purposeless heterosexual relationship with filmmaker Tony Marten (a young filmmaker who is, in turn, absorbed in his own Oedipal ties to his mother) while simultaneously receiving spiritual guidance from Stephen (a hippy turned Anglican priest who plays the part of editor's informant that the prostitute Arabella Calvert fills in Hogg's original—thus offering a provocative if not completely congruent one-to-one exchange between institutional religion and the traffic in women) and remaining in Meg's thrall. And while the murder of Michael Dalzell and his daughter is on some level precipitated by Meg's plan for Jane to become the sole heir to the estate (much diminished though it is through Dalzell's self-indulgence and, presumably, the blackmail of the separatist terrorists), Jane exhibits little desire to enter the social order to which her natural father's wealth and title are connected. Rather, the ostensible motivation for the crimes is, as Meg explains, purely ideological: "This is a paternalistic society. Mr. Dalzell was a symbol of the father of all women. . . . He was the incarnation of capitalism. We have incarnated our disapproval of him" (40). Yet Meg's justification fails to explain the killing of the sister-double who so preoccupies Jane's distorted perceptions. We may assume, however, that she stands between Jane (and, by extension, Meg) and the Dalzell estate; accordingly, the malignant ideologue, who engages Jane in a vampirish sexual encounter (128–35), instigates Ishbel's death through the introduction of a demonic, opposite-sex other named, as in Hogg's novel, Gil-Martin, and through the suggestion that Ishbel is Tony's mistress.

While various elements of lesbian panic that have informed many previously considered texts appear in this inverted simulacrum of the male paranoid gothic, there is, ultimately, little narrative coherence in the sum of the parts. The lesbian panic that results in a double murder is not based on those social and economic conditions that have heretofore influenced the phenomenon. Having been raised by separatist extremists, Jane has little reason to fear the social stigma of ordinary lesbianism, nor does she have much in terms of position or privilege—or male patronage—to lose. Rather, lesbian panic seems motivated here by little more than the megalomaniacal whim of a demonic ideologue. This is, granted, the surface-level dynamic in *The Confessions of a Justified Sinner*. The Calvinist elder Wringhim ironically serves as the conduit through which Gil-Martin takes possession of his son's mind and soul. But because Tennant's revision has, as such postmodern inversions are wont to do, ruptured the structural whole of the original, the narrative cohesion based on male homosocial structures falls to pieces in this female homosocial application—so much so that even the identity of the diabolic force becomes hopelessly muddied. Tennant's Gil-Martin is introduced as the invisible, male, quasisexual consort of Meg (who assumes, at times, the surname Martin)—a seeming contradiction of her female homosocial/homosexual antipatriarchal identity and ideology. Meg "bequeaths" him to Jane as a male double through homosexual union. But this gender-blurring of demonic identity is compounded by the presence of the similarly named Martens, Jane's lover and his mother, particularly as Mrs. Marten, in the denouement, becomes visually indistinguishable from Meg. If Tennant's novel is to be read as an allegory of contemporary feminist politics, and there is much textual evidence to that effect, who, then, is the devil in this schemata of lesbian panic as diabolical possession? The ideological extremist? The insensitive heterosexual male lover? The perfect lady as possessive mother? Or, as Gil-Martin as personal double suggests, the deluded self? Indeed, are they all equally—and indistinguishably—to blame?

In the concluding "Editor's Note," Tennant offers two possibilities by way of closure in the aftermath of Jane's own mysterious death: the medical explanation that Jane was "a schizophrenic with paranoid delusions" (215) and that Meg and Gil-Martin were all part of her imagination, or the more romantic suggestion—after Hogg—that the devil did, after all, make her do it. By offering such a narrative loophole, Tennant can, in the end, avoid placing direct blame for the violence on an often irrational and potentially dangerous yet politically vulnerable and socially marginalized group; that is, the extremists among 1970s lesbian and radical feminists. Yet the slipperiness of this ending, which doubles back on itself to affirm what it simultaneously denies, demonstrates what Patricia Waugh defines as the "first lesson of postmodernism":

> [I]t is impossible to step out of that which one contests . . . one is always implicated in the values one chooses to challenge. Even if other values exist . . . they cannot be translated into available historical forms of representation nor function as the basis for epistemological critique. . . . To offer critique can only be to challenge from within through rhetorical or narrative disruption. Parodic forms are foregrounded for parody implicitly acknowledges its parasitic dependence on a pre-existing rhetorical mode.
>
> (*Practising Postmodernism*, 33)

Tennant's parody of Hogg in fact *explicitly* acknowledges its dependence on its antecedent; she shows her hand on the penultimate page (222) for the benefit, we may assume, of those who missed the joke—if, indeed, a joke is what it is. For while Tennant has, according to her lights, gleefully subverted to feminist ends the teleology of less malign literary antecedents in such novels as *The Time of The Crack* (1973), *The Last of the Country House Murders* (1974), and *Hotel de Dream* (1976), *The Bad Sister* is, inevitably, implicated in the values of *The Confessions of a Justified Sinner*, an "historical form of representation" that, as Sedgwick has observed, is, in some broad sense, inherently and inevitably homophobic in its mechanisms.[34]

It is scarcely surprising, then, that British radical lesbian critics such as Paulina Palmer have responded so violently to *The Bad Sister*. Palmer, in her denunciation of the novel excoriates "Tennant's representation of feminist community and female relations":

> She describes them as essentially destructive and transgressive. They are depicted as constituting a kind of terrorist subculture which undermines and disrupts, often by violent means, the logocentric, rationalistic domain of patriarchal society. Her treatment of women's community and lesbian relations contains elements which are downright prejudiced and offensive. She sensationalizes them, identifying them with a lurid world of witchcraft, violence, drugs and sado-masochism. In this respect, she does contemporary feminism a disservice, reproducing the misogynistic stereotypes of femininity popularized by a phallocratic culture.
>
> (*Contemporary Women's Fiction*, 143)

The disturbing elements that Palmer notes are certainly at work in the novel. Yet to dismiss Tennant and her novels as "homophobic" is to oversimplify matters considerably.[35] Palmer fails to note that there are *other* representations of lesbianism and feminism in the novel, representations that function as markers of stability in the ever-shifting dreamscape of Jane Wild's wanderings. As Jane leaves and returns to the flat she shares with Tony Marten, she passes a shelter for battered women and Paradise Island, "the most successful lesbian nightclub in London" (51). She repeatedly notes these sites as she passes, finding in the two edifices a "mixture of misfits" (51) with whom she assumes to have little in common; yet the two landmarks are ever-present in her comings and goings, as if they are the signs that reconnect her to reality after her hallucinatory ventures. In dismissing both groups of women—the battered women are, to her mind, receiving their "punishment" for having "copulated with the wrong man" (55), while the lesbians, she believes, perceive her as "unplaceable . . . something ancient and known and at the same time infinitely strange" (54)—Jane eschews the far more positive—and rational—forms of sisterhood that Tennant suggestively introduces into the novel's cultural milieu. Thus Jane Wild's own psychological disorientation is confirmed, ironically, in her relationship to other women outside the patriarchal symbolic order, as she fails to see her own abuse or her own homoerotic desires reflected in her fellow female "others."

Yet if the "problematic" quality of Tennant's novel is not necessarily that of representation, it is certainly one of execution. Her attempt to narrate the conflicts of late twentieth-century women's lives through the medium of a late Romantic male-authored narrative demonstrates the proverbial result of pouring new wine into old skins: Hogg's old narrative ruptures under the strain of a postmodern resetting—perhaps a function of postmodernism in and of itself—while much of the essence, as it were, of Tennant's new content is lost in the transition. As a result, while *The Bad Sister* presents the various facets of lesbian panic, these elements are presented in so oblique and unsystematic a manner—along with residual bits of male homosexual panic from its antecedent text, concerns about the future of 1970s feminism, psychoanalytical discourse, and occult phenomenology—that neither the panic as a matter unto itself nor its causes and effects are readily discerned from a myriad of other issues.

If, in this sense, Tennant's novel falls somewhat short of its ambitious mark, Fay Weldon's *The Heart of the Country* (1987) demonstrates the manner in which earlier male-authored narratives—in this case the novels of Thomas Hardy—can be effectively employed to illustrate the struggles of women in a male-dominated postmodern ethos. By appropriating Hardy's characteristic tropes of chance and accident, pessimistic fatalism, and sexual repression in a narrative focused on a desiring female subject, Weldon's creates a plot in which lesbian panic, violence, and madness are not, as they generally have been, ancillary to heterosexual consummation. Rather, through the testimony of the institutionalized narrator Sonia, the perpetrator of an horrendously violent crime committed in the name of "sisterhood" but stemming from the jealous repression of homoerotic desire coupled with economic exigency, the dynamics of lesbian panic form the central narrative, to which heterosexual ventures play a secondary, if nonetheless causative, role.

Lesbians—and the abstract concept of lesbianism—have long played a significant if minor role in Weldon's novels, functioning as markers of alternatives to the heterosexual narratives her woebegone female protagonists enact.[36] In *The Fat Woman's Joke* (1967), *Female Friends* (1975), *Remember Me* (1976), *Words of Advice* (1977; issued in Great Britain as *Little Sisters*), *Praxis* (1979), and *The Life and Loves of a She-Devil* (1984), lesbianism provides women floundering in the disintegration of traditional patriarchy and institutional heterosexuality with foils, role models, experimental sexual encounters, or objects upon which to focus their all-pervading anxieties. While her characters display a wide variety of responses to the possibility of a sexual encounter with other women, lesbian panic as such is little in evidence in these works, save for a brief yet crucial passage in *Praxis*, in which the eponymous heroine's chronically psychotic mother retreats into a permanent state of catatonia as a result of discovering in her daughter's diary a mostly fictional record of an amorous though innocent encounter with another girl at school. (Significantly, other incidents fictionalized in Praxis's diary entries, such as being raped by the local Anglican vicar—whose act of indecent exposure she did, in fact, witness—have no effect on her mother.) Thus Weldon has established herself, despite a few critical complaints to the contrary, as a sympathetic if not uncritical representer of lesbians and their concerns—concerns that are, in Weldon's narrative cosmos, for the most part those of women in general.[37] And, in her exploration of the conditions and concerns of contemporary women, Weldon, perhaps more than any other novelist in this study, anatomizes the extent to which women's public sexual attachments—as opposed to their private or secret desires and fantasies—are shaped not so much by love or any other altruistic impulse as they are by economic need.

In *The Heart of the Country* Weldon explores the contradictory consequences of society's irrational compulsion to police female sexuality, the rewards and punishments that perpetuate the repression of women, and the benevolent tyranny (and compulsory heterosexuality) of the welfare state. The novel is set in a metaphysical juxtaposition of modern technology and ancient impulses in the shadow of Glastonbury Tor, the legendary burial site of King Arthur in Somerset, the "Outer Wessex" of Hardy's fictions.[38] It chronicles the lives of two apparently ordinary British middle-class married women, Sonia and her erstwhile friend Natalie, who have "left the wives and joined the women" (51) as they fall into the conditions of welfare motherhood after having violated the basic rules of the exchange in women through illicit extramarital affairs. Sonia, in her role as abandoned woman turned murderer, becomes Weldon's postmodern Tess Durbeyfield.[39]

As Jeffrey Weeks notes, the British welfare state, in its original post-World War II configurations, was informed by "a series of fundamental and essentially traditional assumptions about the family and motherhood . . . [and] a dominant concern about the importance of a child being brought up in the proper domestic environment."[40] The government was concerned, above all, "not in any way to encourage illegitimacy, or immorality":

> [S]eparate allowances for deserted, separated or divorced wives, for instance, were only to be paid if the woman could prove she was the innocent party. And there was a pervasive concern . . . to reinforce and encourage marriage; amounting to an ideological reconstruction of marriage as a vital occupation and career, so that "Every woman on marriage will become a new person" [Beveridge Report]. These values were to permeate the whole structure of the Welfare State, making benefits in large part dependent on certain standards of morality. (235)

While the welfare state has become, in effect, a refuge for discarded women—often discarded, as in the cases of Sonia and Natalie, as a by-product of a widespread social departure from "fundamental and traditional assumptions about family and motherhood"—it continues to require on the part of its beneficiaries an obeisance to neo-Victorian ideals of maternity, femininity, and "True Womanhood." Consequently, it establishes a reduced and even penitential alternative mode of institutional heterosexuality. Accordingly, Sonia and Natalie, in order to adapt to the norms of the welfare state, learn to present themselves as wronged women unselfconscious of any transgression, while furtively seeking sexual pleasures outside the visible structures of relationships. These arrangements serve not only as a means of evading the watchful eyes of the social workers but also, ironically, to replicate the covert sexual practices of the women's earlier middle-class existences. Yet, as Sonia observes, the welfare state and its ostensible compulsory celibacy does not allow its dependent women the means to become "new persons" upon marriage, nor does it, in fact, enforce anything remotely resembling morality; rather, it deprives the women of any possibility of human intimacy: "They don't begrudge us a spot of sex—it saves paying the psychiatrists' bills later—it's relationships they can't stand. They reckon the ultimate obscenity is human affection. . . . We, the abandoned mothers of Britain, don't deserve love. We had our chance and we muffed it" (135).

Although accustomed to the comforts and privileges of middle-class domesticity, both women end up living together in a small apartment on the Boxover Estate, a run-down housing project for women on the dole and their children. Sonia, embittered by the betrayal of both her former husband who resigned his job to avoid paying alimony and her married lover who deserted her, comes to detest all men and, by extension, the very structures of heterosexuality. Having gained expertise in negotiating the bureaucracy of the predominantly female-administered welfare system, she attempts to advise the relatively inexperienced Natalie in the art of manipulating the system, primarily to ensure the continuation of their living arrangement. Natalie, by contrast, is appalled by the sheer abjection of her environment and her condition and therefore seeks any means of escape at her disposal. Given her lack of education and work experience, such means are limited to menial jobs or perquisites proffered by affluent men—associates of her absconded husband—in exchange for sexual favors.

Under these circumstances, desire is inextricably linked with economic and other environmental factors. Sonia, from the confines of the mental hospital, admits in retrospect and in third person, "Of course Sonia loved Natalie. Of course she was in love with her"; yet, in order to conform to the mores of the social welfare system, she modifies this seeming admission of lesbianism by adding "Who else was there for her to be in love with?" (129). She makes a curious and irrational distinction between her own state of emotional need and physical desire, a condition she attributes to men's habits of abandonment, and lesbianism:

> Don't misunderstand her. Sonia would no more have *touched* Natalie than have picked up a dog's turd with her bare fingers, even a dog she knew well. She would, that is to say, have considered any kind of physical approach shuddery, and she certainly could not imagine *kissing* Natalie. Sonia would have found the deed embarrassing and disgusting. Sonia was no lesbian. On the other hand—now, how can she explain this to you?—Sonia could quite see herself in the same bed with Natalie, clasped, clasping and intertwined, giving and receiving all kinds of pleasure, in imitation of the act (as she remembered it) with men: in the interests of comfort, consolation, present-quenching excitement and emotional and physical gratification. But not somehow *kissing*. (129)

Sonia's careful distinctions between acts and desires, between gratification and love, attempt not only to reconcile her longing with heterosexuality but also to replicate the convoluted logic of the welfare system.

Immediately after articulating her self-justification, Sonia retreats into the guise of her madness, yet in doing so reveals—if only through juxtaposition—a thoroughly practical reason for denying her lesbianism: "Sonia is a disturbed woman. She does not act the way the consensus agrees that a woman should feel and act. . . . If her children are taken from her she should feel grief. If she takes money from the State she should feel gratitude. If she falls in love with another woman, admit she is a lesbian. Sonia just won't" (129–30). In the earlier *Remember Me*, Weldon has demonstrated through her character Renee the consequences of public self-disclosure for a woman with children on the dole:

> The judge rejected her last application [for custody] on the grounds that Renee could not provide the girls with proper accommodation, though Renee herself believes that the real reason is her avowed bisexuality. My husband's heterosexuality, she wished to say, has been more damaging to our marriage than my homosexuality, but no one seemed interested. He has custody of the girls, and to look after them, employs a succession of au-pair girls, with whom he sleeps if he can.
>
> (*Remember Me*, 150)

A similar fate would await Sonia, although her schoolteacher husband has turned social dropout, were she to confess the nature of her desire. Thus, in her enigmatic grumbling against society, custody of her children, welfare benefits, and lesbianism are associatively linked. Ironically, Sonia's articulation of this connection comes only once she is institutionalized and consequently beyond the possibility of having any physical connection to any of the three.

Once Sonia "falls in love" with Natalie, she begins to project her own unarticulated knowledge of her secret homoerotic desire onto everyone else. When Natalie takes a low-paying job out of the sentiment that "it's better than being on the dole," Sonia, sensing on Natalie's part both ingratitude and a rejection of welfare mother "sisterhood," attempts to coerce her to stay by threatening her with eviction: "I asked her where she was going to live because it certainly wasn't going to be with me, because people were saying she and I were lesbians and although I for one didn't have anything against lesbians, I didn't want Stephen to turn up and take away the children because of my immoral life" (157–58). Other than a suggestive remark by Angus, a wealthy local businessman (made outside of Sonia's hearing and possibly a facet of her own unreliable narration), there is little evidence to substantiate her assertions. Yet no sooner has she revealed—through dissimulation—her hidden anxiety and in doing so evoked Natalie's distress, than she attempts to "put my arms around her because I was sorry I'd done it." Natalie, however, pushes Sonia away. Thus rejected, Sonia enters a more active phase of lesbian panic: "I hated her. This love business doesn't flow the same way around all the time. The energy flows the other way and you hate." Consequently, when Natalie departs and accepts Angus's offer of the rent-free tenancy of a four-bedroom luxury flat in return for being his mistress, Sonia attributes the move to Natalie's perceptions of her sexuality: "Angus was a better bargain than sharing with a lesbian lunatic" (158).

Once again, the very practical consideration of the loss of her children becomes a factor in Sonia's apparently irrational rationale. But Sonia would use this threat perversely, as a desperate means to force Natalie not only to stay with her but to deny that she—or they—are or can be seen as lesbian. That Natalie, the object of desire, should deny the existence of that same desire is of the utmost importance to Sonia. As I indicate in my introduction, lesbian panic is most often predicated, on some very basic level, by a fear of loss. Aside from her children, Sonia might be said to have lost all. She is able, albeit perhaps inadvertently in the duress of the moment, to reveal her fear of this seemingly ultimate loss to Natalie, as if to make a pathetic appeal to Natalie's own conceivable maternal anxieties through the threat of others' perceptions of "immorality" (i.e., with Angus); by means of this specter of potential loss she hopes to regain control over the companion whose loss she dreads. Indeed, she subsequently uses this notion of the perceptions of others to threaten Natalie when Harry, the latter's husband, subsequently reappears seeking the custody of his children. Angered by Natalie's new liaison with Angus, Sonia manipulates the information she gives Harry to evoke the same fear she attempts to inspire in Natalie—and simultaneously projects the responsibility for this perception onto Harry: "I could tell. He wanted his abandoned wife to be not only a lesbian but a heterosexual nympho. In other words, he didn't like her very much" (175)

Yet Sonia has an even deeper, more fundamental, and more unspeakable loss to fear: the loss of her children entails for the welfare mother the loss of her status as such. Without her children, Sonia's dependency relationship with the State would end. And, as Sonia's constant rage against men is easily transferred to the usually female social workers, it is evident that the State functions as a husband surrogate to the welfare mother, not only in an economic sense but also, to some extent, in an emotional one as well—with a pronounced homosocial twist. Thus, to lose her children through accusations of lesbianism would mean nothing less than the forfeiture of the homosocially inscribed, dependency-based mode of institutional heterosexuality she wishes to share permanently with Natalie—and, perhaps even more significantly, the relinquishment of the permanent victimage she has embraced and, indeed, cherishes. To admit proscribed sexual desires would be to admit personal agency, a quality incompatible with welfare motherhood and the self-inscribed victimage of one who colludes with the system she claims to abhor.

Consequently Sonia, rather than acting on her desires in any positive fashion, first attempts to heap guilt on Natalie; this failing, she simply indulges herself in paranoia and waits for an opportunity to assign blame to Natalie and to all men for her circumstances and, consequently, her actions. Such an opportunity soon presents itself when Natalie, newly delivered from the abjection of welfare motherhood through her status as mistress, hires the local welfare mothers to participate in the building and presentation of a parade float—a highly incongruous 1950s-style tribute to "Mrs. Housewife Princess"—sponsored by her paramour and the local real estate agent. All involved, including the already disillusioned Natalie, are determined to sabotage this apotheosis of a false myth in which none of them have the luxury of believing any longer. Yet Sonia, who has now added Natalie and Angus to the long list of those she blames for her condition, is not content merely to turn this representation of Ideal Womanhood into a parody; rather, she wishes it to become what she imagines to be a radical feminist polemic. With the rage of a zealot, she conspires with an unwitting fellow welfare mother to douse the effigy of the local real estate agent with gasoline and set it aflame. In doing so, however, she does not disempower the structures responsible for women's oppression but merely victimizes another woman: Flora, a gullible teenaged working-class cleaning woman, who has been coerced into accepting the title of "Mrs. Housewife Princess"—despite her lack of either a house or a husband—is burned to death as the result of Sonia's solipsistic public display of revenge.

Weldon does not offer any easy solutions to Sonia's myriad social and psychological problems. Yet she strongly implies, here and in her other works, that if women were honest with themselves and others in matters of sex, love, and desire, they could at least begin to achieve social equality and personal fulfillment. Lesbian panic in this case is a symptom both of a society that infantilizes women and fears women taking responsibility for themselves and of women themselves internalizing such fears of self-reliance. Yet because no easy solution is, in fact, available while such conditions continue to exist, Weldon ends the narrative with questions rather than closure and renders the issue of Sonia's psychological rehabilitation, in which the construction of her narrative is presumed to play a therapeutic role, as a matter of ambiguity. Sonia reveals that, in the aftermath of the parade float disaster, Natalie rejects Angus and the luxuries he offers. Subsequently, she relinquishes her children to Harry and moves to the caravan adjacent to the local dumpsite, the abode of Bernard, Flora's young, handsome, clever, and impoverished boyfriend. Thus Natalie, who had always formed sexual bonds for purely economic reasons, uncharacteristically elects a mode of heterosexuality based on, we may assume, desire and self-consciousness: "Natalie said she was happier than she had ever been in all her life. She was properly alive at last, she said" (200). Sonia, however, registers her doubts about Natalie's future, then turns to consider her own. Paratactically, she registers what she represents as her own readmission to heterosexuality, the amorous interest, as she sees it, of her psychiatrist, who serves as the auditor of her narrative. While she claims she must reject him because she "must get on with changing the world, rescuing the country" (201), she ends on a note that indicates her own continuing instability and lack of fundamental reliability in her role as narrator.

In her alternately first- and third-person narrative, Sonia attempts to represent herself simultaneously as the innocent victim and the wise fool (or, more precisely, wise madwoman) who subverts the actions of those in power. Thus, she quite improbably assigns herself the standard character types of both the *pharmakos* and the *eiron*. Yet, in her megalomania, she believes herself to be the prime mover in all the events that transpire; everything, she claims, is the result of the curse she puts on Natalie, who, in the last minutes of her middle-class marital prosperity, commits the "special sin of splashing the poor" (14) as she drives her Volvo past Sonia and her children, pedestrians on a rainy morning. Thus Sonia, who sees everyone else in the position of the *alazon*, is herself the most self-deceived, while the feckless and unobtrusive Flora becomes the *pharmakos*, not only of society in general but also as the unwitting scapegoat of Sonia's ill-conceived social protest.[41] That Sonia is not "sane again" (201) by the end of text, despite her protests to the contrary, and that she is not recovered from the causal conditions of her lesbian panic is evinced by the role she assigns Natalie in her narrative. Despite her ostensibly central position in the text, Sonia becomes the secondary figure, effectively decentering herself (both figuratively and literally) in order to make the object of her obsessive desire the romantic heroine. In scenes such as that in which the bedraggled Natalie, at the end of a day of physical labor at the quarry, is pursued along muddy roads by Angus in his Audi and offered material comforts in return for her sexual favors, Natalie resembles nothing so much as a postmodern Tess Durbeyfield preyed upon by Alec d'Urberville.

If *The Heart of the Country* is, in some sense, a revision of Hardy's novel (or, conceivably, several of his novels simultaneously, as is Weldon's *Puffball*), Weldon here avoids the trap into which Tennant falls in *The Bad Sister*. Rather than presenting a systematic translation of Hardy's plot (or plots) that simply reconfigures gender and temporal settings, Weldon uses various Hardian tropes to form the allusory system that undergirds her text. Moreover, in using Hardy, one of the more gynocentric Victorian male novelists, as her antecedent, Weldon need not perform the awkward and, as we have seen, potentially incoherent task of sex-role reversal; the typical Hardian plot focuses on the oppressive conditions of women's lives.[42] Weldon, through the medium of Sonia's "madwoman" testimony, is then able to bifurcate the figure of Tess, whom Northrop Frye numbers among the "whole procession of pathetic female sacrifices in English low mimetic fiction" (38). Sonia is a type of Tess as murderess, while Natalie, who becomes to some extent Sonia's own fictional character, is Tess with a relatively happy ending. As such, they represent postmodern possibilities for retelling this deeply inscribed ur-narrative. In a postmodern ethos, Tess Durbeyfield would never be hanged for killing her seducer; rather, she would be subjected to psychologists and social workers for rehabilitation. So it is for Sonia, who represents herself as betrayed by men, seduced by a woman and, consequently, the murderer of another woman. On the other hand, a postmodern Tess, free from the inhibitions of Victorian moralism, might simply shrug off her past and follow the dictates of her sexual desires, as does Natalie.

That the unquestionably heterosexual Natalie can do so while Sonia, whose sexuality must remain ambiguous, cannot, indicates that Weldon, quite perceptively, finds no solution to offer in the case of lesbian panic, even in a postmodern setting. It might be tempting to find in Sonia's supposed cure an apt closure, a happy ending. Indeed, Sonia eschews a new chance at heterosexuality (provided, of course, that it has actually been offered her), but the extent to which this is a "happy" ending is, I would argue, questionable. A liaison with her psychiatrist, its ethical impracticalities aside, only becomes a consideration on the penultimate page of the novel, immediately following Sonia's revelation of Natalie's ironic happy end. This paratactic arrangement suggests that Sonia, who cannot admit lesbianism, will respond to this development in Natalie's life in like manner: if Natalie can yet form what Sonia would perceive as even one more triangulation (for Sonia has already seen Natalie's alliances in multiple triangular terms), she, too, can demonstrate that she does not need Natalie and, hence, that she is "sane again." Yet her contemplation of a relationship with Dr. Mempton, in a chapter entitled "Resolutions," seems little more that a rhetorical trope presented for the purpose of its rejection. But before Sonia makes her pronouncement of her intention of "changing the world," her rhetoric disintegrates into a revelation of her actual state: "Look at me! Puffy face, puffy hands, twitching. That's the drugs. I talk too much. I am full of hate and self-pity. He knows that, better than anyone" (200).

Accordingly, as we may assume from her fanciful suppositions of a rejected heterosexuality, Sonia has hardly resolved the problem of lesbian panic. Indeed, for women who continue to evade personal responsibility and agency, there can be no such resolution. Likewise, Sonia is hardly an apt candidate for the task of reforming society. She becomes, rather, an emblem of a type of overideologized feminist pseudoconsciousness with which Weldon frequently takes exception. As Jenny Newman notes, Weldon, while thoroughly feminist in her outlook, has long represented "feminist ideologues" unsympathetically; in her modern-day morality tales, "Weldon never allows over-reachers like Sonia to exceed what is politically possible with their primitive magic. Women with awakened strengths and energy may wish to change the world, but witchcraft is not a shortcut to ruling it. And it may all be nonsense after all" (193, 204). In this manner, Weldon allows Sonia, as narrator, to provide her own inadequate resolution but all the while tacitly demonstrates that as long as the conditions of women remain as they are—conditions that no one woman can possibly change—there can be no practical resolution to the narrative of lesbian panic. Nevertheless, in *The Heart of the Country* Weldon provides one of the most exacting postmodern representations of the psychology of lesbian panic and its relationship to the harsh economic realities endured by a vast number of women who attempt or who are forced to exist outside the sphere of heterosexual privilege.

As I have discussed previously, in many of her novels Weldon finds a place for lesbians; a secondary place informed by the more central needs of her heterosexual protagonists, but a place nonetheless, a place relatively free from the pervasive angst of lesbian panic. Yet to narrate lesbianism in a manner that moves beyond lesbian panic without devolving into utopian fantasies, ideological polemic, or reconfigurations of heterosexual romance fiction is an accomplishment that has eluded most contemporary women writers. A notable exception is Jeanette Winterson, a critically acclaimed creator of postmodern lesbian narratives over the past decade. As Laura Doan points out, Winterson's lesbian characters, particularly the autobiographical protagonist of *Oranges Are Not the Only Fruit* (1985), look upon a world defined through binary oppositions with "a profound and unshakable conviction that [their] lesbianism is right and that any attempt to condemn or despise [them] . . . constitutes perversion" (137). Thus, she adds, "Winterson totally redefines normal and renders heterosexuality as unintelligible" (138). In her unabashed explication of lesbian life and desire, Winterson might be seen as the fulfillment, some five decades later, of Virginia Woolf's prophetic observation on a woman's ability to write her "very queer knowledge." Winterson has found in the practice of postmodernism the means of reversing and overthrowing the binaries that construct what DuPlessis has aptly called the "cultural and narrative ideology" of heterosexuality ingrained in societal discourse. Yet, while Winterson is surely the most widely read and critically lauded lesbian author since Virginia Woolf, her postmodern perspective on lesbianism—which not only tacitly acknowledges the complicity of lesbianism in the structures it critiques but breaks down what Wendy Brown calls "the moral force that the subject, truth, and normative coproduce" for feminism (78)—has made Winterson a controversial figure for some lesbian and feminist critics alike.[43] As Margaret Reynolds observes with only slight ironic hyperbole, "Winterson's position as the leader of her literary generation delights her passionate adherents and infuriates her passionate detractors. There is no middle ground" (429).

In her early (and now disowned) *Boating for Beginners* (1985), Winterson employed the now traditional postmodern devices of parody, burlesque, and collage to critique the commerciality of organized religion and (through the medium of a lengthy, nearly verbatim passage from Mary Shelley's *Frankenstein* incorporated into her text) the man-made origins of the "divine." While only hinting at lesbian possibilities for its characters, *Boating for Beginners* offers a foretaste of the devastating dissection of religious hypocrisy and homophobia—and the concomitant "normalizing" of lesbianism—that Winterson presents in *Oranges Are Not the Only Fruit*. While institutional religion, Christianity in particular, is generally perceived as a primary source of social prohibitions against homosexuality, few of the novels I consider in this study have directly considered the interaction between the church and the lesbian individual; it is as if they actively deny the pervasive influence of this interaction over their subjects. Winterson, having herself been a child evangelist, unflinchingly examines the relationship between the male-controlled female homosociality of Christian fundamentalism and the official church policy of homophobia and finds an endless cycle in which the former is both the cause and effect of the latter. In the context of Winterson's novel, the church provides a mode of surrogation for women like the narrator's adoptive mother—a woman who "had never heard of mixed feelings" (3)—who flee their own homoerotic desires and submerge their energies in the all-demanding work of religious proselytizing.

But while such a retreat from desire may represent a form of lesbian panic, it is thoroughly peripheral to the narrative, which focuses on the deconversion of the protagonist Jeanette. A messianic child prodigy of obscure parentage with an uncommon gift for rhetorical persuasion, Jeanette holds a place of pride in the church for her numerous conversions to the faith: "If you want to talk in terms of power I had enough to keep Mussolini happy" (124). But when, as she enters adolescence, her evangelism encompasses the conversion of her followers to the "Unnatural Passions" (85) of lesbianism, she is cast out from church, family, and home. Consequently, however, by forswearing the life of a missionary and heeding the call of her sexuality, she becomes a type of the heroine of *Jane Eyre*, a novel whose real ending her mother habitually elided. She is, likewise, an ironic inversion of Hardy's hero in *Jude the Obscure*: by eschewing the rigid binaries of good and evil, natural and unnatural, while embracing the pleasure of passion, she makes her way all the same to the distant and seemingly elusive Oxford: an "ancient city of stone and stone walls that have not fallen yet" (161).

Through an intertextual reconfiguration of the picaresque novel and the conversion narrative, Winterson raises the "coming-out" story, the often trite mainstay of demotic lesbian and gay writing, to a new artistic level. But while *Oranges Are Not the Only Fruit* does, in this way, break new artistic ground in its representation of a facet of lesbianism rife with what D. A. Miller would deem the "disequilibrium, suspense, and general insufficiency" that give rise to the "narratable" (ix), it nonetheless leaves open the question of whether there is narratable lesbian life, not only after lesbian panic but after its opposite possibility, that of self-knowledge and self-acknowledgment, as well. In *The Passion* (1987) and *Sexing the Cherry* (1989), Winterson utilizes a "magic realism" similar to that employed by Angela Carter—perhaps the most notable of British postmodernists—in her late novels. To inscribe lesbian sexuality without resort to the by now traditional device of lesbian panic, Winterson sets these novels in pre-Freudian historical periods (the Napoleonic Wars and the Restoration, respectively) and populates them with quasimythic and often androgynous or transsexual characters who are free to experiment with modes of sexuality unencumbered by the inhibitions of institutional Christianity, medical sexology, economic exigency, or, for that matter, quotidian reality. But while these narratives are aesthetically innovative and do allow for an expression of female homoerotic desire that might prove difficult, if not impossible, in more traditional narrative forms, they provide little in terms of a new narrative model for lesbian life in the late twentieth century.

To this end, Winterson's more recent *Written on the Body* (1992)—which has the unique distinction of calling to mind simultaneously not only Monique Wittig's *The Lesbian Body* and Roland Barthes's *A Lovers' Discourse* but also Erich Segal's *Love Story*—would offer lesbian eroticism itself as the narrative. The first-person narrative of a lesbian Lothario, the novel delineates the protagonist's passionate relationship with Louise, a married woman who is afflicted with an incurable and terminal disease, the loss of this love, and the attempt to regain it. While this narrative strategy has resulted in Winterson's recognition as a best-selling mainstream novelist and has elicited tremendous widespread sympathy for a lesbian narrative, it is not without its problems—its sentimentality and lack of depth psychology aside. Through various oblique references to genitalia and sexual acts, it is clear, to the lesbian reader at least, that the narrative persona is both female and lesbian; Winterson, however, chooses not to name the protagonist or reveal her gender directly, a tactic Maureen Duffy attempted, to rather different ends, in *The Love Child.* This tactic functions, consequently, as a double discourse: the "straight" reader can assume that the acts and relationship described are heterosexual and thereby avoid the psychic inconveniences that, as we have seen through this examination of lesbian panic, might attach to the conscious consumption of lesbian erotica. Conversely, by making little distinction between heterosexual and homosexual desire, Winterson effectively continues along the line of "normalizing" lesbianism she begins in *Oranges Are Not the Only Fruit*, if not completely universalizing it. Simultaneously, however, the objection might be raised that *Written on the Body*, by not directly acknowledging the lesbian, simply contributes to her ongoing "ghosting."[44]

It is, nonetheless, unfair to expect any one author to transform novelistic convention completely and rid it of its long-accrued sexual, cultural, and ideological encumbrances, a task even Virginia Woolf, for all her efforts, knew would not be possible in her lifetime. In the work of one decade, Jeanette Winterson has undoubtedly "pushed the envelope" to further limits than most of her predecessors and contemporaries in terms of narrating lesbianism. She has, moreover, like Maureen Duffy before her, faced the wrath of lesbian critics who fear the loss of their perceived innocence through the deconstruction of a postmodernism that would reveal their implication through their very "otherness" in the ideologies and institutions they critique, who fear the loss of the moral prerogatives of those permanently marginalized and victimized.[45] One can only hope, then, that Winterson and others will continue to explore the means by which lesbianism may be narrated in a postmodern society. For unless we find new narratives to shape societal perceptions of lesbians and their existence, we may never be able to move completely beyond lesbian panic—either in literature or in life.

NOTES

Introduction: Toward an Axiom of Lesbian Panic

1. It is worth noting, in this regard, that panic disorder is more frequently observed in women than in men and that "there is some evidence that marital disruption . . . is commonly accompanied by a higher prevalence of . . . panic disorder" (Wittchen and Essau, 120). This is significant to this study for, as I will discuss further, lesbian panic is often presented in the novel in conjunction with or as a disruption to the traditional courtship and marriage plot.
2. This is, of course, a greatly simplified overview of Sedgwick's model. See *Between Men* (1–5, 21–27); *Epistemology of the Closet* (182–212). See also Rubin (157–210) and Irigaray (170–97).
3. This exchange of men does, of course, exist in numerous speculative or utopian fictions. One possible exception among the works comprising what Elaine Showalter defines as "the Female Tradition" (3) may be Doris Lessing's *The Golden Notebook*, as I shall discuss in chapter 3.
4. See Castle (67–91) for an illustration of how the triangulation Sedgwick defines is reconfigured by the presence of a second woman. The ur-text for this particular mode of erotic triangulation is René Girard's discussion of " 'Triangular' Desire" (1–52) in his 1965 study *Deceit, Desire, and the Novel.* Girard says little about the latently homosexual aspects of his paradigm, other than to demur that, "Nothing is gained by reducing triangular desire to a homosexuality which is necessarily opaque to the heterosexual. If one turned the explana-

tion around, the results would be much more interesting. An attempt should be made to *understand* at least some forms of homosexuality from the standpoint of triangular desire" (47). This curious circularity is, I think, rather disingenuous yet very much in keeping with the zeitgeist of the 1960s. It is hardly "reducing" the paradigm to demonstrate that, in many cases, it *is* a means of expressing a homosexuality that is, either on a conscious or unconscious level, rendered "necessarily opaque" to at least some of the heterosexuals involved in the configuration.

5. On the history and ethos of women's fictions, narrative conventions, and the social pressures brought to bear thereunto, see especially Woolf, *A Room of One's Own*; Moers, *Literary Women*; Showalter, *A Literature of Their Own*, Gilbert and Gubar, *The Madwoman in the Attic*.
6. In this, Miller follows the lead of Todorov. See Todorov, *The Poetics of Prose* (143–78); *Genres in Discourse* (27–38).
7. I use the term "lesbian" advisedly here as the novel predates the common usage of the term to denote female homosexuality. Yet, as Terry Castle notes, "while *Lesbian* and *homosexual* may indeed be neologisms . . . there have always been *other* words—a whole slangy mob of them—for pointing to (or taking aim at) the lover of women" (9). For all intents and purposes, the behaviors of Edgeworth's character Harriot Freke would be identified by present-day readers as unquestionably those of a "butch" lesbian. For a lesbian reading of *Belinda*, see Lisa Moore. See also Katherine Sobba Green (146–52) on Edgeworth and the narrative ideologies and conventions of the courtship plot.
8. For a somewhat different lesbian reading of *Jane Eyre*, see Adrienne Rich.
9. See Ruth Yeazell for a cogent and comprehensive overview of significance of this de riguer unknowingness on the part of the Victorian heroine as a crucial factor in the courtship plot.
10. See in particular Lillian Faderman (17–20, 141–43, 411–15), who makes a distinction between romantic friendship and lesbianism.
11. I thank Wendy Bashant for drawing both this matter and this source to my attention.
12. For extensive discussions of the lesbian in decadent literature and art, see Faderman (277–94), Dijkstra (119–59 passim), and Foster (81–115).
13. See Gayle Greene and Molly Hite regarding this epistemological shift in women's fiction. While neither critic discusses lesbianism as an aspect of these new "stories," they nonetheless provide two very different and useful overviews of various narrative strategies and ideologies in recent novels by women.
14. For an example of the extremes of absurdity that the fear of indefinition connected to the word "lesbian" can evoke, see Castle on "the bizarre hypothetical case of a physically handicapped married woman, unable to have sex with her husband (or anyone else), who considered herself heterosexual, yet uncon-

sciously desired to have sex with women" (14–15). Having explored the lesbian subtexts of contemporary women's writing for some years now, I can only add, sardonically, that I am surprised that a narrative of lesbian panic incorporating the above scenario has not yet been written.

15. For a multifaceted overview on interfaces of lesbianism, postmodern theory, and the most explicit forms of visual and literary representation (i.e., pornography), see Colleen Lamos (85–103).
16. "Romans zijn niet lesbisch. . . . Romans hebben geen seksuele voorkeur. Mensen hebben een seksuele voorkeur. Vrouwen zijn lesbisch, sommige vrouwen, alle vrouwen voor mijn part" (translation mine).

1. "This Very Queer Knowledge": Virginia Woolf's Narratives of Female Erotic Desire

1. See, in particular, studies by Mitchell A. Leaska and Hermione Lee, also those by James Naremore, Avrom Fleishman, Jean Guiget, Alice Van Buren Kelley, Jane Novak, Harvena Richter, and Irma Rantavaara.
2. In order to maintain uniformity with preexisting Woolf criticism, the pagination that appears throughout this text is that of the 1920 Harcourt Brace Jovanovich edition, which has long served as the "standard" edition. I nevertheless believe that the 1992 Penguin edition, which reproduces the original 1915 British text and is augmented with Jane Wheare's exhaustive notes, is a far superior edition and should supersede the former.
3. Louise A. De Salvo's examinations of *The Voyage Out*, particularly her pioneering work *Virginia Woolf's First Voyage: A Novel in the Making*, have been notable exceptions, as has Rachel Blau DuPlessis's *Writing Beyond the Ending*.
4. James Naremore, in analyzing the aesthetic shortcomings of the novel, cites Helen's shift from foreground to background as a primary example of the manner in which "the novel tends to frustrate conventional expectations" (6).
5. The contrast of the relatively erudite Helen and her companionate marriage with the shallowness and slavish marital devotion of most of the other female characters would seem a microcosmic illustration of the philosophy of women and education articulated by Mary Wollstonecraft in her *Vindication of the Rights of Woman*. Moreover, while the Clarissa Dalloway who appears in *The Voyage Out* and a number of Woolf's short stories is not completely consistent with the protagonist of *Mrs. Dalloway*, her overly emphatic avowal of wifely devotion can be interpreted as an overcompensation for repressed lesbianism—her interactions with both Helen and Rachel aboard ship can be read as subliminally flirtatious—characteristic of a woman who would "fail" her husband in the subsequent text.
6. Brimstone also notes that although Woolf feared exposure and attack on account of her "Sapphism" as a result of her writings, her articulation of lesbian subject matter was so subtle that "it is not until recent years that the lesbian

implications have been noted" (93). According to Edward de Grazia, Woolf's sexual preference and practices were so little known to the public during her lifetime that she was thought an appropriate witness to testify on behalf of the merits of *The Well of Loneliness* at Radclyffe Hall's obscenity trial (178–79).

7. The historical events to which Woolf alludes would date the narrative as occurring in 1909. (See Jane Wheare's notes to the Penguin edition.) The 1895 conviction of Oscar Wilde for sodomy under the 1885 Criminal Law Amendment Act (legislation that was further strengthened in 1912) was then relatively fresh in the minds of the outraged public, which would surely include Woolf's British tourists. Under the act, all sexual acts between men were punishable by imprisonment. For a discussion of social attitudes toward both male and female homosexuality, see Jeffrey Weeks (81–121). For a more general discussion of fin-de-siècle sexual mores, see Judith R. Walkowitz (121–71).
8. As no critic has offered more than a cursory explanation of these enigmatic and, from my perspective, crucial passages, and because these three different versions do not appear together in any one published text, I am reproducing them here in toto, despite their considerable length.
9. For an examination of the medical sexologists' perceptions of lesbianism and its presumed threat to the very fabric of civilization, particularly as it affected the visual arts of the late nineteenth and early twentieth centuries, see Dijkstra, 119–59.
10. For a thoughtful discussion of the analogies between *The Voyage Out* and *Heart of Darkness*, see Shirley Neuman (57–76); Fleishman (1), Naremore (45), and Zwerdling (306) also address this issue. That Woolf was aware of these correspondences is evinced in a morbidly humorous and self-reflexive allusion in the penultimate chapter of *The Voyage Out*. Arthur Venning, attempting to communicate the news of Rachel's death to the deaf Mrs. Paley, exasperatedly shouts, "Miss Vinrace. . . . She's dead" and only with great effort can "prevent himself from bursting into laughter" (361).
11. Several critics, particularly Naremore and McDowell, argue that Terence and Rachel consummate their relationship in the earlier jungle scene in which the couple becomes engaged, although no sexual act is directly represented. Consequently, both criticize Woolf for the "inadequacy" of her "treatment of sexuality," a "fault" that is "deeply grounded in a view of experience that Virginia Woolf develops with great force and consistency in all her novels" and "implies . . . a reluctance to tell the truth about the body" (Naremore 47). Given Rachel's consistent repugnance at the spectacle of physical sexuality between Susan and Arthur, her valediction that her relationship with Terence was "not the love of man for woman" (247), and the allusion to *Comus* (in which "Sabrina Fair" is called upon to rescue the virginity of the opportuned maiden) that marks the onset of her fatal illness, I would argue instead that the relationship between Rachel and Terence is more metaphysical than physical, like that of a

similar couple, Katherine Hilbery and Ralph Denham in Woolf's subsequent novel *Night and Day*. That neither Naremore nor McDowell recognize the role of lesbianism that is present "with consistency in all her novels," I believe, reveals the problem inherent in privileging heterosexuality in the analysis of Woolf's work. For an alternative perspective that, based on Woolf's early modern sources for *The Voyage Out*, argues that Rachel's virginity is absolutely essential to the plot, see Nancy Topping Bazin (48–56).

12. The bitingly satiric tone in which Woolf narrates the episodes that occur in and around the hotel prior to the boat excursion into the jungle (e. g., the courtship of Arthur and Susan, the visits with Evelyn and Miss Allen, and the dance) shows the author in her most Austenian mode. That Woolf was following the example of her predecessor is suggested not only by her allusions to *Persuasion* early in the text but also in her 1913 essay "Jane Austen," written while *The Voyage Out* was in progress. Woolf's displacement of the action to an exotic locale, where sexual behavior repressed in British society is allowed to surface, recalls Austen's highly ironic explanation in *Northanger Abbey* for the Continental settings of Gothic novels:

    > It was not in them perhaps that human nature, at least in the midland counties of England, was to be looked for. Of the Alps and Pyrenees, with their pine forests and their vices, they might give a faithful delineation; and Italy, Switzerland, and the South of France, might be as fruitful in horrors as they were there represented. . . . But in the central part of England there was surely some security . . . in the laws of the land, and the manners of the age. . . . There, such as were not as spotless as an angel, might have the dispositions of a fiend. But in England it was not so.
    >
    > (200).

13. For an analysis of the stratagem of ignorance, see Eve Kosofsky Sedgwick, "Privilege of Unknowing."
14. In *Virginia Woolf's First Voyage*, Louise De Salvo interprets Rachel's death through Sappho's "Ode to Aphrodite," which appears earlier in the text. DeSalvo sees her "leap into watery pools," a reference to both her fevered hallucinations and the "Sabrina Fair" passage Terence reads to her from *Comus*, "as a self inflicted phantasied punishment for the Sapphist life, as a way for Rachel to escape Helen's Sapphist tyranny, or as a parallel to Sappho's own suicide by drowning because she suddenly and inexplicably found herself in love with a man, in love with Phaon" (134).
15. Jane Marcus explores the Shakespearean and Mozartean comic antecedents of *Night and Day* in *Virginia Woolf and the Languages of the Patriarchy* (18–35).
16. See Castle (67–74, 250–52); Sedgwick, *Between Men* (21–27), *Epistemology of the Closet* (185–88). An alternative fourfold configuration can be delineated in *Night and Day*; the fourth term of Cassandra can be added to the original

William Rodney-Katharine-Ralph triangle. In terms of narrative, this "conflict" has a "satisfactory" resolution in the sense that Cassandra gladly relieves the growing mutual dissatisfaction marking the engagement of Katharine and Rodney—thus freeing Katharine to give her full attention to the *other* triangulation in which she is involved.

17. See Castle (28–65) for an exhaustive study of the various modes of "lesbian ghosting" as a narrative device.
18. Phyllis Rose offers an explanation of the frustrations *Night and Day* offers readers and critics alike:

> Rodney, Denham, and Katharine sort out their passions and plan their future over tea, in taxis, by the fire, in walks along the Embankment, and overthrow the accepted social order (that engagements are not broken, that the abandoned woman does not help her ex-fiancé to find a new bride, that great poets' granddaughters do not marry lawclerks) so discreetly and placidly that one hardly knows anything of moment has happened. *Night and Day* is a pleasant book to read, but nothing in it makes one breathe more quickly or disturbs one's mind when the book is put away. It shows what sheer intelligence and determination can produce in the way of a novel, and also their limitations.
>
> (96).

19. Woolf's ambivalent relationship with and artistic debt to Richardson and her work have been sources of interest and controversy for a number of feminist critics. DuPlessis's assessment that "it may be . . . a case of the Woolfean angel fearing to tread, yet entering into a greater narrative boldness, signaled to her by the Richardsonian fool" is, I believe, an apt one (152). While Richardson employed stream-of-consciousness narrative to represent lesbianism and female bisexuality in the later volumes of *Pilgrimage*, particularly *Dawn's Left Hand* (1931), it is noteworthy that she did so *after* Woolf did so in *Mrs. Dalloway* (1925) and *To the Lighthouse* (1927). For discussions of the Woolf-Richardson connection, see Kaplan (76–83), Showalter (261–62), Fromm (318–19), and Gillespie (132–51).
20. The phrase "continuous present" is, of course, Gertrude Stein's description of her own narrative technique, and I do not wish to imply a similarity between Stein's and Woolf's style or method. I feel, however, that the term in and of itself can be aptly applied to Woolf's own method of collapsing past and present, resulting in a past that is as much a part of the present as the present itself is. Makiko Minow-Pinkney has provided a concise grammatical appraisal of the conflation of tense in Woolf's technique: "The tense system of . . . scenes from the past is inconsistent. Since the characters' present is given, in traditional narrative style, in the past tense, their past should presumably be in the pluperfect, but this is not the case. . . . [In a typical scenario, the] discourse [of

the past] returns to [the] present, but the tense remains the same as that used in the remembered scene; from a formal point of view, past and present are indistinguishable" (56). Minow-Pinkney goes on to add that Woolf was "somewhat anxiously" aware of her pronounced tendency to rely on present participles in creating these affects (57), but that, as Woolf herself observed, "I find them very useful in . . . *Mrs. D*" (*Writer's Diary* 66).

21. The history and origins of the homosexual connotation of "queer," both as adjective and noun, have yet to be adequately defined. The 1971 edition of *The Oxford English Dictionary*, while noting that the origins of the word in even its denotative sense of "strange, odd, peculiar, eccentric" are "obscure," makes no mention of "queer" in relation to homosexuality, even as a pejorative or informal usage. (The same edition also gives no definition of "lesbian" other than "of or pertaining to the island of Lesbos. ") Woolf nevertheless uses "queer" with some frequency in *Mrs. Dalloway* and in other texts, and the contexts in which she chooses to employ the word are generally, if not always, those in which a double-entendre could easily be discerned.
22. Minow-Pinkney observes that the commanding and "masculine" Lady Bruton, a relatively minor character in the narrative, functions as an embodiment and "mediation of the antagonist qualities" of socially privileged Clarissa Dalloway and the aggressively physical Doris Kilman (75). This synthesis of conflicting "lesbian" types in a woman whose closest relationship, perhaps not surprisingly, is with her devoted female secretary, goes far to explain Clarissa's extreme responses to Lady Bruton's actions and her almost obsessive attraction to and repulsion by this character with whom she "seldom met" (106).
23. Minow-Pinkney provides an insightful Kristevan semiotic interpretation of Woolf's representation of Clarissa's room and the implications of medical science therein (66–70). See also Patricia Ondek Laurence (148ff) regarding Woolf's use of the Victorian concept of female illness as protest and disruption.
24. Even the reference to her "failures" at Constantinople is suggestive. The ancient Byzantine capital that forms the nexus between the European and Asian worlds, between Pauline Christianity and Hellenism, is the site of the hero[ine]'s sexual metamorphosis in Woolf's subsequent novel, *Orlando*.
25. This passage is indeed oft-cited and oft-discussed. For alternative readings of this passage by other lesbian critics, see, in particular, Teresa de Lauretis (236–39), Judith Roof ("The Match in the Crocus" 100–16), and Paula Bennett (235–59),
26. Here, as elsewhere in *Mrs. Dalloway*, flowers are associated with lesbian desire. Given that we can place this garden scene in the early 1880s, given the clues of ages and historical events Woolf provides, this metaphorical association corresponds closely with the floral images of lesbians, both in their own writings of the period (e. g., Renée Vivien's *The Muse of the Violets*) and in representations in "decadent" literature and graphic arts. See Dijkstra (235–40 and passim).
27. Emily Jensen emphatically argues this point and sees Clarissa's marriage as a

form of "respectable suicide" that both parallels and contrasts with Septimus's more direct and violent self-destruction (162–67). This 1983 article on *Mrs. Dalloway* remains, I believe, one of the best argued and most intelligent lesbian analyses of the novel to date.

28. See Shirley Nelson Garner (328) for a perceptive discussion of the parallels between this interlude, terminated by Peter's sarcastic "star-gazing" remark, and the erotic episode between Katharine and Mary in *Night and Day*, interrupted by "a joke about star-gazing, which destroyed their pleasure" (61).
29. Jensen points out that both Peter and Sally recall and repress the thought of their earlier competition for Clarissa's affections and attentions through their memories of intimacy with one another at Bourton (165). Woolf's consciousness of the potency of Clarissa's phrase is obvious in her highly manipulative letter of October 18, 1932, to her lover Vita Sackville-West. After expressing her jealousy over Sackville-West's tryst in the Alps with another woman, Woolf attempts to provoke jealousy by broadly hinting at the possibility of a second triangle comprised of herself, Sackville-West, and Elizabeth Bowen. She signs off, with no transition and feigned nonchalance, "Anyhow my Elizabeth comes to see me, alone, tomorrow . . ." (De Salvo and Leaska 362, ellipses original).
30. This, I would suggest, is the function as well of the minor "queer" characters in the novel, whose own romantic or sexual histories go unrevealed and unremarked. The presumably independent Miss Pym in her florist shop, connected with the "lesbian" image of flowers (see n. 27 above); the "strong martial woman," Lady Bruton, who successfully synthesizes her "masculinity" with her class status (109); and Milly Brush, Lady Bruton's secretary (who is "capable of everlasting devotion, to her own sex in particular" [106]) all suggest lesbian possibilities far less self-abnegating or self-destructive than the fates of the three protagonists. Their relatively unstressed presence in the text, moreover, indicates not only a certain "normalcy" of lesbian existence but also its relative commonness and its occurrence among all classes.
31. See, in particular, J. Hillis Miller's 1970 and 1985 studies of the novel. Suzette A. Henke (138–41) provides a more specifically homosexual reading of these parallels.
32. For a discussion of the class dynamics of *Mrs. Dalloway*, see Alex Zwerdling (120–143).
33. Septimus's case of homosexual panic, arising from experiences acquired and traumas sustained primarily in the military, perhaps the most deeply demarcated site of male homosocial sexual politics and one of the primary enforcers of traditional social constructions of masculinity, corresponds far more closely to Sedgwick's paradigm than to mine. Indeed, were he not the product of a female author, surely Septimus would find a place in *The Epistemology of the Closet*. My point here is not to dispute Sedgwick; rather, I am exploring the manner in which Clarissa Dalloway comes to self-knowledge by the end of the

novel through her intuitive recognition of kinship and similarity with a character so very different from herself. In doing so, I trust that the differences between male homosexual panic and lesbian panic are quite evident.

34. Mitchell A. Leaska notes that despite common critical assumptions about the war-related causes of his illness, "nowhere in the novel is there any evidence the Septimus's psychological state is the result of shell shock" (114n.). Indeed, this diagnosis, one the physicians would readily apply, seems simply another manifestation of an inability/refusal, demonstrated by Rezia and others in the novel, to comprehend the source of the complaint behind the ravings.
35. See Dijkstra (10–24).
36. For an exhaustive explication of Septimus's hallucinatory ramblings with reference to their latent homosexual implications, see Leaska (104–12).
37. How or why the conservative and nationalistic Richard Dalloway would hire a woman with political views so at odds with his own as a teacher and companion to his daughter, apart from his assessment that "she was very able, had a really historical mind" (11), is never really explained and should be interpreted, I believe, as an indication of his basic indifference to and distance from even the other members of his household—despite the flowers he presents to his wife (without being able to tell her he loves her). It is this solipsistic indifference, perhaps, resembling a nondemandingness, which determines Clarissa's choice of a marriage partner.
38. See Dijkstra (152–59 and passim) and Lillian Faderman, *Surpassing the Love of Men* (254–94) on fin-de-siècle representations of lesbianism; Jeanette Foster (149–92, 240–341) on mid-century "sinister" lesbian figures; Faderman, *Odd Girls and Twilight Lovers* (230–35) on post-Stonewall codes of lesbian "political correctness."
39. For a historicized examination of shopping and consumerism in *Mrs. Dalloway*, see Reginald Abbott (193–216).
40. Clarissa's source of enlightenment is, needless to say, not wholly empirical. While a type of ineffable "clairvoyance" or "telepathy" between characters has to some extent been accepted by critics as a given in Woolf's novels, few have attempted to define it more than vaguely. Both Miller and Henke, from very different perspectives, delineate this psychic interaction—based on Miller's identification of the song of the old woman in the subway station as Richard Strauss's "Allerseelen" (All Souls' Day)—as a secular variation on the Roman Catholic theological concept of the Communion of Saints. Yet, given Woolf's indifference (if not antipathy) toward traditional Christianity, this explanation is not completely convincing. Instead, I would suggest, the phenomenon might, in part, be understood as a manifestation of the contemporary interest in spiritualism, a frequently woman-centered belief system of communication between and among the living and the dead. (Suggestively if, perhaps, figuratively, Erich Auerbach calls the narrative voices in *To the*

Lighthouse "spirits" [532]). It is, moreover, similar to Quakerism (which Woolf knew through her aunt Caroline Emelia Stephen, a Quaker theologian) in many aspects of its belief in private revelation. Numerous and diverse lesbian authors of the fin-de-siècle and modern periods, including Marie Corelli, Henry Handel Richardson, May Sinclair, Radclyffe Hall, H. D., Bryher, and Vita Sackville-West, were adherents of or influenced by spiritualism, theosophy, or other quasireligious forms of personal spiritual revelation. While no work has yet analyzed the particular attraction spiritualism has held for lesbians, I would suggest that the absence of a male priesthood, the lack of a formal hierarchy or organization, and the focus on the individual as the medium of revelation are possible explanations. See Jane Marcus (115–35) on Woolf and Caroline Emelia Stephens; see Suzanne Raitt, *Vita and Virginia* (117–45) on Sackville-West and spiritualism; and Alex Owen on women and spiritualism in general.

41. Suzette Henke (136) cites deleted passages from Woolf's holograph notes and fragments indicating that Peter had been well aware of the homoerotic nature of the relationship between Sally and Clarissa and indicating that the conclusion, although represented as part of Peter's consciousness, is very much a shared moment between Peter and Sally.
42. The resonance of "deadlock" in the phrase "wedlock plot" is intentional on Boone's part (1).
43. Mrs. Ramsay enacts the sort of domestic power play John Stuart Mill observes in *The Subjection of Women*: "An active and energetic mind, if denied liberty, will seek for power; refused the command of itself, it will assert its personality by attempting to control others" (238).
44. The lesbian element of *To the Lighthouse* has been minimized or obscured, particularly in feminist readings, by an insistence on reading the relationship between Mrs. Ramsay and Lily Briscoe as that of mother and daughter. This, no doubt, stems from Woolf having based the Ramsays on her own parents and from Woolf's own life as a rather closeted lesbian artist. As a result, however, the relationship between the two women is often reduced to an indefinite and problematic semi-incestual struggle between generations. I believe that the Freudian concept of the pre-Oedipal concept (on which I comment more in my discussion of Elizabeth Bowen's novels in chapter 3) has been overused by a number of Woolf's critics, often as a means of avoiding a discussion of the lesbianism present in Woolf's novels on its own terms. This is not to say that a Freudian analysis of Woolf is inappropriate (despite the protests of certain lesbian Woolf critics who maintain it is); rather, it strikes me as a questionable means of examining certain homoerotic attachments in Woolf's fictions that are *not* mother-daughter relationships. For an apt lesbian critical response to one such reading of Woolf (i. e., Elizabeth Abel's pre-Oedipal reading of *Mrs. Dalloway*), see Abraham (146–52).

45. Much critical debate has transpired in the past over the merits and demerits of Mrs. Ramsay as an individual. It is outside the scope of my argument to take a partisan stand on this issue; yet I think the limitations of Mrs. Ramsay's erudition and her conventional wisdom are quite obvious. For a history of this debate and a more balanced, historicized view of Mrs. Ramsay's character and marriage, see Jane Lilienfeld (148–69).
46. On the function of the spinster/lesbian figure in Woolf's fictions, see Sybil Oldfield (85–103).
47. This is not to say that Woolf's philosophy of androgyny approaches the condition of a truth acknowledged by either lesbian or heterosexual feminist critics. Surely an overview of what Terry Castle terms "the literature of lesbianism" (as opposed to the more restrictive concept of "lesbian literature") reveals a wide variety of lesbians who are not androgynous and, for that matter, female androgynes who are not lesbian. Additionally, the usefulness and worth of Woolf's concept was the subject of considerable debate among early feminists, particularly in relation to the notion of a rather essentialist view of the "feminine." For a discussion promoting Woolf's ideals, see Heilbrun; for an opposing view, see Elaine Showalter (263–97).
48. On the "significant syntax" with which Woolf narrates Mrs. Ramsay's death, see Heilbrun (161).
49. The extent to which this masking of lesbianism is a either a mode of self-censorship or, in light of the obscenity trial of *The Well of Loneliness*, contemporary with the writing of *Orlando*, a ruse to avoid censorship is, I think, debatable. Hall's novel was hardly the only text of the period to represent lesbianism or, in the terminology Hall accepted from the sexologists, "inversion." The legal objections to *The Well of Loneliness* arose primarily from its special pleading for homosexuality and from the fact that its protagonist, despite her obvious misery, was not suitably punished for her transgression. Subtle representations of lesbianism by Woolf and other authors (see n. 6 above) often went unnoticed, either by the reading public or by the critics. While Woolf was certainly willing to support Hall's defense, she found that this lugubrious and melodramatic novel, as her correspondence with Sackville-West indicates, left much to be desired artistically. Because Woolf surely saw Sackville-West's "androgynous" life as a narrative for which no conventional mode existed, the use of an elaborate fantasy may have been the only feasible means at her disposal, regardless of the disposition of Hall's case. See De Salvo and Leaska (271, 279–81, 293n. 3) and de Grazia (178–93 passim).
50. On the relationship between patriarchal privilege, hypermasculinity, and fascism in *Between the Acts* and Woolf's essays, see Patricia Klindienst Joplin (215–18) and Nora Eisenberg (255).
51. See Sedgwick (*Epistemology* 19–21) on the legal "justification" of violence arising from homosexual panic.

2. *"Are You a Lesbian, Mumbo?": Freudian Discourse, Shame, and Panic in Postwar Prefeminist Fiction*

1. See Hermione Lee (58–61) for a discussion of Bowen's influences in *The Hotel.* See also Patricia Craig (53) on Woolf's response to Bowen's novel.
2. Or, as Allan E. Austin wistfully observes in respect to Bowen's early novels, "when not one of the novels culminates in love, let alone marriage, we have an indication of what the novel of manners has become in the context of this disoriented century" (13). This assumes, of course, that the novel of manners is, generally speaking, a variant of the courtship plot. In fairness to Austin, whom I have taken to task in chapter 1, it should be noted that he discerns the various lines of homoerotic attraction in Bowen's novels, a matter that most of her female/feminist critics have chosen to elide completely (or, in the case of Harriet Blodgett, to demonize). In this sense, his relatively unheralded study of the author's works might be deemed superior to most. Unfortunately, Austin routinely obfuscates these alignments as soon as he reports them, through euphemism and vagueness (e.g., Mrs. Kerr is simply described as "a 'dark' character whose true nature for one reason or another is not readily discernible" (13), without any attempt being made to discern what that "true nature" might be. On the influence of the First World War on this novel, see also Heather Bryant Jordan (23–27).
3. It is hardly accidental that the novel Sydney is seen "enjoying" shortly before this incident is *Jude the Obscure*. Her unreflecting rush toward an ill-matched marriage with a churchman threatens to follow the pattern of Sue Bridehead's marriage to Phillotson and Sue's subsequent "breakdown from an original, incisive intellect to the compulsive reiteration of the principles of conduct of a mid-Victorian marriage manual" in Hardy's novel (Boumelha 141). As the product of a later generation, however, Sydney is, unlike Sue, able to reverse herself and escape a tragic end.
4. Some critics have read this passage as Sydney's refutation of the "cruel and unfair" Mrs. Kerr. The passage itself, taken as a whole, would, I believe, mitigate such a reading; the most marked "cruelty and unfairness" in the text is surely that which plays an essential role, so to speak, in "all that was latently English," whether in James Milton or in other characters. To position Mrs. Kerr as the villainess in this text would seem either a critical distortion or, worse, a demonization of her sexuality. See Austin (20) and, in particular, Blodgett (30–38).
5. Bowen, in fact, had no children and was already married at the time she wrote *The Hotel*. See Hoogland (302–03, 342 n. 24, 25) on these biographical fallacies as well as others of a more pernicious "heterocentric and lesbophobic" variety.
6. It is worth noting that *The Well of Loneliness* was suppressed in Great Britain only; a similar obscenity case in the United States was thrown out of court in

1929. While banned in the author's own country, the novel was a best-seller in most others and was widely translated. For a concise yet detailed account of the legal aspects of the trial and their ramifications, see de Grazia (165–208). For a detailed overview of fictional representations of female "sex variance" in the years following the trial, see Foster (288–328). It is noteworthy how few of the works Foster surveys are by British authors.

7. Baker provides an extremely useful examination of noncanonical British women's writing in the decade and a half following the Second World War and in doing so provides pertinent insights into a body of works almost completely ignored by feminist critics. Of particular interest are her overview of the sociological and cultural conditions informing this literature (1–24) and, for the purposes of this study, her analysis of characterizations of "Odd Women" (66–85). For a thorough sociological study of British women during this period, see Elizabeth Wilson.

8. Townsend Warner does, however, utilize an extended form of triangulation (indeed, quadrangulation and an exchange of men (or, more precisely, *a man*) in *Summer Will Show*. On this configuration, see Castle (66–91).

9. For a highly metaphorical reading of Renault's novel, see Julie Abraham (61–65). Terry Castle, on the other hand sees both *The Friendly Young Ladies* and *Olivia* as narrative examples of the "ghosted" lesbian (41–45).

10. On this developmental transition, the so-called pre-Oedipal phase, see Freud, "Female Sexuality" (*SE* 21:221–46) and "Femininity" (*SE* 22:113–17). While not directly concerned with this phenomenon, Freud's essay "The Psychogenesis of a Case of Homosexuality in a Woman" (*SE* 18:145–72) is also vital to an understanding of his representation of lesbianism as failure and lack.

11. Several of Murdoch's novels of the early and mid-1960s, particularly *An Unofficial Rose* (1962), as well as *The Unicorn* (1963), *The Italian Girl* (1964) and *The Time of the Angels* (1966) have significant lesbian characters and subplots. While I do not examine the novels of Iris Murdoch here under the rubric of lesbian panic—Murdoch's lesbian subplots strike me as almost too singular in their purpose and execution to fit comfortably in this framework—they are certainly deserving of a focused and thoughtful lesbian critique.

12. An exception is Nina Auerbach's analysis of *The Prime of Miss Jean Brodie* in *Communities of Women* (167–91). Both Velma Bourgeois Richmond (23) and David Lodge acknowledge the possibility of a lesbian interpretation of the protagonist's motivations, but subsequently leave the suggestion unexamined. Lodge, for instance, offers an alternative suggestion that Jean Brodie's actions might be "a sublimation of . . . the experience of menopause, which would be particularly traumatic for a spinster, and would explain many of the vagaries of her behaviour," but goes on to argue that a "religious interpretation has the most force" (168). A notable (and isolated) lesbian commentary on *The Golden Notebook* comes from Adrienne Rich, who quoted Lessing's protagonist's

hypothesis on the origin of lesbianism as the epigraph to her groundbreaking essay "Compulsory Heterosexuality and Lesbian Existence." For Rich's further comments on the text, see Bulkin (181–82).

13. A parodic reductum ad absurdio of such a female reversal of Freud's paradigm is the basis of Fay Weldon's relatively obscure first novel, *The Fat Woman's Joke.* While there is no overt lesbianism in the narrative, virtually all of the characters, both male and female, all of whom are hell-bent on the self-expression of their heterosexuality with one another, constantly cite lesbianism as the motivation of virtually every action on the part of the various female characters.
14. Some critics have cited parallels between *The Prime of Miss Jean Brodie* and an earlier Scottish novel, James Hogg's *Private Memoirs and Confessions of a Justified Sinner*, particularly in their representation of the corrupting relationship between a pernicious Calvinist pedagogue and a devoted student. As I discuss in the following chapter—in relation to Emma Tennant's *The Bad Sister*, a novel pointedly based on Hogg's—Eve Kosofsky Sedgwick has identified both *Confessions of a Justified Sinner* and Robert Lewis Stevenson's *The Strange Case of Dr. Jekyll and Mr. Hyde* (to which both *The Prime of Miss Jean Brodie* and Tennant's *Two Women of London* have been compared) as novels of male homosexual panic. While thoroughly eliding the homoerotic elements of the works, Trevor Royle (154–57) offers a useful overview of the common grounding in Scottish Calvinist history and culture of the narratives by Hogg, Stevenson, and Spark.
15. Lesbian girlhood as an entity unto itself has received little critical or analytical attention to date. Teresa de Lauretis's recent and exhaustive study, *The Practice of Love*, which seeks to move beyond Freudian and Lacanian suppositions about what constitutes lesbianism, perversion, and, indeed, "normalcy," is a most welcome and, I believe, revolutionary initial step toward an understanding of this phenomenon.
16. For other critical interpretations of the doppelgänger relationship between Jean Brodie and Sandy, see, in particular, Joseph Hynes (69–80); see also Royle (159–61) and Richmond (24–26).
17. Ironically, filmmakers, along with certain critics, have found it more expedient to interpret Spark's narrative along political lines while eliding its sexual (or, more precisely, the nonheterosexual) elements. A case in point is the 1969 film version, which brought actress Maggie Smith an Academy Award for her portrayal of its protagonist. In this highly reductive adaptation, Jean Brodie is primarily a self-deluded fascist ideologue whose behavior could be remedied by a [hetero]sexual awakening (an idea reemphasized by Rod McKuen's theme song), an experience that her students (particularly Sandy) are quite capable of achieving while she, to her own perdition, does not. As such, the struggle between Sandy and Miss Brodie becomes one of the generation gap more than anything else, which, given the political and cultural climate of the late 1960s,

is hardly surprising. Nor is it surprising in this context that Sandy's conversion and vocation are completely elided.

18. See, in particular, Lodge (164–73). Parallels can be drawn between Sandy's conversion and that of Nicholas Farringdon in Spark's previous novel, *The Girls of Slender Means*. A relatively tortured and profoundly sensitive character of uncertain sexual orientation, Nicholas becomes, after a particularly traumatic experience, a Roman Catholic missionary priest who is eventually martyred. For Sandy and Nicholas, the asexual life of a Catholic religious, with the structures of permanently vowed celibacy as a sign of devotion and dedication, provides a useful if extreme means of resolving the conflicts of their socially or personally unacceptable sexuality. See Alan Massie (101–05) for a comparison of these two characters.
19. See Norman Page (40–42), Lodge (155–58), Richmond (17–18).
20. The sheer volume of critical commentary on *The Golden Notebook* obviates any attempt to categorize or enumerate individual examples of such criticism, nor would such an attempt be particularly meaningful in terms of this study. Nevertheless, several texts are useful in presenting a feminist view and, in general, a consideration of the novel's structure as a means of articulating the protagonist's sexual and psychological experience. These include Betsy Draine (69–88), Gayle Greene (105–29), Molly Hite (55–102), Roberta Rubenstein (71–112), Mary Ann Singleton (83–130), and Claire Sprague (65–84). Additionally, N. Katherine Hayles (236–64) offers a provocative examination of the novel's form through the application of chaos theory.
21. For a thoughtful and deeply considered discussion of what *The Golden Notebook* might mean to the individual female reader, particularly in the context of the early 1960s, see Jean McCrindle (43–56).
22. See, for example, Lorna Sage (*Doris Lessing*, 51–52), Claire Sprague (69–71).
23. This is not to say that there is any consensus among critics as to which is the "central" or, for that matter, the "true" text or ending. N. Katherine Hayles, taking an approach à la Baudrillard, proposes that the ending of "Free Women" is a simulacrum, "a copy that has no original" in which "reality and our representations of it have collapsed into the same space" (263, 264). While I would suggest that this is even more so the case with the alternate ending offered by "The Golden Notebook," Hayles's point is well taken. Indeed, the disappearance of reality per se, if not the absolute collapse of reality and representations thereof into one another, might be said to be a common feature of the narrative strategies of lesbian panic. More problematic, I think, are the critiques that privilege "The Golden Notebook" over "Free Women 5" (in which "Molly gets married and Anna has an affair" [553]). These generally cite the transformative power in the movement from writer's block to madness to creativity by means of [hetero]sexual healing and, as such, celebrate the woman-as-artist thematic ploy frequent in earlier feminist criticism. This apotheosis of the surrealistic "The

Golden Notebook" over the realistic "Free Women 5" is, perhaps, understandable, given the apparent capitulation on the part of both Anna and Molly to the pressures of the patriarchy that inform the conclusion. At the same time such critiques, by rendering "Free Women" a secondary text, tend to reduce the relationship between Anna and Molly to an artistic "secret sharer"/"Madwoman in the Attic" variation on the Jungian notion of the "shadow" and thus, by making Molly a mere projection of Anna's divided self-consciousness, effectively obviate the rather obvious homoerotic connection between the two. (See, for example, Sprague [66–73]).

24. See Craig (131–37), Lee (206), and Sullivan (142–49). Blodgett, while addressing *The Little Girls* at length, finally surmises that it "is not a major novel. A shorter tale promising less would have been better fiction" (74). Phyllis Lassner, by contrast, refutes these novels by elision, devoting no more than a few sentences to either in her study (24, 139–40, 162–63).
25. *The Little Girls*, as many critics have noted, is replete with allusions to Shakespeare's play and a host of other sources. See Austin (62–64), Kenney (89–92), Lee (204). Additionally, Blodgett (68–74) provides an exhaustive examination of allusions and archetypes in the novel.
26. I am greatly indebted to Hoogland's exhaustive discussion of *Eva Trout* (206–290), the only study to date that analyzes the novel from a lesbian perspective. My basic argument, however, differs greatly from hers, which focuses in part on the quest for the absent mother and is deeply concerned with the Freudian female pre-Oedipal complex. While I applaud Hoogland's efforts, I must ultimately conclude that the use of the latter, as I have argued regarding its use in analyzing Woolf's novels, tends to be a self-defeating strategy that erases the story of lesbianism at the heart of these texts, and I must ultimately agree with Teresa de Lauretis that lesbian critics must resist the desire to "keep on playing in the pre-Oedipal sandbox" (31). On the problematics of lesbian pre-Oedipal interpretation, see de Lauretis (81–148).
27. See Freud (*SE* 21:152–58). For a comprehensive overview of female fetishism, see Gamman and Makinen; on the peculiarly lesbian mode of fetishism, see De Lauretis (226–49).
28. On the "mannish lesbian," see Esther Newton (557–75) and Teresa de Lauretis (203–53).
29. For a provocative and exhaustive overview of this Freudian type in modernist literature, see Marcia Ian.
30. See, for example Lee (205–06) and Craig (135). See also Hoogland (209–12) for an analysis of and response to this criticism.
31. In so defining *Eva Trout*, I am distinguishing it from even earlier lesbian postmodern texts such as Brigid Brophy's *The King of a Rainy Country* and Maureen Duffy's *The Microcosm*, novels that I discuss in the subsequent chapter. While Brophy and Duffy employ relatively rudimentary postmodern

modalities in an attempt to create narratives that move beyond the limitations of the lesbian panic model, Bowen's novel is, I propose, one of the first to present lesbian panic as the central narrative in a postmodern text.

32. While *A Friend from England* is the most intensively homoerotic of Brookner's novels, this is not to say that female/female obsession is absent from her other works. As John Skinner observes in his analysis of *A Friend from England*, the protagonist's constant criticisms of the object of her interest "echo those of various Brookner protagonists . . . towards women they regard as spoilt, parasitic or childishly irresponsible" (114). The negativity of Brookner's characters' perceptions of other women functions, I would suggest, as a means of their disavowing their erotic attraction.
33. Michiko Kakutani (16) argues that such self-deception on the part of the unreliable narrator is precisely what this novel is about.
34. Brookner herself states her protagonists "obey all nineteenth-century rules of morality and duty and seriousness, dedication and devotion without realising that these are important but anachronistic qualities." Their downfalls, she adds, result from their assumption about the extent of their options in life, a mistake she also attributes to most of her peers: "The choice is never unlimited, that's the twentieth-century mistake, whereas the nineteenth century was more realistic. You can do this *or* that, not an unlimited number of things. . . . I find the moral position of many modern novelists ridiculous, as if you could start editing your life halfway through—and doing something for which you're unprepared" (Kenyon 20–21). This characteristically indirect argument may not adequately describe the crises confronted—or avoided—by Rachel Kennedy, but it does demonstrate Brookner's own antipathy toward postmodernism.

3. *"The Proper Name for Things": The Lesbian in Postmodern Women's Fiction*

1. In her lucid overview *Practising Postmodernism/Reading Modernism*, Patricia Waugh discusses the shifting definitions of "Postmodernism" (3–7) as well as the difficulties inherent in interpreting postmodernism as an historical period (37–48).
2. See Hite, *The Other Side of the Story*; and Waugh, *Feminine Fictions: Revisiting the Postmodern* and *Practising Postmodernism*. For a more "traditional" examination of contemporary women's narrative that finds little congruence between postmodernism and feminism (and that summarily—and troublingly, I feel—dismisses writers such as Bainbridge as "not feminist" [25]), see Gayle Greene. A good if incomplete overview of women's writing since the 1940s may be found in Lorna Sage.
3. See *Feminine Fictions* (126–27, 168–78). I am basically in agreement with Waugh's categorizations, differing with her only in the case of Muriel Spark,

primarily for reasons of Spark's sensibilities regarding sexuality, as I discuss in the previous chapter and in the following paragraph.

4. For an idea of the vast array of literary and cultural entities that might be deemed examples of "lesbian postmodernity," see the various essays in Laura Doan, ed., *The Lesbian Postmodern*.
5. See Jeffrey Weeks (232–48).
6. The characters' shared affinity for the poetry of Charles Baudelaire (the title of the novel is taken from "Je suis comme le roi d'un pays pluvieux" in *Les fleurs du mal*) is in itself a tacit allusion to one of the creators of the image of the "decadent" lesbian in nineteenth-century French literature. (See Jeannette Foster [76–78, 104–114 passim] and Lillian Faderman [*Surpassing the Love of Men*, 268–73].) Given this extreme model, homosexuality, particularly lesbianism, becomes both highly attractive and completely forbidding to Brophy's protagonists, especially to Neale, who imagines the diva Helena Buchan as "gloriously bi-sexual . . . with three concubines and four lovers" (221).
7. It is only with critical hindsight that we are able to see Brophy's novel as an early postmodern text. Her critics in the mid-1950s, quite expectedly, faulted this technique as an example of her artistic immaturity. Charles J. Rolo, for example, found the novel "as a whole . . . far from being a success: it is somewhat disjointed, lacking in coherence, and at times not sufficiently convincing" (89). Curiously, Rolo, who found the scenes with Finkelheim "comedy of the choicest order," failed to see (or, at least, to report) the homosexual/lesbian subtext.
8. Some notable examples of the homoerotic girls' school novel are Colette's *Claudine à l'école*, Henry Handel Richardson's *The Getting of Wisdom*, Dorothy (Olivia) Strachey's *Olivia*, and Christa Winsloe's *The Child Manuela*. Certain "women's college" novels, such as Gertrude Stein's *Fernhurst*, can be seen as an extension of this subgenre. Brophy subsequently contributed a Firbankian parodic novel to this tradition; *The Finishing Touch*, which might be deemed the comic version of the tragic *Olivia*, presents a sexually voracious lesbian headmistress who, with the cooperation of her equally jaded students, manages to carry on her school—and her *affaires*—with relative impunity.
9. See Terry Castle (43n.) for a discussion of this scene as an example of cross-dressed masquerade as a convention in the homoerotic girls' school novel.
10. See Castle (59).
11. The use of the French "impuissant," which can be translated as "powerless" or "impotent" (in a sexual sense), recalls Baudelaire's poem. Early in the novel, Neale, styling himself the "king of a rainy country," quotes a portion of the original in French to Susan : "I only know: Je suis comme le roi d'un pays pluvieux, Riche mais impuissant." (24) in response to her inquiry as to whether he is withholding something from her. Given his apparent latent homosexuality, which he seems unwilling to reveal or act upon, "impuissant" takes on the con-

notation of powerlessness, while his ongoing nonsexual relationship with Susan also suggests impotence. Conversely, François, who admits his homosexuality, can assert that he is not "impuissant" in either sense and that one condition is not analogous with the other.

12. Mozart's opera, which is based on the second play of Beaumarchais's Figaro trilogy, does not relate the further and unfortunate adventures of Cherubino. In the third play, *La mère coupable* (The Guilty Mother), Cherubino is killed in military service and the countess gives birth to his posthumous child, indicating that the page has, in fact, accomplished Neale's desires. Brophy, however, follows Mozart in her scenario; thus Neale does not die but must, eventually, find a different role to play. Simultaneously, through Neale's utterly bootless attempt at heterosexual aggression, Brophy takes issue, as she does in *Mozart the Dramatist*, with Kierkegaard's observation that Cherubino is "Don Giovanni in youth" (105), an issue Brophy subsequently explores in her novel *The Snow Ball.*
13. According to Beaumarchais, "this part can only be played . . . by a young and very pretty woman" (222). On the lesbian valences of this and other cross-dressed opera roles, see Elizabeth Wood (27–66) and Margaret Reynolds ("Ruggiero's Distractions" 132–51); on the performance of gender that is mistaken for reality, see Judith Butler (24–25).
14. Brophy is clearly aware of the slippage between representations of mother-daughter bonds and those of homosocial/homoerotic affection. She writes in *Mozart the Dramatist* that, under the conditions of noblesse oblige, "Susanna is, so to speak, the Countess's proletarian daughter"; she adds, however, that "they decline to be trapped in either the social conventions or the code of inverted chivalry. . . . It is the strength of their affection for one another which gives the opera its rarity and touchingness. At the same time, it is Susanna's and the Countess's affection which makes the opera a revolutionary document" (113). Brophy further compares the Countess and Susanna with the quasilesbian prototypes Chloe and Olivia ("Sometimes women do like women") in Virginia Woolf's *A Room of One's Own*: "In fact, it was not the first time [women liked women in literature]. There is no doubt that Susanna and the Countess like one another" (113). One might add that the sexually ambiguous Cherubino provides the erotic linkage between the two.
15. Most of these writings are reprinted in Brophy's *Don't Never Forget: Collected Views and Reviews.*
16. On the relationship between consumer capitalism and cultural expressions of sexuality, see Judith Williamson, *Consuming Passions.* Other than *The Microcosm*, the most notable among 1960s British novels that utilize stylistic or formal experimentation in their representation of lesbianism is Ann Quin's *Three.* The more common form of representing lesbianism in women's writing of the period, however, was the grubby realism that informs Shena Mackay's *The*

Music Upstairs and Lynne Reid Banks's *The L-Shaped Room*. On Ann Quin's fictions see Margaret Crosland (192–97).

17. In her 1988 afterword to the Virago edition, Duffy discloses that *The Microcosm* began not as a novel but rather as a documentary "treatment of female homosexuality which would delineate the state of the heart in the early sixties when we were presumably in the middle of a sexual revolution towards a more open society." To this end, Duffy tape-recorded interviews with a cross-section of the patrons of The Gateways, a well-known London lesbian bar. When informed that "no reputable [publishing] house would commission me to write a non-fiction book on such a risky subject" (289), Duffy followed her agent's suggestion that her research serve as the basis of a work of fiction. On the ethos and clientele of The Gateways, as well as many other insights into lesbian life in 1960s Britain, see Val Wilmer (162–66, 170–73).
18. For historical overviews of butch/femme roles, see Lillian Faderman (*Odd Girls* 159–87), Joan Nestle (100–09), Esther Newton (281–93); for theoretical perspectives on these gender constructs, see Sue-Ellen Case (294–306), Judith Butler (122–24), and Colleen Lamos (85–103).
19. Barbara Grier, writing under the pseudonym "Gene Damon," was from 1966 to 1972 the poetry and fiction editor of *The Ladder*, the publication of the Daughters of Bilitis, an organization of lesbians whose primary goals included mainstream acceptance of homosexuality through lesbian adoption of middle-class values. As such, her initial enthusiasm for *The Microcosm*, which ultimately eschews the limits of separatist, subcultural isolationism, is understandable. Her later views on Duffy are, I believe, more a reflection of political change than of literary judgment. Subsequent to the demise of *The Ladder*, Grier became one of the founders of Naiad Press, one of the most prolific publishers of lesbian popular fiction. On the Daughters of Bilitis see Faderman, *Surpassing the Love of Men* (377–91) and *Odd Girls* (148–50, 190–93).
20. Some of the so-called "pulps," however, particularly those written by lesbians, managed to rise above these limitations. Only recently have lesbian scholars begun to assess their significance in the creation of lesbian popular culture. See Faderman, *Odd Girls* (146–48); Diane Hamer (47–75); and Angela Weir and Elizabeth Wilson (95–114).
21. Bonnie Zimmerman examines lesbian-feminist popular fiction as bildungsroman in "Exiting from the Patriarchy" (244–57) and offers a comprehensive historical analysis of the subgenre in *The Safe Sea of Women*, a work whose title, taken from June Arnold's novel *Sister Gin* (xiii), stands in ironic contradistinction to Duffy's image of the tidepool in *The Microcosm*. "Lesbian Nation" is the term Jill Johnston gave to the ideal of a utopian, separatist society replete with an newly invented mythology and free from the influence and presence of men, an ideal numerous lesbians in the United States, Great Britain, and Europe attempted to achieve during the 1970s by "dropping out" of society in

the manner of the 1960s hippies. See Johnston, Zimmerman, *The Safe Sea of Women* (121–26), and Faderman, *Odd Girls* (215–45)

22. Stimpson's categorization of *Lover* as a "modernist" text derives in part from her comparison of Harris's novel with those of Djuna Barnes but stands without elaboration and remains, I believe, somewhat problematic. This assessment, dating from 1982, does, however, predate any widespread acknowledgment on the part of feminist critics that postmodernism and feminism could coexist. For a later consideration of this issue, see Stimpson (184–89).
23. For a painfully revealing account of the personal and ideological machinations of the early lesbian feminist publishing business—a realm in which the personal and the political were often indistinguishably merged—see Bertha Harris's introduction to the 1993 New York University Press reprint of *Lover* (xvii-lxxviii).
24. On the extent to which *Change* is "a very exactly autobiographical novel," see Rachel Gould (18).
25. See, for example, Lyndie Brimstone's otherwise excellent "Keepers of History" (23–46).
26. On male homosexuality and homosexual panic as an originary factor and ongoing influence in the Gothic, see George E. Haggerty, "Literature and Homosexuality in the Late Eighteenth Century," and "The Gothic Novel, 1764–1824"; and Sedgwick, *Between Men* (83–117). On the conventions of the female Gothic and their relation to illicit [hetero]sexual desire, see Ann Ronald (176–86); Nina da Vinci Nichols (187–206); and Cynthia Griffin Wolff (207–23). See also Elizabeth MacAndrews's thorough study of the Gothic tradition. While the figure of the vampire *qua* lesbian has been relatively insignificant in canonical or semicanonical literature, this character has surely loomed large in film; see Andrea Weiss (84–108).
27. Quoted on the back dust jacket cover of the first U.S. edition of *Harriet Said*, published by George Braziller (New York, 1973). The "famous case" to which Symons alludes is the murder of Honora Parker by two fifteen-year-old girls, her daughter Pauline and her daughter's friend Juliet Hulme (who, as was recently revealed, is now Anne Perry, the noted British murder mystery writer). The case has been the focus of much renewed interest as the result of Peter Jackson's 1994 film *Heavenly Creatures*, which was based on the diary kept by the girls in the months prior to the slaying. In light of the film, it is worth noting the extent to which Bainbridge actually deemphasizes by elision the homoerotic aspects of the girls' relationship—in the film Pauline Parker is shown being subjected to psychiatric testing and treatment for demonstrating lesbian tendencies—while at the same time closely paralleling the original, factual story. Rather than fault Bainbridge for this elision, one must instead attempt to comprehend just how "unspeakable" lesbianism was at the time of its composition, so much so that it could not be represented outright even in her

"indecent" novel. For a lesbian analysis of the Parker-Hulme case, see Glamuzina and Laurie.

28. The narrator is only once called by any name in the novel. When Harriet espies Peter Biggs at the fairgrounds the two girls are visiting, she shouts to her friend, "He's here, Sister Ann" (52). This appellation recalls the song "Here we go again Sister Jane" (22) that the narrator earlier sings to herself and, given the theatrical quality of both "namings," probably does not indicate the name of the narrator. Rather, Harriet calling the narrator "Sister Ann" while announcing Mr. Biggs's approach may be a tacit allusion to the character by that name in the English fairy tale known as "Mr. Fox," a violent variation on the Bluebeard story and the basis for Fay Weldon's novel *Words of Advice*. On the original fairy tale, see Maureen Duffy (*Erotic World of Faery*, 376).
29. Hence, despite their having internalized the concept of lesbianism and the social stigma attached thereunto, the word "lesbian" is not included in the girls' vocabulary, just as it does not appear in the works of D. H. Lawrence. In her flirtations with locally interned Italian prisoners of war and her narrative of an adventure with a young man in Wales, Harriet presents herself as the heroine of an ersatz version of Lawrence's *The Virgin and the Gipsy*; the triangulation of the two girls and the decrepit, aging Peter Biggs might be seen as a grotesque, parodic inversion of Lawrence's own novella of lesbian panic. For a well-considered discussion of the problematic representation of homoerotic desire in Lawrence's fictions, see Vincent P. Pecora (718–25 passim).
30. See Sedgwick, *Between Men* (90–96).
31. I am aware that Fredric Jameson makes a particular distinction between parody and pastiche in postmodern cultural contexts, positing that pastiche is "a neutral practice of . . . mimicry, without any of parody's ulterior motives, amputated of the satiric impulse, devoid of laughter and of any conviction that alongside the abnormal tongue you have momentarily borrowed, some healthy linguistic normality still exists. Pastiche is thus blank parody, a statue with blind eyeballs" (17). I am also aware that other critics do not necessarily draw such fine distinctions between the two. Indeed, in the novels of Emma Tennant, such distinctions may be ultimately beside the point. Tennant frequently blurs categorizations in her texts, indulging at times in the sort of stylistic patchwork characteristic of the musical *pasticcio* (a word derived from the Italian for "pie") that seems to celebrate what it imitates while simultaneously satirizing it. At other times, often within the same text, the borrowing is, as I later discuss, quite apparently complicit in what it poses itself to critique. Whether or not Tennant's parody is the "neutral practice" of pastiche, then, is ultimately a matter of critical interpretation: to some poststructuralist critics, this indefiniteness might be seen as a matter of faulty execution (for which Tennant has often, at times justly, been taken to task), while to some feminist critics it might provide evidence of her subversive intent. It is, at any rate, an

issue with which Tennant herself seems little concerned. For Tennant's own views on her works, see Kenyon (*Women Writers Talk*, 175–87). For a discussion of postmodernism and various parodic modes (i.e., collage, pastiche, burlesque, and parody) in the writings of contemporary British female novelists (not including Tennant), see Carol McGuirk (944–54). I thank Colleen Lamos for calling my attention to this matter.

32. See Showalter (105–18) for an analysis of homosexual panic in Stevenson's *The Strange Case of Dr. Jekyll and Mr. Hyde*. Showalter, who deems *Two Women of London* a "brilliant feminist version" of the original, also offers a discussion of Tennant's novel (124–25). See also Sedgwick on Stevenson (*Epistemology* 188–89).
33. See Julia Kristeva (19–106).
34. In her analysis of the group of Gothics that she identifies as "embodying strongly homophobic mechanisms," which includes *The Confessions of a Justified Sinner*, Sedgwick offers a caveat: "This is not to say that either the authors . . . or the overall cultural effects of the novels, were necessarily homophobic" (92), a sentiment that, as I subsequently detail, I share regarding Emma Tennant.
35. To deem Tennant homophobic also overlooks the function of lesbianism in her other novels. In *The Adventures of Robina*, for example, her Moll Flanders-like protagonist reflects (with faux eighteenth-century orthography) that had she followed her early impulses to love another woman: "I might have spared many hours of suffering; and many Crimes, indeed, which were committed for Men or to Spite them, when the love of a *Madonna* was all I truly sought in my Existence" (115). In *Sisters and Strangers*, Tennant's sardonic and intertextual "seven ages of woman" tale, moreover, the last and, presumably, more advanced stages in a woman's life are lesbian. It is worth noting that while writing *The Bad Sister* Tennant reviewed *Sita*, Kate Millett's autobiographical novel of psychological disintegration and abjection in the course of a lesbian relationship. Tennant, who had admired Millett's earlier feminist work, wondered, "What has come over Ms. Millett, brave civil rights champion and . . . a warm and intelligent person? Is this what happens to people when they have an unhappy love affair? Is this what she's trying to tell us? Or is it important for her that her followers, those women who are still trying desperately to hold the aircraft in the air, should understand that their goddess has feet of clay? Certainly she's chosen a dicey moment to tell us that she feels old and finished." (Lambert 711–12). This reaction to Millett, who chose to "drop out" from feminist activism and retreat to a lesbian separatist commune, is, I believe quite palpable in Tennant's critique of separatism as paranoid delusion in *The Bad Sister* and is conceivably compounded by the quasiterroristic tactics adopted by certain British radical lesbian separatists over the past two decades, activities that, until recently, relatively few lesbian critics have been willing to question or criticize openly (see Andermahr [149, 151–52n and passim]). Thus Palmer, writing from a self-proclaimed "radical feminist" position (*Contemporary Women's*

Fiction, 168), is also caught up in Waugh's "first lesson of Postmodernism" in her own implication of that which she critiques.

36. I examine these characters at length in "'Women Like Us Must Learn to Stick Together': Lesbians in the Novels of Fay Weldon," forthcoming in *British Women Writing Fiction*, ed. Abby H. P. Werlock (Tuscaloosa: University of Alabama Press, 1997).
37. See, for example, Palmer, *Contemporary Women's Fiction* (37–38, 73–75, 99, 101–102), and *Plotting Change* (59–62); Harriet Blodgett (754–56 passim).
38. "Glaston," Hardy's fictive Glastonbury, and the Mendip Hills serve as settings not only in *The Heart of the Country* but also in "A Trampwoman's Tragedy," which F. B. Pinion calls one of Hardy's "most sensational tales" (122). The narrative poem, which involves a transient woman, the uncertain paternity of her child, the murder of "the other man," and the execution of her lover, has echoes in Weldon's own "Wessex" novels. See Hardy, *Collected Poems* (182–85); and Lea (295–303).
39. Weldon has, in her career as a screenwriter, adapted a number of canonical novels for British television. Additionally, she has written a stage version of Hardy's *Tess of the d'Urbervilles*. See K. G. Wright (67–69).
40. On the creation and ethos of the British welfare state, see also Peter Hennessy (119–82) and Kenneth O. Morgan (36–42, 61–65, 173–74, 424–28).
41. In this manner Sonia resembles Ruth Patchett in Weldon's *The Life and Loves of a She-Devil*. See my article, "A Comic Turn, Turned Serious" (255–57). On the traditional deployment of these character types, see Northrop Frye (148–49, 172–76, 226–32)
42. Various incidents in *The Heart of the Country* resonate to Hardy's *The Mayor of Casterbridge*. For example, Sonia's curse echoes the curse the envious (and by that time downwardly mobile) Michael Henchard brings down on Donald Farfrae, just as the public exposition of Natalie's adulterous relationship with Angus during the fatal progress of the float echoes *Casterbridge*'s "skimmity-ride"—albeit to a far different end. Hardy, moreover, provides some of the more interesting examples of lesbian panic in the male-authored Victorian novel. The most notable occurs in his first novel, *Desperate Remedies*, in which Cynthia, an aging grande dame, befriends a guileless younger woman, also named Cynthia, whose father was once the older woman's lover. Multiple triangulations occur in this plot, including the older woman's attempt to forge an erotic bond between her illegitimate son and the younger woman. Included in the narrative is a particularly odd encounter—in bed—between the two women that begs for an in-depth Freudian interpretation. Also of note are the dynamics of the relationships between and among women in both *A Laodicean* and *The Woodlanders*, the latter of which also involves an elaborate exchange of men. On Hardy's representations of women's lives, see Penny Boumelha, Rosemarie Morgan, and the various essays in Margaret R. Higonnet, ed.

43. For a cogent and concise discussion of the feminist "problem" with postmodernism, particularly in reference to Winterson's novels, see Doan (139–41). See also n. 2, above.
44. See Castle (59).
45. For a veritable syllabus of Winterson's offenses against the tenets of radical lesbianism—which range from publishing with a mainstream (hence patriarchal) publisher to insensitivity to members of the working class (despite their homophobia) in *Oranges Are Not the Only Fruit*—see Rebecca O'Rourke.

WORKS CITED

Abbott, Reginald. "What Miss Kilman's Petticoat Means: Virginia Woolf, Shopping, and Spectacle." *Modern Fiction Studies* 38.1 (1992): 193–216.

Abel, Elizabeth. "Narrative Structure(s) and Female Development: The Case of *Mrs. Dalloway*." *The Voyage In: Fictions of Female Development*. Ed. Elizabeth Abel, Marianne Hirsch, and Elizabeth Langland. Hanover: University Press of New England, 1983, 161–85.

———. *Virginia Woolf and the Fictions of Psychoanalysis*. Chicago: University of Chicago Press, 1989.

Abraham, Julie. *Are Girls Necessary?: Lesbian Writing and Modern Histories*. New York: Routledge, 1996.

Andermahr, Sonya. "The Politics of Separatism and Lesbian Utopian Fiction." *New Lesbian Criticism: Literary and Cultural Readings*. Ed. Sally Munt. New York: Columbia University Press, 1992, 133–152.

Auerbach, Erich. *Mimesis: The Representation of Reality in Western Literature*. Trans. Willard R. Trask. Princeton: Princeton University Press, 1953.

Auerbach, Nina. *Communities of Women: An Idea in Fiction*. Cambridge: Harvard University Press, 1978.

———. *Ellen Terry: Player in her Time*. New York: Norton, 1987.

Austen, Jane. *Northanger Abbey*. The Oxford Illustrated Jane Austen 5. Oxford: Oxford University Press, 1965.

Austin, Allen E. *Elizabeth Bowen*. Rev. Ed. Boston: Twayne, 1989.

Bainbridge, Beryl. *The Bottle Factory Outing. Beryl Bainbridge Omnibus*. London: Duckworth, 1989, 301–475.

———. *Harriet Said. Beryl Bainbridge Omnibus*. London: Duckworth, 1989, 7–152.

Baker, Niamh. *Happily Ever After?: Women's Fiction in Postwar Britain 1945–60*. New York: St. Martin's, 1989.

Bakhtin, M. M. *The Dialogic Imagination: Four Essays*. Trans. Caryl Emerson and Michael Holmquist. Austin: University of Texas Press, 1981.

Banks, Lynn Reid. *The L-Shaped Room*. London: Chatto, 1960.

Barnes, Djuna. *Nightwood*. New York: New Directions, 1960.

Barr, Marleen S. *Feminist Fabulation*. Iowa City: University of Iowa Press, 1992.

Barreca, Regina. *Untamed and Unabashed: Essays on Women and Humor in British Literature*. Detroit: Wayne State University Press, 1994.

Barthes, Roland. *Writing Degree Zero*. Trans. Annette Lavers and Colin Smith. New York: Hill and Wang, 1968.

Baudelaire, Charles. *The Flowers of Evil and Spleen*. Trans. William H. Crosby. Brockport, N.Y.: B O A Editions, 1991.

Bazin, Nancy Topping. *Virginia Woolf and the Androgynous Vision*. New Brunswick: Rutgers University Press, 1973.

Beaumarchais, Pierre-Augustin Caron de. *The Barber of Seville and The Marriage of Figaro*. Trans. John Wood. Harmondsworth: Penguin, 1964.

Bennett, Paula. "Critical Clitoridectomy: Female Sexual Imagery and Feminist Psychoanalytic Theory." *Signs* 18 (1993): 235–59.

Blodgett, Harriet. "Fay Weldon." *British Novelists Since 1960*. Ed. Jay L. Halio. Detroit: Gale, 1983, 750–59.

———. *Patterns of Reality: Elizabeth Bowen's Novels*. The Hague: Mouton, 1975.

Bold, Alan. *Muriel Spark*. London: Methuen, 1986.

Boone, Joseph Allen. *Tradition Counter Tradition: Love and the Form of Fiction*. Chicago: University of Chicago Press, 1987.

Boumelha, Penny. *Thomas Hardy and Women: Sexual Ideology and Narrative Form*. Madison: University of Wisconsin Press, 1985.

Bowen, Elizabeth. *The Heat of the Day*. Harmondsworth: Penguin, 1962.

———. *The Hotel*. Harmondsworth: Penguin, 1984.

———. *The Last September*. Harmondsworth, Penguin, 1987.

———. *The Little Girls*. Harmondsworth: Penguin, 1982.

Briggs, Asa. *A Social History of England*. Harmondsworth: Penguin, 1985.

Brimstone, Lyndie. " 'Keepers of History': The Novels of Maureen Duffy." *Lesbian and Gay Writing: An Anthology of Critical Essays*. Ed. Mark Lilly. London: Macmillan, 1990.

———. "Towards a New Cartography: Radclyffe Hall, Virginia Woolf and the Working of Common Land." *What Lesbians Do in Books*. Ed. Elaine Hobby and Chris White. London: The Women's Press, 1991.

Brontë, Charlotte. *Jane Eyre*. New York: Norton, 1987.

Brookner, Anita. *A Friend from England.* New York: Pantheon, 1987.

Brophy, Brigid. *Don't Never Forget: Collected Views and Reviews.* New York: Holt, 1966.

———. *The Finishing Touch.* London: Gay Men's Press, 1987.

———. *The King of a Rainy Country.* London: Virago, 1990.

———. *Mozart the Dramatist: The Value of His Operas to Him, to His Age, and to Us.* Rev. ed. London: Libris, 1988.

———. *"The Snow Ball" and "The Snow Ball and The Finishing Touch".* Cleveland: World, 1964.

Brown, Wendy. "Feminist Hesitations, Postmodern Exposure." *differences* 3 (1991): 63–84.

Bulkin, Elly. "An Interview with Adrienne Rich." *Critical Essays on Doris Lessing.* Ed. Claire Sprague and Virginia Tiger. Boston: G. K. Hall, 1986, 181–82.

Butler, Judith. *Gender Trouble: Feminism and the Subversion of Identity.* New York: Routledge, 1990.

Case, Sue-Ellen. "Toward a Butch-Femme Aesthetic." *The Lesbian and Gay Studies Reader.* Ed. Henry Abelove, Michèle Aina Barale, and David M. Halperin. New York: Routledge, 1993.

Castle, Terry. *The Apparitional Lesbian: Female Homosexuality and Modern Culture.* New York: Columbia University Press, 1993.

Caughie, Pamela L. *Virginia Woolf and Postmodernism: Literature in Quest and Question of Itself.* Urbana: University of Illinois Press, 1991.

Colette, [Sidonie Gabrielle]. *Claudine à l'école.* Paris: A. Michel, 1978.

Compton-Burnett, Ivy. *More Women Than Men.* London: Eyre and Spottiswoode, 1951,

Cook, Blanche Wiesen. " 'Women Alone Stir My Imagination': Lesbianism and the Cultural Tradition." *Signs* 4 (1978–79): 718–39.

Craig, Patricia. *Elizabeth Bowen.* Harmondsworth: Penguin, 1986.

Cramer, Patricia. "Notes from Underground: Lesbian Ritual in the Writings of Virginia Woolf." *Virginia Woolf Miscellanies: Proceedings of the First Annual Conference on Virginia Woolf.* Ed. Mark Hussey and Vara Neverow-Turk. New York: Pace University Press, 1992.

Crosland, Margaret. *Beyond the Lighthouse: English Women Novelists in the Twentieth Century.* New York: Taplinger, 1981.

De Grazia, Edward. *Girls Lean Back Everywhere: The Law of Obscenity and the Assault on Genius.* New York: Vintage, 1993.

De Lauretis, Teresa. *The Practice of Love: Lesbian Sexuality and Perverse Desire.* Bloomington: Indiana University Press, 1994.

DeSalvo, Louise A. Introduction to *The Voyage Out.* By Virginia Woolf. New York: Signet, 1991.

———. *Virginia Woolf: The Impact of Childhood Sexual Abuse on Her Life and Work.* Boston: Beacon, 1989.

———. *Virginia Woolf's First Voyage: A Novel in the Making.* Totowa: Rowman and Littlefield, 1980.

———. and Mitchell A. Leaska, eds. *The Letters of Vita Sackville-West to Virginia Woolf.* New York: Morrow, 1985.

Dijkstra, Bram. *Idols of Perversity: Fantasies of Feminine Evil in Fin-de-Siècle Culture.* New York: Oxford University Press, 1986.

Doan, Laura. Preface. *The Lesbian Postmodern.* New York: Columbia University Press, 1994.

———. "Jeanette Winterson's Sexing the Postmodern." *The Lesbian Postmodern.* Ed. Laura Doan. New York: Columbia University Press, 1994, 137–55.

Draine, Betsy. *Substance Under Pressure: Artistic Coherence and Evolving Form in the Novels of Doris Lessing.* Madison: University of Wisconsin Press, 1983.

Duffy, Maureen. *Capital.* London: Jonathan Cape, 1975.

———. *Change.* London: Methuen, 1987.

———. *The Erotic World of Faery.* London: Cardinal, 1989.

———. *Londoners: An Elegy.* London: Methuen, 1983.

———. *The Love Child.* New York: Knopf, 1971.

———. *The Microcosm.* New York: Penguin/Virago, 1990.

———. *That's How It Was.* London: Hutchinson, 1962.

———. *Wounds.* London: Cape, 1969.

DuPlessis, Rachel Blau. *Writing Beyond the Ending: Narrative Strategies of Twentieth-Century Women Writers.* Bloomington: Indiana University Press, 1985.

Edgeworth, Maria. *Belinda.* Oxford: Oxford University Press, 1994.

Eisenberg, Nora. "Virginia Woolf's Last Word on Words: *Between the Acts* and 'Anon.'" *New Feminist Essays on Virginia Woolf.* Ed. Jane Marcus. Lincoln: University of Nebraska Press, 1981, 253–66.

Faderman, Lillian. *Odd Girls and Twilight Lovers: A History of Lesbian Life in Twentieth-Century America.* New York: Columbia University Press, 1991.

———. *Surpassing the Love of Men: Romantic Friendship and Love between Women from the Renaissance to the Present.* New York: Morrow, 1981.

Farwell, Marilyn R. *Heterosexual Plots and Lesbian Narratives.* New York: New York University Press, 1996.

Fleishman, Avrom. *Virginia Woolf: A Critical Reading.* Baltimore: Johns Hopkins University Press, 1975.

Foster, Jeannette H. *Sex Variant Women in Literature.* Tallahassee: Naiad, 1985.

Freud, Sigmund. *The Complete Psychological Works.* Trans. and ed. James Strachey. 24 vols. London: Hogarth Press, 1953–74.

Fromm, Gloria Glikin. *Dorothy Richardson, a Biography.* Urbana: University of Illinois Press, 1977.

Frye, Northrop. *The Anatomy of Criticism: Four Essays.* Princeton: Princeton University Press, 1957.

Gamman, Lorraine, and Merja Makinen. *Female Fetishism.* New York: New York University Press, 1995.

Garner, Shirley Nelson. " 'Women Together' in Virginia Woolf's *Night and Day.*" *The (M)other Tongue: Essays in Feminist Psychoanalytic Interpretation.* Ed. Shirley Nelson Garner, Claire Kahane, and Madelon Sprengnether. Ithaca: Cornell University Press, 1985.

Gilbert, Sandra M., and Susan Gubar. *The Madwoman in the Attic: The Woman Writer and the Nineteenth-Century Literary Imagination.* New Haven: Yale University Press, 1979.

Gillespie, Diane Filby. "Political Aesthetics: Virginia Woolf and Dorothy Richardson." *Virginia Woolf: A Feminist Slant.* Ed. Jane Marcus. Lincoln: University of Nebraska Press, 1983.

Girard, René. *Deceit, Desire, and the Novel.* Trans. Yvonne Freccero. Baltimore: Johns Hopkins University Press, 1965.

Glamuzina, Julie, and Alison J. Laurie. *Parker and Hulme: A Lesbian View.* Ithaca: Firebrand, 1995.

Gordon, Lyndall. *Virginia Woolf: A Writer's Life.* New York: Norton, 1984.

Gould, Rachel. Interview with Maureen Duffy. *Guardian,* October 5, 1983: 13.

Green, Katherine Sobba. *The Courtship Novel 1740–1820: A Feminized Genre.* Lexington: University Press of Kentucky, 1991.

Greene, Gayle. *Changing the Story: Feminist Fiction and the Tradition.* Bloomington: Indiana University Press, 199l.

Grier, Barbara [Gene Damon]. *Lesbiana: Book Reviews from The Ladder.* Reno: Naiad, 1976.

Guiget, Jean. *Virginia Woolf and Her Works.* Trans. Jean Stewart. London: Hogarth, 1965.

Haggerty, George E. "The Gothic Novel, 1764–1824." *Columbia History of the British Novel.* Ed. John Richetti et al. New York: Columbia University Press, 1994, 220–26.

———. "Literature and Homosexuality in the Late Eighteenth Century: Walpole, Beckford, and Lewis." *Studies in the Novel* 18 (1986): 341–52.

Hall, Radclyffe. *The Well of Loneliness.* London: Jonathan Cape, 1928.

Hamer, Diane. " 'I Am a Woman': Ann Bannon and the Writing of Lesbian Identity in the 1950s." *Lesbian and Gay Writing: An Anthology of Critical Essays.* Ed. Mark Lilly. London: Macmillan, 1990.

Hanscombe, Gillian, and Virginia L. Smyers. *Writing for Their Lives: The Modernist Women 1910–1940.* London: The Women's Press, 1987.

Hardy, Thomas. *Collected Poems.* New York: Macmillan, 1925.

———. *Desperate Remedies.* New York: St. Martin's, 1977.

———. *A Laodicean.* London: Macmillan, 1951.

———. *The Mayor of Casterbridge.* Boston: Houghton Mifflin, 1962.

———. *Tess of the d'Urbervilles*. Boston: Houghton Mifflin, 1960.

———. *The Woodlanders*. New York: Oxford University Press, 1981.

Harris, Bertha. *Lover*. New York: New York University Press, 1993.

Harrison, Bernard. "Muriel Spark and Jane Austen." *Critical Essays on Muriel Spark*. Ed. Joseph Hynes. New York: G. K. Hall, 1992, 131–150.

Hayles, N. Katherine. *Chaos Bound: Orderly Disorder in Contemporary Literature and Science*. Ithaca: Cornell University Press, 1990.

Heilbrun, Carolyn G. *Toward a Recognition of Androgyny*. New York: Norton, 1982.

Henke, Suzette A. "Mrs Dalloway: The Communion of Saints." *New Feminist Essays on Virginia Woolf*. Ed. Jane Marcus. Lincoln: University of Nebraska Press, 1981, 125–47.

Hennessy, Peter. *Never Again: Britain, 1945–1951*. New York: Pantheon, 1994.

Higonnet, Margaret R., ed. *The Sense of Sex: Feminist Perspectives on Hardy*. Urbana: University of Illinois Press, 1993.

Hite, Molly. *The Other Side of the Story: Structures and Strategies of Contemporary Feminist Narratives*. Ithaca: Cornell University Press, 1989.

Hogg, James. *The Private Memoirs and Confessions of a Justified Sinner*. London: Oxford University Press, 1969.

Hoogland, Renée C. *Elizabeth Bowen: A Reputation in Writing*. New York: New York University Press, 1994.

Hynes, Joseph. *The Art of the Real: Muriel Spark's Novels*. Rutherford: Fairleigh Dickinson University Press, 1988.

Ian, Marcia. *Remembering the Phallic Mother: Psychoanalysis, Modernism, and the Fetish*. Ithaca: Cornell University Press, 1993.

Irigaray, Luce. *This Sex Which Is Not One*. Trans. Catherine Porter with Carolyn Burke. Ithaca: Cornell University Press, 1985.

Jagose, Annamarie. *Lesbian Utopics*. New York: Routledge, 1994.

James, Henry. "The Beast in the Jungle." *The Short Stories of Henry James*. Ed. Clifton Fadiman. New York: Random House, 1945, 548–97.

Jameson, Fredric. *Postmodernism, or, The Cultural Logic of Late Capitalism*. Durham: Duke University Press, 1991.

Jensen, Emily. "Clarissa Dalloway's Respectable Suicide." *Virginia Woolf: A Feminist Slant*. Ed. Jane Marcus. University of Nebraska Press, 1982, 162–79.

Johnson, Anne Janette. "Beryl Bainbridge." *Contemporary Authors*. Ed. Deborah A. Straub et al. Vol. 24, New Revision Series. Detroit: Gale, 1988, 29–33.

Johnston, Jill. *Lesbian Nation*. New York: Simon and Schuster, 1973.

Joplin, Patricia Klindienst. "Feminism and Fascism in Virginia Woolf's *Between the Acts*." *Virginia Woolf: A Collection of Critical Essays*. Ed. Margaret Homans. Englewood Cliffs, N.J.: Prentice Hall, 1993, 210–26.

Jordan, Heather Bryant. *How Will the Heart Endure: Elizabeth Bowen and the Landscape of War*. Ann Arbor: University of Michigan Press, 1992.

Kaplan, Sydney Janet. *Feminist Consciousness in the Modern British Novel.* Urbana: University of Illinois Press, 1975.

Kakutani, Michiko. "Genteel Predators." *New York Times*, February 20, 1988: 16.

Kelley, Alice Van Buren. *The Novels of Virginia Woolf: Fact and Vision.* Chicago: University of Chicago Press, 1973.

Kenney, Edwin J., Jr. *Elizabeth Bowen.* Lewisburg: Bucknell University Press, 1975.

Kenyon, Olga. *Women Writers Talk.* New York: Carroll and Graf, 1989.

———. *Women Novelists Today: A Survey of English Writing in the Seventies and Eighties.* New York: St. Martin's, 1988.

Kristeva, Julia. *Revolution in Poetic Language.* Trans. Margaret Waller. New York: Columbia University Press, 1984.

Lambert, Georgia L. "Emma Tennant." *British Novelists Since 1960.* Ed. Jay L. Halio. Detroit: Gale, 1983, 708–15.

Lamos, Colleen. "The Postmodern Lesbian Position: *On Our Backs.*" *The Lesbian Postmodern.* Ed. Laura Doan. New York: Columbia University Press, 1993.

Lassner, Phyllis. *Elizabeth Bowen.* Savage, Md.: Barnes and Noble, 1990.

Laurence, Patricia Ondek. *The Reading of Silence: Virginia Woolf in the English Tradition.* Stanford: Stanford University Press, 1991.

Lawrence, D. H. *The Fox.* New York: Viking, 1965.

———. *The Rainbow.* Harmondsworth: Penguin, 1981.

———. *The Virgin and the Gipsy.* New York: Knopf, 1930.

Lea, Hermann. *Thomas Hardy's Wessex.* London: Macmillan, 1913.

Leaska, Mitchell A. *The Novels of Virginia Woolf from Beginning to End.* New York: John Jay, 1977.

Lee, Hermione. *Elizabeth Bowen: An Estimation.* London: Vision, 1981.

———. *The Novels of Virginia Woolf.* New York: Holmes and Meier, 1977.

LeFanu, Joseph Sheridan. "Carmilla." *Best Ghost Stories of J. S. LeFanu.* Ed. E. F. Bleiler. New York: Dover, 1964, 274–339.

Lessing, Doris. *The Golden Notebook.* New York: Simon and Schuster, 1962.

Light, Alison. *Forever England: Femininity, Literature, and Conservatism between the Wars.* London: Routledge, 1991.

Lilienfeld, Jane. " 'Where the Spear Plants Grew': The Ramsays' Marriage in *To the Lighthouse.*" *New Feminist Essays on Virginia Woolf.* Ed. Jane Marcus. Lincoln: University of Nebraska Press, 1981, 148–67.

Lodge, David. "The Use and Abuses of Omniscience: Method and Meaning in Muriel Spark's *The Prime of Miss Jean Brodie.*" *Critical Essays on Muriel Spark.* Ed. Joseph Hynes. New York: G. K. Hall, 1992, 151–73.

MacAndrew, Elizabeth. *The Gothic Tradition in Fiction.* New York: Columbia University Press, 1979.

Mackay, Shena. *The Music Upstairs.* London: Virago, 1989.

Marcus, Jane. *Virginia Woolf and the Languages of Patriarchy*. Bloomington: Indiana University Press, 1987.

Massie, Alan. "Calvinism and Catholicism in Muriel Spark." *Muriel Spark: An Odd Capacity for Vision*. Ed. Alan Bold. London: Vision, 1984, 94-107.

McCrindle, Jean. "Reading *The Golden Notebook* in 1962." *Notebooks/ Memoirs/ Archives: Reading and Rereading Doris Lessing*. Ed. Jenny Taylor. Boston: Routledge, 1982, 43–56.

McDowell, Frederick P. W. " 'Surely Order Did Prevail': Virginia Woolf and *The Voyage Out*." *Virginia Woolf: Revaluation and Continuity*. Ed. Ralph Freedman. Berkeley: University of California Press, 1980.

McGuirk, Carol. "Drabble to Carter: Fiction by Women, 1962–1992." *Columbia History of the British Novel*. Ed. John Richetti et al. New York: Columbia University Press, 1994, 939–65.

Meese, Elizabeth A. *[Sem]erotics: Theorizing Lesbian: Writing*. New York: New York University Press, 1992.

Meulenbelt, Anja. *De Bewondering*. Amsterdam: Van Gennep, 1987.

Mill, John Stuart. *The Subjection of Women. Mill and Taylor: Essays on Sex Equality*. Ed. Alice Rossi. Chicago: University of Chicago Press, 1970.

Millard, Barbara C. "Beryl Bainbridge." *British Novelists Since 1960*. Ed. Jay L. Halio. Detroit: Gale, 1983, 38–49.

Miller, D. A. *Narrative and its Discontents: Problems of Closure in the Traditional Novel*. Princeton: Princeton University Press, 1981.

Miller, J. Hillis. "*Mrs. Dalloway*: Repetition as the Raising of the Dead." *Critical Essays on Virginia Woolf*. Ed. Morris Beja. Boston: Hall, 1985.

Minow-Pinkney, Makiko. *Virginia Woolf and the Problem of the Subject*. New Brunswick: Rutgers University Press, 1987.

Moers, Ellen. *Literary Women: The Great Writers*. Garden City: Doubleday, 1976.

Moore, Lisa. " 'Something More Tender Still than Friendship': Romantic Friendship in Early-Nineteenth-Century England." *Feminist Studies* 18 (1992): 499–520.

Moore, Madeline. *The Short Season Between Two Silences: The Mystical and the Political in the Novels of Virginia Woolf*. Boston: Allen and Unwin, 1984.

Morgan, Kenneth O. *The People's Peace: British History 1945–1989*. Oxford: Oxford University Press, 1990.

Morgan, Rosemarie. *Women and Sexuality in the Novels of Thomas Hardy*. London: Routledge, 1988.

Mozart, Wolfgang Amadeus. *Le Nozze di Figaro*. Libretto by Lorenzo da Ponte. With Kiri Te Kanawa, Lucia Popp, Frederica von Stade, Samuel Ramey, Thomas Allen, and Kurt Moll. Cond. Georg Solti. London Phil. Orch. London 410 150–2, 1982.

Murdoch, Iris. *The Italian Girl*. New York: Viking, 1964.

———. *The Time of the Angels*. New York: Viking, 1966.

———. *The Unicorn*. New York: Viking, 1963.

———. *An Unofficial Rose.* New York: Viking, 1962.

Naremore, James. *The World Without a Self: Virginia Woolf and the Novel.* New Haven: Yale University Press, 1973.

Nestle, Joan. "Butch-Fem Relationships: Sexual Courage in the 1950s." *A Restricted Country.* Ithaca: Firebrand, 1987.

Neuman, Shirley. "*Heart of Darkness* , Virginia Woolf and the Spectre of Domination." *Virginia Woolf: New Critical Essays.* Ed. Patricia Clements and Isobel Grundy. London: Vision, 1983.

Newman, Jenny. " 'See Me as Sisyphus, But Having a Good Time': the Fictions of Fay Weldon." *Contemporary British Women Writers: Narrative Strategies.* Ed. Robert E. Hosmer, Jr. New York: St. Martin's, 1993.

Newton, Esther. "The Mythic Mannish Lesbian: Radclyffe Hall and the New Woman." *Signs* 9 (1984): 557–75.

Nichols, Nina da Vinci. "Place and Eros in Radcliffe, Lewis, and Brontë." *The Female Gothic.* Ed. Juliann E. Fleenor. Montreal: Eden, 1983, 187–206.

Norton, G. Ron, John R. Walker, and Colin A. Ross. "Panic Disorder and Agoraphobia: An Introduction." *Panic Disorder and Agoraphobia: A Comprehensive Guide for the Practitioner.* Ed. Norton, Walker, and Ross. Pacific Grove: Brooks/Cole, 1991, 4–15.

Novak, Jane. *The Razor Edge of Balance: A Study of Virginia Woolf.* Coral Gables: University of Miami Press, 1975.

O'Connor, Noreen, and Joanna Ryan. *Wild Desires and Mistaken Identities: Lesbianism and Psychoanalysis.* New York: Columbia University Press, 1995.

Oldfield, Sybil. "From Rachel's Aunts to Miss La Trobe: Spinsters in the Fiction of Virginia Woolf." *Old Maids to Radical Spinsters: Unmarried Women in the Twentieth-Century Novel.* Ed. Laura L. Doan. Urbana: University of Illinois Press, 1991, 85–103.

O'Rourke, Rebecca. "Fingers in the Fruit Basket: A Feminist Reading of Jeanette Winterson's *Oranges Are Not the Only Fruit.*" *Feminist Criticism: Theory and Practice.* Ed. Susan Sellers, Linda Hutcheon, and Paul Perron. Toronto: University of Toronto Press, 1991.

Owen, Alex. *The Darkened Room: Women, Power, and Spiritualism in Late Victorian England.* London: Virago, 1989.

Page, Norman. *Muriel Spark.* New York: St. Martin's, 1990.

Palmer, Paulina. "Contemporary Lesbian Feminist Fiction: Texts for Everywoman." *Plotting Change: Contemporary Women's Fiction.* Ed. Linda Anderson. London: Edward Arnold, 1990, 43–64.

———. *Contemporary Women's Fiction: Narrative Practice and Feminist Theory.* Jackson: University Press of Mississippi, 1989.

Pecora, Vincent P. "D. H. Lawrence." *Columbia History of the British Novel.* Ed. John Richetti et al. New York: Columbia University Press, 1994, 715–39.

Pinion, F. B. *A Hardy Companion.* London: Macmillan, 1968.

Pullin, Faith. "Autonomy and Fabulation in the Fiction of Muriel Spark." *Muriel Spark: An Odd Capacity for Vision*. Ed. Alan Bold. London: Vision, 1984, 71–93.

Pynchon, Thomas. *The Crying of Lot 49*. New York: Harper and Row, 1986.

Quin, Ann. *Three*. New York: Scribner, 1966.

Raitt, Suzanne. Introduction to *Night and Day*. By Virginia Woolf. Oxford: Oxford University Press, 1992.

———. *Vita and Virginia: The Work and Friendship of V. Sackville-West and Virginia Woolf*. Oxford: Oxford University Press, 1993.

Rantavaara, Irma. *Virginia Woolf and Bloomsbury*. Helsinki: Annales Academiæ Scientiarium Fennicæ, 1953.

Renault, Mary. *The Friendly Young Ladies*. New York: Pantheon, 1985.

Reynolds, Margaret. "Ruggiero's Deceptions, Cherubino's Distractions." *En Travesti: Women, Gender Subversion, Opera*. Ed. Corinne E. Blackmer and Patricia Juliana Smith. New York: Columbia University Press, 1995, 132–51.

———. ed. *The Penguin Book of Lesbian Short Stories*. Harmondsworth: Penguin, 1994.

Rich, Adrienne. "Compulsory Heterosexuality and Lesbian Existence." *Powers of Desire: The Politics of Sexuality*. Ed. Ann Snitow, Christine Stansell, and Sharon Thompson. New York: Monthly Review Press, 1983, 177–205.

———. "Jane Eyre: The Temptations of a Motherless Woman." *On Lies, Secrets, and Silence, Selected Prose, 1966–1978*. New York: Norton, 1979.

Richardson, Dorothy. *Dawn's Left Hand. Pilgrimage* IV. London: Virago, 1979.

Richardson, Henry Handel. *The Getting of Wisdom*. New York: Dial, 1981.

Richmond, Velma Bourgeois. *Muriel Spark*. New York: Frederick Ungar, 1984.

Richter, Harvena. *Virginia Woolf: The Inward Voyage*. Princeton: Princeton University Press, 1970.

Rolo, Charles J. "Reader's Choice." *Atlantic Monthly* 199, no. 4 (April 1957): 82–85.

Ronald, Ann. "Terror-Gothic: Nightmare and Dream." *The Female Gothic*. Ed. Juliann E. Fleenor. Montreal: Eden, 1983, 176–86.

Roof, Judith. *Come as You Are: Sexuality and Narrative*. New York: Columbia University Press, 1966.

———. "Lesbians and Lyotard: Legitimation and the Politics of the Name." *The Lesbian Postmodern*. Ed. Laura Doan. New York: Columbia University Press, 1994, 47–66.

———. *A Lure of Knowledge: Lesbian Sexuality and Theory*. New York: Columbia University Press, 1991.

———. "The Match in the Crocus: Representations of Lesbian Sexuality." *Discontented Discourses: Feminism/Textual Intervention/Psychoanalysis*. Ed. Marleen S. Barr and Richard Feldstein. Urbana: University of Illinois Press, 1989, 100–16.

Rose, Phyllis. *Woman of Letters*. San Diego: Harcourt, 1978.

Royle, Trevor. "Spark and Scotland." *Muriel Spark: An Odd Capacity for Vision*. Ed. Alan Bold. London: Vision, 1984, 147–66.

Rubenstein, Roberta. *The Novelistic Vision of Doris Lessing: Breaking the Forms of Consciousness*. Urbana: University of Illinois Press, 1979.
Rubin, Gayle. "The Traffic in Women: Notes Toward a Political Economy of Sex." *Toward an Anthropology of Women*. Ed. Rayna Reiter. New York: Monthly Review Press, 1975, 157–210.
Rule, Jane. *Lesbian Images*. Trumansburg, N.Y.: Crossing Press, 1982.
Sadler, Lynn Veach. *Anita Brookner*. Boston: Twayne, 1990.
Sage, Lorna. *Doris Lessing*. London: Methuen, 1983.
———. *Women in the House of Fiction: Post-War Women Novelists*. New York: Routledge, 1992.
Sedgwick, Eve Kosofsky. *Between Men: English Literature and Male Homosocial Desire*. New York: Columbia University Press, 1985.
———. *Epistemology of the Closet*. Berkeley and Los Angeles: University of California Press, 1990.
———. "Privilege of Unknowing." *Genders* 1 (1988): 102–24.
Showalter, Elaine. *A Literature of Their Own: British Women Novelists from Brontë to Lessing*. Princeton: Princeton University Press, 1977.
———. *Sexual Anarchy: Gender and Culture at the Fin de Siècle*. Harmondsworth: Penguin, 1990.
Singleton, Mary Ann. *The City and the Veld: The Fiction of Doris Lessing*. Lewisburg: Bucknell University Press, 1977.
Skinner, John. *The Fictions of Anita Brookner*. New York: St. Martin's, 1992.
Smith, Patricia Juliana. " 'A Comic Turn, Turned Serious': Fay Weldon's *The Life and Loves of a She-Devil*." *The Explicator* 51 (1993): 255–57.
Snitow, Ann Barr. "The Front Line: Notes on Sex in Novels by Women, 1969–1979." *Women: Sex and Sexuality*. Ed. Catharine R. Stimpson and Ethel Spector Person. Chicago: University of Chicago Press, 1980, 158–74.
Spark, Muriel. *The Girls of Slender Means*. New York: Perigee, 1982.
———. *The Prime of Miss Jean Brodie*. New York: Plume, 1984.
Sprague, Claire. *Rereading Doris Lessing: Narrative Patterns of Doubling and Repetition*. Chapel Hill: University of North Carolina Press, 1987.
Stein, Gertrude. *Fernhurst. Fernhurst, Q.E.D., and Other Early Writings*. New York: Liveright, 1971.
Stevenson, Robert Louis. *Dr. Jekyll and Mr. Hyde*. New York: Bantam, 1981.
Stimpson, Catharine R. *Where the Meanings Are: Feminism and Cultural Spaces*. New York: Routledge, 1988.
Strachey, Dorothy ["Olivia"]. *Olivia*. London: Virago, 1987.
Sullivan, Walter. "A Sense of Place: Elizabeth Bowen and the Landscape of the Heart." *Sewanee Review* 84 (1976): 142–49.
Tennant, Emma. *The Adventures of Robina, by Herself: Being the Memoirs of a Débutante at the Court of Queen Elizabeth II*. London: Faber, 1986.
———. *The Bad Sister*. London: Faber, 1989.

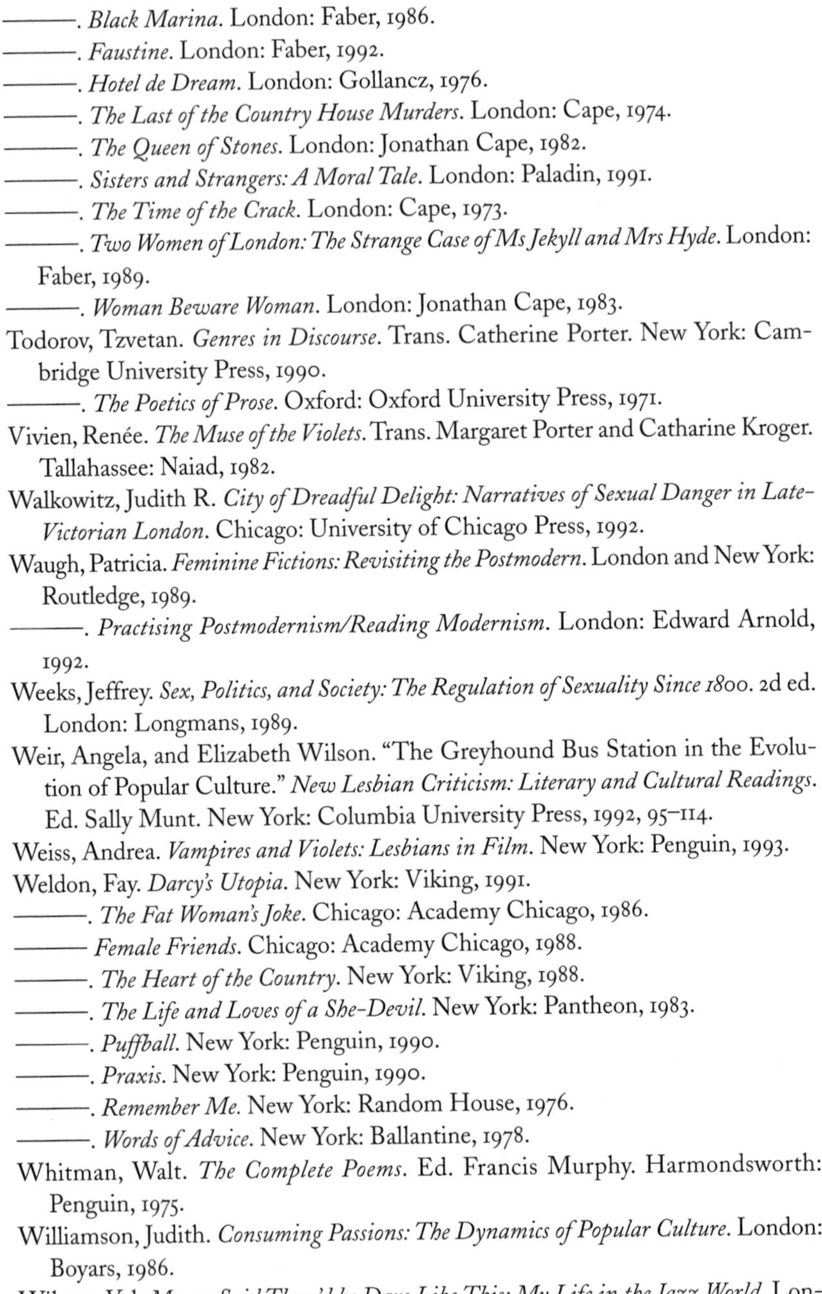

———. *Black Marina*. London: Faber, 1986.
———. *Faustine*. London: Faber, 1992.
———. *Hotel de Dream*. London: Gollancz, 1976.
———. *The Last of the Country House Murders*. London: Cape, 1974.
———. *The Queen of Stones*. London: Jonathan Cape, 1982.
———. *Sisters and Strangers: A Moral Tale*. London: Paladin, 1991.
———. *The Time of the Crack*. London: Cape, 1973.
———. *Two Women of London: The Strange Case of Ms Jekyll and Mrs Hyde*. London: Faber, 1989.
———. *Woman Beware Woman*. London: Jonathan Cape, 1983.
Todorov, Tzvetan. *Genres in Discourse*. Trans. Catherine Porter. New York: Cambridge University Press, 1990.
———. *The Poetics of Prose*. Oxford: Oxford University Press, 1971.
Vivien, Renée. *The Muse of the Violets*. Trans. Margaret Porter and Catharine Kroger. Tallahassee: Naiad, 1982.
Walkowitz, Judith R. *City of Dreadful Delight: Narratives of Sexual Danger in Late-Victorian London*. Chicago: University of Chicago Press, 1992.
Waugh, Patricia. *Feminine Fictions: Revisiting the Postmodern*. London and New York: Routledge, 1989.
———. *Practising Postmodernism/Reading Modernism*. London: Edward Arnold, 1992.
Weeks, Jeffrey. *Sex, Politics, and Society: The Regulation of Sexuality Since 1800*. 2d ed. London: Longmans, 1989.
Weir, Angela, and Elizabeth Wilson. "The Greyhound Bus Station in the Evolution of Popular Culture." *New Lesbian Criticism: Literary and Cultural Readings*. Ed. Sally Munt. New York: Columbia University Press, 1992, 95–114.
Weiss, Andrea. *Vampires and Violets: Lesbians in Film*. New York: Penguin, 1993.
Weldon, Fay. *Darcy's Utopia*. New York: Viking, 1991.
———. *The Fat Woman's Joke*. Chicago: Academy Chicago, 1986.
——— *Female Friends*. Chicago: Academy Chicago, 1988.
———. *The Heart of the Country*. New York: Viking, 1988.
———. *The Life and Loves of a She-Devil*. New York: Pantheon, 1983.
———. *Puffball*. New York: Penguin, 1990.
———. *Praxis*. New York: Penguin, 1990.
———. *Remember Me*. New York: Random House, 1976.
———. *Words of Advice*. New York: Ballantine, 1978.
Whitman, Walt. *The Complete Poems*. Ed. Francis Murphy. Harmondsworth: Penguin, 1975.
Williamson, Judith. *Consuming Passions: The Dynamics of Popular Culture*. London: Boyars, 1986.
Wilmer, Val. *Mama Said There'd be Days Like This: My Life in the Jazz World*. London: The Women's Press, 1989.

Wilson, Elizabeth. *Only Halfway to Paradise: Women in Postwar Britain 1945–68*. London: Tavistock, 1980.
Winterson, Jeanette. *Boating for Beginners*. London: Minerva, 1990.
———. *Oranges Are Not the Only Fruit*. New York: Atlantic Monthly, 1987.
———. *The Passion*. New York: Vintage, 1987.
———. *Sexing the Cherry*. New York: Atlantic Monthly, 1989.
———. *Written on the Body*. London: Jonathan Cape, 1992.
Winsloe, Christa. *The Child Manuela*. Trans. Agnes Neill Scott. New York: Farrar, 1933.
Wittchen, Hans-Ulrich, and Cecilia A. Essau. "The Epidemiology of Panic Attacks, Panic Disorder, and Agoraphobia." *Panic Disorder and Agoraphobia: A Comprehensive Guide for the Practitioner*. Ed. Norton, Walker, and Ross. Pacific Grove: Brooks/Cole, 1991, 103–49,
Wittig, Monique. *The Lesbian Body*. Trans. David Le Vay. Boston: Beacon, 1986.
Wolff, Cynthia Griffin. "The Radcliffean Gothic Model: A Form for Feminine Sexuality." *The Female Gothic*. Ed. Juliann E. Fleenor. Montréal: Eden, 1983, 207–23.
Wollstonecraft, Mary. *Vindication of the Rights of Woman*. Harmondsworth: Penguin, 1975.
Wood, Elizabeth. "Sapphonics." *Queering the Pitch: The New Gay and Lesbian Musicology*. Ed. Philip Brett, Elizabeth Wood, and Gary C. Thomas. New York: Routledge, 1994, 27–66.
Wood, Michael. "The Contemporary Novel." *Columbia History of the British Novel*. Ed. John Richetti et al. New York: Columbia University Press, 1994, 961–88.
Woolf, Virginia. *The Diary of Virginia Woolf*. Ed. Anne Olivier Bell. 5 vols. San Diego: Harcourt, 1977–84.
———. Introduction to *Mrs. Dalloway*. New York: Modern Library, 1928.
———. "Jane Austen." *The Essays of Virginia Woolf*, vol. 2, 1912–1918. Ed. Andrew McNeillie. San Diego: Harcourt, 1987.
———. *Mrs. Dalloway*. New York: Harcourt, 1981.
———. *Melymbrosia: An Early Version of The Voyage Out*. Edited by Louise A. DeSalvo. New York: New York Public Library, 1982.
———. "Modern Fiction." *Granite and Rainbow: Essays*. Ed. Leonard Woolf. New York: Harcourt, 1958.
———. *Night and Day*. New York: Harcourt, 1925.
———. *Orlando*. New York: Harcourt, 1928.
———. "Professions for Women." *The Death of the Moth and Other Essays*. New York: Harcourt, 1942, 235–42.
———. *A Room of One's Own*. New York: Harcourt, 1929.
———. "Speech before the London/National Society for Women's Service, January 21, 1931." *The Pargiters: The Novel-Essay Portion of The Years*. Ed. Mitchell A. Leaska. New York: Harcourt, 1978, xxvii-xliv.

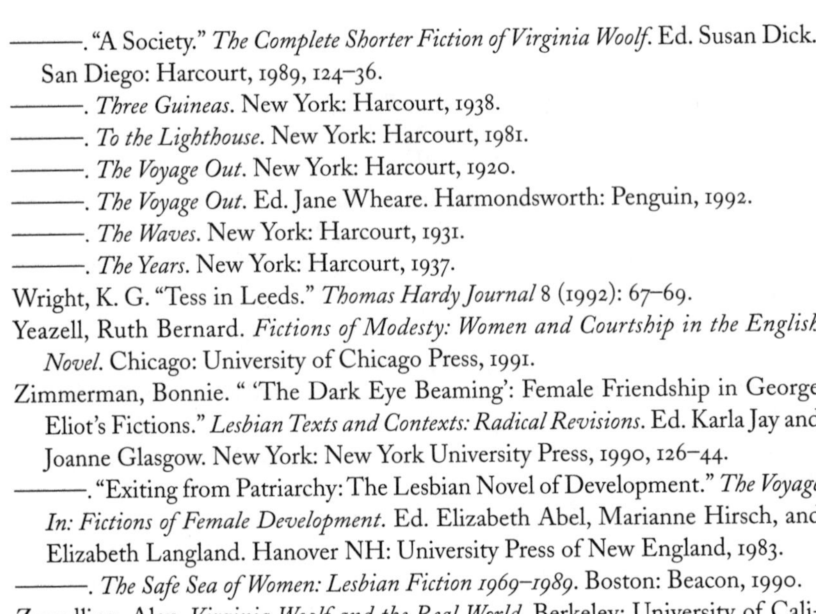

———. "A Society." *The Complete Shorter Fiction of Virginia Woolf.* Ed. Susan Dick. San Diego: Harcourt, 1989, 124–36.

———. *Three Guineas.* New York: Harcourt, 1938.

———. *To the Lighthouse.* New York: Harcourt, 1981.

———. *The Voyage Out.* New York: Harcourt, 1920.

———. *The Voyage Out.* Ed. Jane Wheare. Harmondsworth: Penguin, 1992.

———. *The Waves.* New York: Harcourt, 1931.

———. *The Years.* New York: Harcourt, 1937.

Wright, K. G. "Tess in Leeds." *Thomas Hardy Journal* 8 (1992): 67–69.

Yeazell, Ruth Bernard. *Fictions of Modesty: Women and Courtship in the English Novel.* Chicago: University of Chicago Press, 1991.

Zimmerman, Bonnie. " 'The Dark Eye Beaming': Female Friendship in George Eliot's Fictions." *Lesbian Texts and Contexts: Radical Revisions.* Ed. Karla Jay and Joanne Glasgow. New York: New York University Press, 1990, 126–44.

———. "Exiting from Patriarchy: The Lesbian Novel of Development." *The Voyage In: Fictions of Female Development.* Ed. Elizabeth Abel, Marianne Hirsch, and Elizabeth Langland. Hanover NH: University Press of New England, 1983.

———. *The Safe Sea of Women: Lesbian Fiction 1969–1989.* Boston: Beacon, 1990.

Zwerdling, Alex. *Virginia Woolf and the Real World.* Berkeley: University of California Press, 1986.

INDEX

Between Men ~ Between Women

Lesbian and Gay Studies

Lillian Faderman and Larry Gross, Editors

Rebecca Alpert, *Like Bread on the Seder Plate*

Edward Alwood, *Straight News: Gays, Lesbians, and the News Media*

Corinne E. Blackmer and Patricia Juliana Smith, editors, *En Travesti: Women, Gender Subversion, Opera*

Alan Bray, *Homosexuality in Renaissance England*

Joseph Bristow, *Effeminate England: Homoerotic Writing After 1885*

Beverly Burch, *Other Women: Lesbian Theory and Psychoanalytic Narratives*

Claudia Card, *Lesbian Choices*

Joseph Carrier, *De Los Otros: Intimacy and Homosexuality Among Mexican Men*

Terry Castle, *Noël Coward and Radclyffe Hall: Kindred Spirits*

John Clum, *Acting Gay: Male Homosexuality in Modern Drama*

Gary David Comstock, *Violence Against Lesbians and Gay Men*

Laura Doan, editor, *The Lesbian Postmodern*

Allen Ellenzweig, *The Homoerotic Photograph: Male Images from Durieu/Delacroix to Mapplethorpe*

Lillian Faderman, *Odd Girls and Twilight Lovers: A History of Lesbian Life in Twentieth-Century America*

Linda D. Garnets and Douglas C. Kimmel, editors, *Psychological Perspectives on Lesbian and Gay Male Experiences*

Richard D. Mohr, *Gays/Justice: A Study of Ethics, Society, and Law*

Sally Munt, editor, *New Lesbian Criticism: Literary and Cultural Readings*

Timothy F. Murphy and Suzanne Poirier, editors, *Writing AIDS: Gay Literature, Language, and Analysis*

Noreen O'Connor and Joanna Ryan, *Wild Desires and Mistaken Identities: Lesbianism and Psychoanalysis*

Don Paulson with Roger Simpson, *An Evening in the Garden of Allah: A Gay Cabaret in Seattle*

Judith Roof, *Come As You Are: Sexuality and Narrative*

Judith Roof, *A Lure of Knowledge: Lesbian Sexuality and Theory*

Claudia Schoppmann, *Days of Masquerade: Life Stories of Lesbians During the Third Reich*

James T. Sears and Walter L. Williams, editors, *Overcoming Heterosexism and Homophobia: Strategies That Work*

Alan Sinfield, *The Wilde Century: Effeminacy, Oscar Wilde, and the Queer Moment*

Jane Snyder, *Lesbian Desire in the Lyrics of Sappho*

Chris Straayer: *Deviant Eyes, Deviant Bodies: Sexual Re-Orientations in Film and Video*

Ruth Vanita, *Sappho and the Virgin Mary: Same-Sex Love and the English Literary Imagination*

Thomas Waugh, *Hard to Imagine: Gay Male Eroticism in Photography and Film from Their Beginnings to Stonewall*

Kath Weston, *Families We Choose: Lesbians, Gays, Kinship*

Kath Weston, *Render Me, Gender Me: Lesbians Talk Sex, Class, Color, Nation, Studmuffins . . .*

Carter Wilson, *Hidden in the Blood: A Personal Investigation of AIDS in the Yucatán*